PLAYING
GOD

ALSO BY MARY JO MCCONAHAY

Maya Roads, One Woman's Journey Among the People of the Rainforest

Ricochet, Two Women War Reporters and a Friendship Under Fire

Tango War, The Struggle for the Hearts, Minds, and Riches of Latin America During World War II

MARY JO McCONAHAY

PLAYING
GOD

AMERICAN CATHOLIC
BISHOPS
AND THE FAR RIGHT

MELVILLE HOUSE
BROOKLYN · LONDON

Playing God: American Catholic Bishops and the Far Right
First published in 2023 by Melville House
Copyright © Mary Jo McConahay, 2022
All rights reserved
First Melville House Printing: January 2023

Melville House Publishing
46 John Street
Brooklyn, NY 11201
and
Melville House UK
Suite 2000
16/18 Woodford Road
London E7 0HA

mhpbooks.com
@melvillehouse

ISBN: 978-1-68589-028-5
ISBN: 978-1-68589-029-2 (eBook)

Library of Congress Control Number: 2022947780

Printed in the United States of America
1 3 5 7 9 10 8 6 4 2
A catalog record for this book is available from the Library of Congress

To the memory of Rev. Bill O'Donnell
(1930–2003)
Social justice activist,
"a bishop's nightmare,"
parish priest

Contents

Introduction

THE EUPHORIA WITH which American Catholic bishops greeted the Supreme Court decision to overturn *Roe v. Wade* reflects how much the prelates claim the victory as their own. This was a victory fifty years in the making. The most conservative among the bishops will continue their efforts, in alliance with far-right Catholic laypeople, like-minded evangelical Christians, and ultraright politicians, to implant a nationalist Christian dispensation in the law and culture of the United States, believing that their own moral point of view ought to reign for everybody, throughout the land.

The posture of America's Catholic bishops is important beyond the Church. They lead 73 million believers in the United States, more than a fifth of the population. Catholics vote (75 percent in 2016), and, since 1952, their vote usually goes to the winning presidential candidate. The active members of the United States Conference of Catholic Bishops (USCCB), 274 men, almost all beyond middle age and white, represent one of the most powerful lobbying groups in America, their Office of Government Relations charged with directing activities "to influence the actions of the Congress." The bishops influence what goes on in every Catholic parish in America.

But these days U.S. bishops do not reflect the global Catholic Church. As a group they are a particularly American species, hierarchical to a fault, and so traditionalist and politically right wing that they are out of step with the current occupant of the Chair of St. Peter, Pope Francis. Named bishops by Pope John Paul II (1978–2005) or by Pope Benedict XVI (2005–2013), the majority of them spotlight dissatisfaction with Francis by opposing him over issues such as whether politicians who support abortion may be denied Holy Communion—the right-wing bishops try to deny Communion to the likes of President Joe Biden and Nancy Pelosi, even though the pope has said he has never denied the Eucharist to anyone. As religious leaders of the wealthiest capitalist country on the planet, they are embarrassed by the pope's full-throated criticism of unfettered capitalism, or they ignore it, a stand that is key to understanding the American bishops' alliance with the monied far right, both Catholic and non-Catholic. They disagree with the pope that bishops should emphasize the importance of *all* pro-life issues, without calling abortion "preeminent" among them. The distance between the United States Conference of Catholic Bishops and the Vatican has placed the U.S. Church on the verge of schism.

POPE FRANCIS, ELECTED in 2013, the first pope from Latin America, possesses an outgoing personality, is open to the press, and is enormously popular with many of the world's 1.3 billion Catholics for his pastoral manner. He has declared that the landmark Second Vatican Council (1962–65), known as Vatican II, presents the Church's ultimate teaching, including insistence that the Catholic Church is not defined by its hierarchy alone, but that laypeople, clergy, and bishops make up the People of God, who are the Church. He stands against reverting to pre–Vatican II customs and practices, such as the Traditional Latin Mass (TLM), a position with which ultra-conservative American bishops disagree.

Some of the U.S. bishops support the vision and priorities of Pope Francis, and many are faithful in letter and spirit to Vatican II. But so intransigent is the conservative majority, and so strong is the financial support for their positions from the wealthy, as well as from allies in political and legal spheres, that American Catholic prelates can be expected to continue to help spearhead the country's rightward lurch toward nationalism and rule that reflects Christian values as only they see them. This remains true whether Pope Francis leaves the papal throne by resignation or in death.

U.S. bishops want to insert their vision of Catholicism into aspects of law and society that go beyond religion. They really don't want separation of church and state if their moral values are missing from politics and culture. Besides anti-abortion legislation and other limits on women's freedom, the most ultraconservative bishops stand for traditional gender roles, and the most radical of their far-right allies promote laws that repress voting by African Americans and Latinos, with little vocal disapproval from the bishops. Members of the USCCB already control a significant part of the U.S. health system, with one in six hospitals nationwide (and 40 percent of hospitals in some states) run by Catholics and subject to directives codified by the bishops: no to contraception, to abortion (to a point that may put the health of miscarrying mothers at risk), to voluntary sterilization, certain hysterectomies and end of life directives, euthanasia, physician-assisted suicide, and gender-affirming care (for transgender people). The bishops' views align with those of the six members of the conservative majority of the U.S. Supreme Court, all of whom were raised Catholic.

This book examines the teaching and public witness of the U.S. Catholic bishops, where they converge with pivotal figures of the far

right, and the Catholic lay rightists who have been key in partnering
with right-wing evangelical Christians in a fifty-year, precisely or-
chestrated campaign to shape the country into a Christian nation that
conforms to their moral views. It looks at the bishops' wealthy corporate and industrial supporters, like Charles Koch and Tim Busch,
who fund the far-right vision under the guise of pursuing civic and
religious freedoms; they spend billions on the idea of a supremely free
market nation without safety, environment, and labor regulation or
guarantees for groups that offend their radical Christian sensibilities,
like LGBTQ+ people. The book shows the role of the most conservative bishops in what they have done or failed to do, in undermining
national priorities like fighting the COVID-19 pandemic and com-
batting the environmental crisis—chipping away at government authority is a hallmark of surging Christian nationalism. And the book
looks at important Catholic legal figures, like Justice Clarence Thomas
and Federalist Society cofounder Leonard Leo, who have rendered the
wall between church and state a mere gossamer curtain, the better for
their version of Christian morality to rule the land.

I HAVE NO animus toward the Catholic Church or its bishops. As
a lifelong Catholic, including years reporting from Latin America, I
have seen the extent to which my coreligionists, including bishops,
have gone, even to the point of martyrdom, on behalf of other people,
and of justice. At the same time, I have always believed the institution
of the Church was worth investigation and critique.

Like other Americans, I was shaken by the events of January 6,
2021. I saw those hours through the eyes and ears of a reporter who
has covered war, religion, and politics, both at home and in autocra-
cies abroad. Now, in my own nation's capital, I watched in horror and
disbelief at one man's exhortation to loyalists to rise up and march
with him to upturn the law. I saw crosses and Bibles side by side

with Confederate flags, nooses, and other symbols of white supremacy connected with ultraright Christianity and Christian nationalism. I tracked the reactions of people on social media and in the alt-right press, including multiple far-right Catholic outlets. I saw how they conflated the figure of a strongman—in this case, Donald Trump, who disdains democratic norms—with Jesus Christ. How the extremists among my coreligionists exuded a sense of embattled Christianity, expressed in comparisons of supposedly repressed U.S. believers with Jews killed by Hitler.

As a reporter, indeed as a Catholic, I felt it was time to look at the U.S. Church as a key institution playing an outsize role in the current, dangerous political moment.

1

Plague of Illusion

Catholic Clerics' Pandemic Attack on the State

DURING THE OUTBREAK of Black Death of the fourteenth century, when 25 million people died in Europe, believers could pray to the Fourteen Holy Helpers, mostly early Church martyrs whose intercession might heal, or at least bring a holy death. Prayer was also prevalent during the COVID-19 pandemic, but unlike residents of medieval Europe at a time when a monolithic Catholicism permeated everything, the faithful in the United States heard mixed messages from their leaders, compounding agony and confusion. The pandemic illustrated the breach between the Church of Pope Francis (which includes most of the faithful) and right-wing U.S. prelates, who used the extraordinary period to dig in their heels against the pontiff at the cost of bringing comfort to their flocks. It also showed how the most conservative bishops attempted to chip away at Washington's authority—and responsibility for public health—at a time of crisis.

In Rome, Pope Francis modeled the caring shepherd in addresses
and tweets, appearing truly grieved as COVID tore through Italy,
the first European country with a major outbreak. On the evening
of March 27, 2020, the eighty-three-year-old pontiff walked alone
in light rain in an empty St. Peter's Square, and, with the help of an
aide, climbed the steps of the grand basilica to deliver an address *urbi
et orbi*, to the city and the world. COVID was spreading. A global
audience watched the pope speak on live television:

> For weeks now it has been evening. Thick darkness has gathered
> over our squares, our streets and our cities; it has taken over our
> lives, filling everything with a deafening silence and a distressing
> void, that stops everything as it passes by; we feel it in the air, we
> notice in people's gestures, their glances give them away. We find
> ourselves afraid and lost.

CONTRAST THIS PAPAL message, compassionate and addressed
to all, with those of key ultraconservative U.S. bishops and their allies,
who have been at war against Francis since his election in 2013. The
rightist prelates sometimes treated public health mandates as an attack
on their authority, as if they were in competition with Dr. Anthony
Fauci and the Centers for Disease Control and Prevention (CDC), vying with health experts and civil authorities for influence. At the same
time, by taking their own authoritarian path during the pandemic, the
clerics could assert themselves in opposition to the attitude of their
nemesis, Pope Francis.

The gospel on the day of the pope's address recounted the story
of the sudden storm on the Sea of Galilee that terrified the fishermen disciples, until Jesus calmed the wind and reproved the men for
losing faith.

"Like the disciples in the Gospel we were caught off guard by an unexpected, turbulent storm," the pope said. "We have realized that we are on the same boat, all of us fragile and disoriented, but at the same time important and needed, all of us called to row together."

Solidarity and cooperation, however, appeared far from the minds of some U.S. bishops.

THE PRINCE OF SAN FRANCISCO

ARCHBISHOP SALVATORE CORDILEONE personified the princes of the Church who took a stand against government directives, and against the pope's counsel to heed health authorities. In the summer of 2020, after San Francisco mayor London Breed assigned strict COVID rules for religious gatherings—arguably one of many local mandates that kept hospitalizations and deaths among the lowest in the country—the city's archbishop protested in public messages and theatrical outbursts. Cordileone used the kind of language that fanned the fires of the culture wars, in which one side—conservative and supposedly beleaguered—regards itself as upholding traditional values to the scorn of a powerful elite. Cordileone made sure that spectacle accompanied the message.

On a September Sunday, hundreds answered a call from the archbishop to assemble in a plaza in front of City Hall, to show resistance to the mayor's limits on how many people could worship in the same place—fifty outdoors, one at a time inside a closed building. For over an hour, old and young came on foot, on bicycles, in wheelchairs, or pushing strollers, carrying signs distributed by the archdiocese, as well as signs they had made by hand, in Spanish and English: FREE THE MASS; IN GOD WE TRUST—BE NOT AFRAID. One large cloth banner carried by two men read: HONOR FIRST AMENDMENT—RESPECT RIGHT OF CHURCH.

Three local parishes sent Eucharistic processions, in which a priest solemnly carries a consecrated host through the streets in a golden monstrance under a four-cornered canopy, preceded by acolytes swinging censers of smoking incense and followed by parishioners. Cordileone, also carrying a monstrance, appeared in the plaza as the elegant figure San Franciscans have come to expect, in a long ivory cape over his vestments and an ivory stole with gold fringe. People wore white T-shirts given out before the procession, marked on the back with a line drawing of a simple church and a legend that took a swipe at exceptions to restrictions for essential workers: WE ARE ES-SENTIAL, they read. From the Beaux Arts City Hall, many proceeded to the gleaming ultramodern-looking Cathedral of St. Mary of the Assumption, about half a mile away. They took their places on chairs or stood in an outdoor patio to hear Masses said at white-covered tables by various priests, called upon by Cordileone to concelebrate— thus honoring the letter if not the spirit of the fifty-person limit on outdoor worship events.

In his homily, Archbishop Cordileone made it clear that he felt he held the trump card. Love of God and neighbor must "take precedence over the human-made law of the state when government would ask us to turn our backs on God," he said. Behind him rose the huge white cathedral, whose design has been controversial since it was finished in 1971, some admiring its capacity (2,400) and modernist design, others jokingly dubbing it Our Lady of the Maytag because its roof of hyperbolic paraboloids evoked the inside of a washing machine. Cordileone asked the faithful why people were permitted to shop at swank stores at 25 percent capacity, "but only one of you at a time is allowed to pray inside of this great cathedral, your cathedral?"

Those friendly toward Archbishop Salvatore Cordileone have described him as "humble" or use a nickname, Sal. His coat of arms—

every bishop has one—includes the image of a red crab for the Cordileone family line of hard-working fishermen, a paternal grandfather in Sicily and his father in California. Humility does not mark Cordileone's liturgical appearance, however. He chooses the dressy end of the spectrum with vestments of lacy sleeves and gold thread, a throwback to the time when splendor was a hallmark of the hierarchy, a reminder to ordinary people of the distance between them and princes of the Church. There are no sumptuary laws that forbid such choices, but they contrast with those of Pope Francis, who did away with the luxuriant trappings of predecessors from the first moments after election, when he stepped out on the famous St. Peter's Square balcony to greet waiting crowds in his signature plain white cassock. Cordileone's messaging before the San Francisco cathedral dripped with grievance. He insisted that during COVID, Catholics suffered "willful discrimination" from authorities. "Our blessed Lord is openly mocked to the gleeful grins of the cultural elites," he said. "It is because of our Catholic faith that we are being put at the end of the line." Yet all houses of worship were held to the same rules.

San Francisco shops, malls, restaurants, and other workplaces were subject to health and capacity guidelines, too, but Cordileone implied that to be a Catholic was to be a victim of conspiracy by government and its allies, that the matter was personal. He was echoing the language of Christian nationalists who maintain that certain laws—such as those that guarantee equal rights for LGBTQ+ people—put believers under attack, infringing on their freedom of religion. Cordileone said that San Francisco had "abandoned God."

"It has become clear to me that they just don't care about you," he insisted to the Catholics listening outside the cathedral. "To them you are nothing, to them you don't matter. Let me repeat that: to City Hall, *you don't matter.*"

WARRIORS

CORDILEONE'S LINES CAME directly from the Christian nationalism playbook, in which conspiratorial thinking reinforces an
idea of "us versus them." Cordileone once worked in the Vatican under Cardinal Raymond Burke, considered the leader of U.S. Catholic
traditionalists, who uses the same kind of language, for instance, when
he calls opposition to large-scale Muslim immigration "the responsible exercise of one's patriotism." Burke told a 2019 pro-life conference in Rome that Muslims would take over the United States because
"Christians are not reproducing themselves," a reference to contracep-
tive use.

As a young priest in Rome, Salvatore Cordileone studied canon
law, and in 1995 he was named as assistant at the Supreme Tribunal
of the Apostolic Signatura, the Church's highest court, led by Burke.
When Cordileone was named a bishop in 2002, Burke presided as co-
consecrator at his investiture in San Diego, Cordileone's hometown.
In 2009, Raymond Burke became one of the most powerful church-
men in Rome when Pope Benedict XVI promoted him to lead the
Congregation for Bishops, which virtually determines the selection of
new prelates all over the world. When Benedict resigned in 2013 and
Francis took over, however, the new pope demoted him.

Pope Francis is a champion of the reforms of the Vatican II council
meant to bring the Church into the modern world, emphasizing mercy
over judgment, while Burke, a strict constructionist who is among the
most conservative U.S. bishops, considers that Vatican II brought "a
loss of respect for church law," even "chaos"; he prefers the pre-council
ritual in Latin, which the pope discourages. Burke and the new pontiff are oil and water. Just before his demotion, the cardinal reinforced
his reputation as a culture warrior, saying of Pope Francis: "One gets
the impression, or it's interpreted this way in the media, that he thinks

we're talking too much about abortion, too much about the integrity of marriage as between one man and one woman. But we can never talk enough about that."

In 2018, when Archbishop Carlo Maria Viganò, the former pontifical vicar to the United States appointed by Benedict XVI, issued a public letter calling on Pope Francis to resign, Burke and Cordileone, along with Tulsa Bishop David Konderla, were among the first to support him. Without defending Pope Francis, or even mentioning him, Cordileone praised Viganò effusively, saying the archbishop had labored during his five-year (2011–16) Washington tenure "at great personal sacrifice and with absolutely no consideration given to furthering his 'career.'"

Today Cardinal Raymond Burke, who once served as archbishop of St. Louis, remains a leader among ultraconservative U.S. Catholics. It seems that Cordileone wants to be in his league. Both took advantage of the opportunity presented by COVID to posit Church authority against that of the state.

Before Burke came down with the virus in August 2021—he was on a ventilator for days at the Mayo Clinic and survived—he was an anti-vaxxer who said the government had nefarious intentions in distributing the vaccine: "There is a certain movement to insist that now everyone must be vaccinated against the coronavirus, and even that a kind of microchip needs to be placed under the skin of every person, so that at any moment, he or she can be controlled regarding health and regarding other matters, which we can only imagine as a possible object of control by the state," he said in a homily.

In November 2021, Cordileone, who had been saying Mass and distributing Holy Communion without a mask since the beginning of the pandemic, and shaking hands with the poor at free breakfasts, revealed that he wasn't vaccinated either. Pope Francis had long urged taking the vaccine as an "act of charity," or love for others, to prevent

the spread of the virus, and expressed impatience with those who refused. But Cordileone told the *San Francisco Chronicle*'s podcast *It's All
Political* that he considered getting the shot "a personal choice." His
own "immune system is strong," Cordileone told host Joe Garofoli,
with little apparent concern that, without vaccination, the archbishop
could carry the virus and infect others. If he felt symptoms, he would
stay home, he said, adding, incorrectly, that "people who are asymp-
tomatic can't spread it." Cordileone echoed the vaccine skepticism
championed by the far right. The vaccinations approved by the government to prevent the COVID-19 virus "are not really vaccines," he
said, again incorrectly, and followed with a non sequitur: "[The] shots
actually don't give any immunity at all. They give protection."

IN THE MEDIEVAL plague years there was no question of where
the ultimate social and political authority lay in Europe: the Roman
Catholic Church. Catholicism was the homogenous matrix of everyday life; for an ordinary person to doubt the logic or right intentions
of a consecrated hierarch was almost inconceivable. It would have
been like questioning the order of the known universe. COVID-19,
which has killed more than 6 million people globally since it was first
recognized in early 2020, is not the Black Death, which killed 75
million between 1347 and 1351 by conservative estimates. And the
Catholic Church today is not just separate from the state, it is only
one religion among many, albeit the largest single denomination in
the United States.

    Yet bishops like Cordileone, and laypeople who follow them, speak
as if we were still living in the fourteenth century, when religion was
hegemonic, and any given cleric was likely to be considered the font
of knowledge and truth. Today we know better than to trust our very
selves unquestioningly to our faith leaders, who themselves are only

human. And scientific facts are available for the asking, when they do not come in a torrent by way of the media. Ultraconservative Catholics fail greatly when they try to attribute blame for the pandemic on anything besides facts that can be scientifically proven.

This wasn't always the way. The sudden illness and death that came with the medieval plague—the ailing died overnight, a doctor arriving at a house might fall sick and expire before the patient he was treating—was so mysterious in its origins that some people were convinced by equally perplexed clerics that the infestation could only be punishment from an angry God, dissatisfied with a sinful people. History records processions of hundreds to plead for divine mercy, gatherings of prayerful multitudes that inadvertently spread the disease. In his *urbi et orbi* address at the beginning of the pandemic, when its mystery was greatest, Pope Francis, who studied science and began his adult life as a chemist, spoke not a word of just desserts or punishment, but instead, about the emergence of a moment for striving for a common good.

In the United States, however, conservative religious media beat a different drum. The news director of the Alabama-based Eternal Word Television Network (EWTN), Raymond Arroyo, entertained vaccination skeptics on his show, *The World Over*, reputed to be seen in 350 million homes across the globe. Arroyo's special "Papal Posse" segments feature critics of Pope Francis. In these, Arroyo sits in a dapper-looking suit and tie against a cityscape lit in the night, his dark hair combed back behind a receding hairline, asking guests about the pope's "mixed messaging" on themes such as abortion and communion, for instance (Francis opposes abortion, but does not support U.S. bishops who call for forbidding the Eucharist to Catholic politicians who support abortion). He nods sagely, or raises his eyebrows over a closed-mouth smile, at the comments of guests who may be pictured to his left and right, as if their opinions differed from their host's, which they do not. Sometimes Arroyo jumps in with answers to his own questions, which can be snide when commenting on the opinions of the pope.

For Arroyo during the COVID pandemic, those who received vaccinations were objects of derision. "[All] I see is people dancing and doing TikTok videos of themselves getting shot in the arm," Arroyo said early in the vaccination campaign, ridiculing people who were relieved to be living in less fear of the virus.

Another prominent voice in conservative media, R. R. Reno, the Catholic editor of the religious journal *First Things*, published by the Institute on Religion and Public Life—founded in 1989 "to confront the ideology of secularism"—seemed to jump back seven hundred years in thought during the height of the pandemic when he suggested it was a mistake to give priority to life on earth by masking up and going into lockdown. Instead, we should give priority to the everlasting life that is ours when we die. The response to our twenty-first century plague, Reno suggested, is coming from a confused disquiet that marks our modern civilization. "There are many things more precious than life," he wrote, criticizing politicians who waged "an ill-conceived crusade against human finitude and the dolorous reality of death."

STOP THE VACCINE. SAVE A BABY.

CATHOLICS ARE EXPECTED to regard all life as sacred. They campaign against capital punishment and abortion, and on behalf of the poor and the environment. Of these key issues, Catholic leaders in the United States, more than any other country, are obsessed—there is no other word—with abortion. That preoccupation during the COVID pandemic linked them to evangelical Christians in a special way, providing a primary reason to war against the COVID shots: a fetal cell line that originated in an abortion fifty years ago was used in creating the serum. Those Catholics who militated against Pope Francis anyway were further reinforced in their defiance of him because Francis encouraged vaccination.

In November 2020, when news had broken that COVID-19 vaccines were imminent, Joseph Brennan, bishop of 1 million Catholics in the 35,000-square-mile Diocese of Fresno, California, warned the faithful not to "jump on the vaccine bandwagon." The origin of the shots was morally unacceptable, he said in a widely publicized video. The Church disagreed. Cells derived from elective abortions have been used since the 1960s to manufacture vaccines, including today's vaccines against rubella, chicken pox, hepatitis A, and shingles. They have also been used to make drugs against diseases including hemophilia, rheumatoid arthritis, and cystic fibrosis. The Congregation for the Doctrine of the Faith, the Vatican office responsible for safeguarding the doctrine on faith and morals, said Catholics should seek "ethically irreproachable Covid-19 vaccines" when available, but that the vaccines in general, especially given the life-and-death situation presented by COVID, were "morally acceptable." In a television interview in January, Pope Francis said, "I believe that, ethically, everyone has to get the vaccine." It was important for the common good. Not to do so, he said, was "suicidal."

Less than three weeks after Bishop Brennan's "bandwagon" warning, he apologized for "confusion" caused by his remarks, differentiating himself from rightists like Cordileone, Burke, and others who never sought to deny or clarify their false pronouncements. The Pfizer and Moderna vaccines were permissible, Bishop Brennan said, because they used "illicit materials" only to a small extent in their testing phase, not in their development or composition. He repeated the view already hammered out by the National Catholic Bioethics Center, considered conservative, and the Vatican: the person who gets the shot is an end user "far removed" from the original "moral evil of abortion." Brennan didn't say so, but dozens of over-the-counter products found in medicine cabinets today such as Tylenol, Tums, Benadryl, Claritin, and Maalox used the same decades-old fetal cell lines as the COVID vaccines did during research. On December 10, Brennan gave the green light in California's agricultural heartland: Catholics could get their shots in good conscience.

Four months later, in March 2021, the chairman of the United States Conference of Catholic Bishops (USCCB) Committee on Doctrine, Bishop Kevin C. Rhoades of Fort Wayne, Indiana, made it official. "All the COVID vaccines recognized as clinically safe and effective can be used . . . there's no more need to turn down a vaccine," Rhoades said in a YouTube video.

Ultrarightists, however, stood by falsehoods they had popularized. After Cardinal Burke survived the virus, he never suggested that vaccination might be a good idea after all, or expressed regret that he missed taking the shots. He thanked Our Lady of Guadalupe for a miracle. He never withdrew his assessment that the "mysterious Wuhan virus . . . [was] used by certain forces, inimical to families and to the freedom of states, to advance their evil agenda."

The stick-to-your-guns attitude was not limited to hierarchy, but maintained among a number of ordinary parish priests who, of course, could look to the rightist bishops for affirmation. Take Rev. Michael Panicali, who attended the Stop the Steal (Save America) rally on January 6, 2021, in Washington, D.C., with other "prayerful people" and "patriots," as he told his local diocesan newspaper. Nine months later, the Brooklyn priest stood in the white marble pulpit at St. Mark Roman Catholic Church, telling the congregation, "You are under absolutely no obligation to take a vaccine that is made, produced, manufactured, tested even in the most remote ways with aborted, fetal cells. Do not let anyone tell you otherwise."

TOGETHER IN RESISTANCE

STANDS LIKE THAT of Panicali aligned alt-right Catholics with radical Christian evangelicals who condemn abortion to the point of rejecting vaccines, blame evil spirits for COVID-19, and call loudly upon prayer to combat the virus because only God, not vaccines invented by man, can beat the devil.

Throughout the pandemic, the popular evangelical religious broadcaster Marcus Lamb promoted the views on the global Christian broadcasting network he owned, Daystar, one of the largest of its kind in the world. Lamb, born in Cordele, Georgia, trim and vibrant in his sixties, with salt-and-pepper hair and a chinstrap beard and always nattily dressed, used his practiced powerful delivery to tell millions of viewers over the months, falsely, that vaccines were "killing your immune system." Instead of the shots, he said, "we can pray, we can get ivermectin and budesonide and hydroxychloroquine," thus recommending, in order, an anti-parasitic used for animals; a treatment for Crohn's disease, a condition in which the body attacks the lining of the digestive tract; and a medication used against malaria caused by mosquito bites. The CDC and the Food and Drug Administration warned against using these products against the virus. As Lamb lay struggling with terminal COVID-19 in 2021 (he died on November 30), his son Jonathan said on Daystar that his father's condition was due to an evil force angered because the elder Lamb promoted alternatives to the vaccine. "There's no doubt in my mind that this is a spiritual attack from the enemy," said Jonathan Lamb. "And he's doing everything he can to take down my dad."

As COVID raged, Fr. Panicali, Cardinal Burke, the evangelical Protestant Daystar network, and other far-right religious voices mixed spirituality with fear in the same way and promoted theories about conspiracies against Christians. Cordileone had played upon Catholic fear of being attacked as a moral minority by a "godless" municipal cabal in his "Free the Mass" homily. Archbishop Viganò authored yet another public letter, this one arguing that the pandemic was being exploited by evil forces in order to create a one-world government, cautioning that an "odious technological tyranny" would "allow centuries of Christian civilization to be erased under the pretext of a virus."

Religious vaccine skeptics and those who claimed a pandemic plot against believers, whether concocted by the government or the devil, reinforce the Christian nationalism movement. Centered on the belief that God intended America to be a Christian nation, both radical-right Catholics and evangelical Protestants are adherents. They claim the current U.S. political and administrative system is not that of a Christian nation, but an excessively secular one, and do what they can—what they feel they must—to undermine it. During the pandemic, this meant stirring resistance against federal and local health mandates and the distribution of vaccines.

Sometimes bishops used Catholic precepts to exert their authority over government regulations that limited numbers at houses of worship, shaming the faithful who were being cautious about gathering with others to sing and pray. For Catholics, Sunday Mass is an obligation; many clergy opted to follow health guidelines by televising or live-streaming services, but others did not, or stopped remote masses after a few weeks or months. By September 2020, Milwaukee's archbishop Jerome Listecki had had enough, even though the number of virus cases, and deaths, continued unabated. He told his flock in ten counties that physically missing Sunday Mass was a sin, and that "fear of getting sick, in and of itself, does not excuse someone from the obligation." The proclamation left Catholics in the difficult position of deciding whether to protect their health in a crowd—though Listecki said social distancing and masks were advised—or knowingly committing an offense against God. The elderly and "those caught up in the grips of fear" might be excused, Listecki said, as if caution in the face of COVID were a weakness.

Listecki's brother bishop in Springfield, Illinois, Thomas John Paprocki, who had been vaccinated, said other Catholics may refuse the shots based on the right to freedom of conscience. He, too, declared that Sunday Mass in person was not optional. But Paprocki went a step further. He allowed worshippers to attend Mass without face coverings. Immediately after Illinois governor J. B. Pritzker, with COVID surging, issued an indoor mask mandate, Paprocki said, "The obligation to attend Holy Mass on Sundays and holy days of obligation is paramount since eternal life is the most important consideration," allowing no exception for those who objected to exposing themselves to unmasked fellow worshippers.

PANDEMIC LOCKSTEP: CONSERVATIVE BISHOPS AND THE SUPREME COURT

WHILE COVID CONTINUED to spread in the late spring and summer of 2020, the Supreme Court considered cases that were important for churchgoers. California and Nevada had temporarily limited the number of people allowed at houses of worship, and the Supreme Court approved. Chief Justice John Roberts, in the majority, said that elected authorities—not unelected judges—must have the flexibility to make decisions about public health, drawing on medical expertise. The pandemic restrictions of the two states appeared "consistent with the free exercise clause of the First Amendment," Roberts wrote.

When Justice Ruth Bader Ginsburg died in September, things changed. Even before Ginsburg was buried, President Trump met with the conservative Catholic law school professor Amy Coney

Barrett and decided to name her as Ginsburg's replacement. Going forward, Supreme Court decisions on church attendance during the pandemic might have been written by rightist bishops themselves.

Roman Catholic Diocese of Brooklyn v. Andrew M. Cuomo was one of Barrett's first cases. The new justice joined the other two Trump appointees, Neil Gorsuch and Brett Kavanaugh, and veteran court conservatives Samuel Alito and Clarence Thomas to reverse the previous COVID church-attendance cases. Concurring with the majority, Gorsuch, like the other justices, ignored the particular risks of indoor religious gatherings—proximity of worshippers singing and praying aloud—while his aggrieved-sounding language echoed precisely the voice of Archbishop Cordileone at his "Free the Mass" event.

"At least according to the Governor, it may be unsafe to go to church, but it is always fine to pick up another bottle of wine, shop for a new bike, or spend the afternoon exploring your distal points and meridians," the justice wrote. "The only explanation for treating religious places differently seems to be a judgment that what happens there just isn't as 'essential' as what happens in secular spaces."

New COVID-era cases would be decided in favor of religious petitioners who wanted relaxed limits on indoor attendance, virus or no virus.

RUN, BISHOP, RUN

JUST AS SUPREME Court justices are not supposed to allow politics to affect their legal decisions, bishops are not supposed to politicize their guidance to the faithful. Bishops, too, can be opinion leaders, especially in times of crisis like the pandemic. They write commentaries in *The New York Times* and *The Washington Post*, publish their own columns in diocesan media, appear on Catholic and non-

Catholic media. Tradition and the official U.S. bishops' conference, the USCCB, hold that Catholics should involve themselves in civic life, but also that clergy do not tell the faithful how to vote or engage in political affairs. Instead, as the conference says in its official resource on citizenship, "Our purpose is to help Catholics form their consciences in accordance with God's truth." It is a noble sentiment often honored in the breach.

One way conservative bishops may get around expressing overtly political opinions is by condoning the words of others. Bishop Joseph Strickland of Tyler, Texas, is a paragon of the form.

In 2020, Strickland supported a youthful-looking rabble-rouser from Wisconsin, Rev. James Altman, pastor of St. James the Less Parish in La Crosse. Trained as a lawyer, Altman had been misleading his congregation about the COVID vaccine and promoting Republican Party positions. His bishop, William Callahan of La Crosse, warned Altman to stand down, but from one thousand miles away in Texas, Joe Strickland undermined the La Crosse prelate by giving Altman his seal of approval.

"Do not be anyone's guinea pig," said one of Altman's parish bulletins. Amid listings of Mass times, usher assignments, and ads from local businesses, a stark alert warned: "God is still the best doctor and prayer is still the best medicine." Altman played upon the Christian nationalism tropes of fear and distrust of government. "If the Injection actually worked, the Godless powers would not have to mislead nor threaten you to take it," the bulletin said. Altman called the anti-COVID shots "an experimental use of a genetic altering substance that modifies YOUR BODY—YOUR Temple of the Holy Spirit. It is NOT a vaccine, and the use of that word bears False Witness to the Truth."

This was not the first time Rev. James Altman provoked attention. During the presidential campaign of 2020, he made a slick video that went viral, proclaiming that "you cannot be a Catholic and be a Democrat." He praised Donald Trump, "a pro-life President with a Catholic wife," for his "ideas on national sovereignty and national borders." The ten-minute performance, with shots of Altman perorating before a backlit crucifix, cut between beauteous scenes of mountains, clouds, and the art deco statue of Christ the Redeemer above Rio de Janeiro, unrolled to the music of Beethoven's Symphony No. 7 in A Major, op. 92. It received more than 1.3 million views. The video also trashed Black Lives Matter, DACA recipients—the young people brought illegally to the country as babies who are trying to regularize their status—and maligned, by name, the first African American cardinal, Wilton Gregory of Washington, D.C., for failing to denounce abortion as a war against Black births.

Bishop Strickland reached out to his 58,000 Twitter followers to support the Wisconsin priest. "As the Bishop of Tyler I endorse Fr Altman's statement in this video," Strickland wrote. "My shame is that it has taken me so long. Thank you Fr Altman for your COURAGE. If you love Jesus & His Church & this nation . . . pleases HEED THIS MESSAGE."

Bishops may disagree with each other, but it is out of bounds for one diocesan prelate, like Strickland, to openly question how another, like the La Crosse bishop, disciplines his own clergy. That is effectively what Strickland did with his support for Altman, who refused his own bishop's request to resign. Altman hired a canon lawyer to defend his cause. At a procession of Altman admirers, Rev. Richard Heilman, a regular on podcasts of the military-themed right-wing Catholic group United States Grace Force, compared the "courageous" priest to the Allied soldiers who landed at Normandy.

In July 2021, Altman was removed from his parish, his priestly functions suspended. Almost immediately, he began a countrywide speaking spree, giving interviews to right-wing Catholic media, attending the high-end annual Napa Institute meeting of big-name conservative Catholics, and headlining a Michigan event organized by the radical Catholic group Church Militant. In Dallas, he offered a blessing to the powerful Conservative Political Action Conference (CPAC). As a lead-in to a speech by President Trump, Altman prayed, "So now and always, let us realize our help is in the name of the Lord, who actually did make heaven and earth, and that's all the science we need to know."

Other priests have openly doubted the vaccines and said that Catholics cannot in good conscience vote for Democrats because their party platform supports abortion. But for sheer showmanship, Altman beats all. He raised $650,000 from supporters on Catholic crowdfunding sites, enough to buy a new house in the La Crosse diocese, donate $100,000 to an organization called the Coalition for Canceled Priests, and have cash left over for legal fees. In continuing videos and appearances, he called the insurrection of January 6 a "false flag operation," accused Pope Francis of betraying God "like Judas," termed mask wearers "Godless vermin," and said the Jews of Warsaw brought the Holocaust upon themselves by failing to fight against abortion.

Fr. James Altman "is in trouble for speaking the truth," Strickland tweeted in May 2021. "I continue to support him for speaking the truth in Jesus Christ. He inspires many to keep the faith during these dark days."

NAMED TO THE episcopacy in 2012 by Pope Benedict XVI, Joseph Strickland stood out at first because he was a jogger, and savvy about media, with a blog called *RunFatherRun*. Announcing the appointment, Vatican Radio described the Fredericksburg, Texas, native as being on the cutting edge of U.S. clerics, "one of North America's new generation of blogging priests."

The silver-haired Strickland, who maintains the runner's lean frame in his sixties, first jumped into the rightist limelight by supporting someone who used even more radical language than he did in 2018. That was when Viganò, the former papal nuncio to the United States, falsely accused Pope Francis of covering up sex abuse charges of a ranking cardinal and demanded the pope resign. Within hours Strickland wrote a statement of support for Viganò—not the pope—and ordered it distributed at all the Masses in his diocese. Soon after, Strickland said Pope Francis's acceptance of civil unions for gay couples was only an "opinion," and called the pope "dangerous" for saying so. In 2020, Bishop Strickland threw in his lot with many Church rightists when he began celebrating the Traditional Latin Mass (TLM), which is discouraged by Pope Francis and not the norm in Catholic churches, but a hallmark of traditionalist practice. The bishop admitted that he had never learned how to offer the Mass in Latin in seminary, but only recently had decided to take it up. (Altman also celebrated the TLM in La Crosse.)

With the coming of COVID-19, Bishop Strickland joined radical evangelical anti-vaxxers, and ultraconservative bishops like Cordileone, in resisting the recommendations of health authorities. On Twitter, he established a kind of ongoing anti-vaccine theology in 280 characters at a time. "ANY vaccine available today involves using murdered children before they could even be born," said one tweet. Vaccine mandates, he told the YouTube interviewer Rev. Mark Goring, take away "our God-given freedom to make those choices for ourselves." Strickland compared his mandate resistance to the refusal of sixteenth-century philosopher Thomas More to recognize Henry VIII as leader of the Church of England, which would mean denying the pope. Thomas More, executed for treason, his head set on a pike, is revered by Catholics as a saint.

All the people shall shout with a great shout, and the wall of the city shall fall down flat, and the people shall ascend up every man straight before him.

—Joshua 6:5, on the destruction of Jericho

BISHOP JOSEPH STRICKLAND has also backed personalities who spout the language of the QAnon conspiracy. Adherents believe the claims of an anonymous, Bible-quoting "Q," who began to drop social media messages in 2017 claiming that a cabal of Satan-worshipping, cannibalistic members of a world elite operate a global child sex-trafficking ring and conspire against Donald Trump, who will one day defeat them. A 2021 Public Religion Research Institute survey determined that a quarter of white evangelicals and Mormons (and 16 to 17 percent of Catholics) believe in the conspiracy. QAnon posits a "deep state" network of government, finance, and industry figures that operates secretly against Trump's agenda; connections of some of the conspiracy's followers with violence, including at the Capitol on January 6, 2021, have led the FBI to consider them a domestic terrorist threat.

QAnon believers attack COVID as a hoax, and malign COVID vaccines as a "deep state" form of control. The lead speaker at a 2021 QAnon conference in Las Vegas, For God & Country: Patriot Double Down, drew Bishop Strickland's attention. Jim Caviezel, the Catholic actor who played Jesus Christ in Mel Gibson's controversial (for charges of anti-Semitism) 2004 film, *The Passion of the Christ*, spread lies about COVID, and denigrated the pope for what he called an attitude of liberal "appeasement."

"You can take our lives, but you can never take our freedom," Caviezel shouted, quoting a line from another Mel Gibson film, *Braveheart*.

Bishop Strickland praised the actor's eighteen-minute speech as

"HISTORIC," tweeting a link with a commendation: "All need to listen to this speech." An earlier anti-vaxxer gathering attended by Caviezel ended with burning a pyre of medical masks.

In May 2020, Strickland was the only U.S. bishop to condone a manifesto written by Archbishop Viganò that condemned obligatory mask wearing and other COVID measures. Viganò claimed that the rules had been levied to create "panic among the world's population with the sole aim of permanently imposing unacceptable forms of restriction on freedom." Anyway, the archbishop said, COVID wasn't that serious. There were "growing doubts . . . about the actual contagiousness, danger, and resistance of the virus."

Viganò also seems to have drunk the QAnon potion. He was once intimately connected to U.S. bishops as the pope's apostolic nuncio, and continues to be lionized in rightist Catholic media. The position he held in Washington, equivalent to the ambassador representing the Holy See, has been long respected as a unique diplomatic position linking U.S. Catholics and the Vatican. Appointed by Pope Benedict XVI, Viganò advised Benedict about U.S. episcopal candidates during the years that Benedict appointed conservatives like Strickland, Cordileone, and Michael Barber of Oakland, or elevated others to higher rank. Viganò remains a beacon for U.S. Catholics opposed to Pope Francis. He had considered his transfer from Rome to Washington as a kind of punishment for exposing corruption in the Vatican. Once he was in the United States, as theologian Massimo Faggioli, of Villanova University, told *TIME* magazine, Viganò spent time cultivating relationships with conservative American Catholics who oppose Pope Francis.

A LETTER VIGANÒ wrote to Trump in June 2020 used the jargon and memes of the QAnon conspiracy—"children of light" versus the "offspring of the Serpent," etc. He compared the alleged "deep state" to the supposed existence of a heretical "deep Church." The mysterious Q posted the Viganò letter to 8kun, a fringe social media site, and former Trump advisor Michael Flynn, who also uses QAnon language in public talks, tweeted it. Trump gave Viganò's followers a virtual embrace by retweeting the letter and saying he was "honored" by it. Viganò has since said COVID does not exist, and that the vaccination campaign is "Satanic action against God."

Christian nationalists who oppose COVID health measures and use conspiracy language are inevitably the same who support the claim that President Trump won the 2020 election. On December 12, 2020, Viganò and Strickland joined thousands of evangelical Christians, Catholics, and a few sympathetic Jews who gathered on the National Mall at a Stop the Steal rally called by the Christian group Jericho March to support the falsehood that Trump was robbed of reelection through fraud. The idea of the event was to recall the Biblical story of the Israelite army marching around the walled city of Jericho, then watching as God demolished the city's defenses so the Israelites could conquer. Participants marched around the Supreme Court seven times. The message: true believers would circle the corrupt institutions of the U.S. government, which spread the "hoax" that Trump lost the election, and the government with all its "deep state" would fall. Before a stage, the crowds cheered the words of one personality after another, including Michael Flynn and MyPillow CEO Mike Lindell, who laced their brief messages with prayer, and radio host Alex Jones, who did not.

On a mammoth screen set up before the throng to receive virtual participants by video links, Viganò explained the biblical Jericho story. When Bishop Strickland's turn came, he appeared in half profile gazing at a crucifix. His words of prayer were not partisan or inflammatory, but a blessing to a warm-up for the January 6 rally, which became the violent march on the Capitol.

On the day the mob attacked, the Jericho March website declared, "This is bigger than one election . . . This is about protecting free and fair elections for the future and saving America from tyranny." While much of America reacted in shock to images of rage and destruction at the Capitol, the Jericho March Twitter account sent out a screenshot of Trump condemning Vice President Mike Pence, who certified the Electoral College votes. It was a "sad day in America," said the tweet, bemoaning not the violence, but Pence's refusal to help Trump overturn the election.

It is tempting to regard Cordileone, Burke, Viganò, Altman, and the retweeting fellow traveler Bishop Strickland as clerics on the fringe, but they are provocative, and their regular exposure on big media like Fox News, and on conservative Catholic media, gives them an audience of millions. They are speaking to a population increasingly ready to believe conspiracy theories. Dr. Robert Pape, a professor of political science at the University of Chicago who specializes in national and international security affairs, has researched the records of more than seven hundred people arrested during the attack on the Capitol and determined that, far from fringe actors, the individuals moved to violence to "Stop the Steal" were decidedly "mainstream." Over half were business owners or held white-collar jobs, including as doctors, lawyers, and architects. About 25 percent had college degrees, and 15 percent had served in the military, not far from national percentages (30 percent and 10 percent respectively). They are the kind of folks likely to sit next to you in the pew.

For forty-eight hours before the January 6 riot, websites carried an interview with Viganò by former Trump strategist Steve Bannon, the alt-right Catholic culture warrior, who asked the archbishop what would happen if the United States failed to expose "now . . . the coordinated theft of our election?"

Viganò spoke unequivocally. The country, he said, would be "wiped out from history."

Comfort ye, comfort ye my people.

—Song of Solomon 40:1

OF ALL THE worldly tasks of ordained clergy and consecrated religious, attending the sick and the anguished must be among the greatest, for how often does a person turn to a padre or a favorite nun, seeking wisdom or at least solace in times of stress and hopelessness?

During the pandemic, stories emerged of clergymen risking their health, and sometimes dying after infection, to anoint COVID patients in extremis. Some Catholic bishops stretched rules on the last rites, which, by Church law, require proximity to the dying to touch the forehead with blessed oil. With COVID, where bishops allowed, a priest could administer the sacrament from beyond a door, or a Plexiglas shield, for instance. The nurse holds a phone to the patient's ear, the sick person's blood pressure goes down, and they die less isolated than they might be, the words of prayer—sometimes refashioned to include the names of loved ones who cannot be present—the last they hear.

This capacity to comfort, one might say the responsibility to provide peace and understanding to troubled souls, was particularly violated by bishops and clergy who split from Church counsel and papal example during the pandemic. They inspired fear and division instead, with misinformation. To the extent that such voices were motivated by opposition to Pope Francis, or beholden to an ultraconservative political vision that overwhelms common sense, they have been culpable at least of grievous dereliction of a basic duty, the shepherd's responsibility to care for his sheep.

Massimo Faggioli, the Villanova University professor of the history of Christianity, moved to the United States from Italy in 2008, during the campaign that led to the election of Barack Obama. "The intertwining of church and politics immediately caught my interest," said Faggioli in the introduction to one of his many books, *Joe Biden and Catholicism in the United States*. Faggioli became one of the preeminent analysts of specifically U.S. Catholicism, interpreting it for a wide audience in the United States and abroad. Teaching at Villanova, he watched the COVID pandemic—and the U.S. bishops' reaction to it—unfold as he wrote for a host of Italian and pan-European publications, and, in English, for *Commonweal*, *La Croix International*, and *The Tablet* of London.

"One of the classical definitions of a bishop in Latin was *defensor civitatis*, which refers to one who is in charge of defending the community, especially in times of war, emergency and social political crisis," Faggioli told Brian Fraga, who has written often on the pandemic for the *National Catholic Reporter*. "That is something that seems to me many of them have lost." Faggioli suggests U.S. Catholic prelates came up short during the pandemic, failing to act while priests in their charge spread false information about vaccines. Many bishops encouraged cooperation with health care protocols, but others remained silent when their own brethren boosted conspiracy theories, as if they were affected not by prudential silence but by fear of speaking out in a politicized atmosphere. The USCCB as a group hardly took the lead in encouraging vaccination but said in a late 2020 statement, "In view of the gravity of the current pandemic and the lack of availability of alternative vaccines, the reasons to accept the new COVID-19 vaccines from Pfizer and Moderna are sufficiently serious to justify their use, despite their remote connection to morally compromised cell lines."

Americans' individualistic idea of freedom may have blurred the bishops' understandings of their role to defend the common good, said Faggioli. "The most serious problem is that they have forgotten what it means to be a bishop in the Catholic Church, which is different than being the corporate manager in a firm that is only interested in what's good for the firm. That has been astonishing to me."

IN JANUARY, 2022, Archbishop Cordileone traveled from San Francisco to New York to say a High Mass in Latin in Lower Manhattan's Old St. Patrick's Cathedral, which had been built in 1815, only a few years after the last colonial-era anti-Catholic laws were rescinded. The church might as well have been chosen as a symbol of the COVID-era defiance and defensiveness of Cordileone, who apparently still had not been vaccinated. To discourage nativist gangs who attacked early-nineteenth-century Catholics, the first parishioners of the old cathedral had holes punched in the wall surrounding the grounds where they could set muskets to defend life and property, should they come under attack.

For more than a century after the Old St. Patrick's wall went up, the nativist movement colloquially called the Know Nothings, men (mostly) who claimed a pureblooded pedigree of Protestant Anglo-Saxon stock, rejected, sometimes violently, all Catholics, and Catholics in general were suspect as being un-American, sidelined from shaping national policy. That all changed as Catholics grew in number, bishops during World War I united as a national body, and, after the mid-twentieth century, the political agendas of prominent Catholics like Paul Weyrich, William Simon, Leonard Leo, Clarence Thomas, and others overlapped with those of the most conservative U.S. bishops to make their marks on Catholic—and U.S.—history.

2

Christianizing America

The Roots of the Religious Right

A MIDWESTERNER WHOSE face and figure were so unremarkable he might disappear in a crowd, whose name is unknown to most Americans, did more than anyone else to create the radical U.S. religious right. Paul Weyrich, who died in 2008 at age sixty-six, lived and breathed politics but never held public office. He brought Catholics and white evangelical Protestants together as a voting bloc to support Christian principles but believed that the fewer people who voted in elections overall the better, because history showed that the broader the voter turnout, the less likely that conservative candidates and causes win. "I don't want everybody to vote," he told a gathering of pastors in 1980.

"Elections are not won by a majority of people. They never have been from the beginning of our country, and they are not now," Weyrich said, adumbrating voter repression efforts of the 2020s. Only certain people—those who agreed with him, who wanted to restore Christian values at the highest levels of government—should be encouraged to vote.

From the 1970s to the 2020s, laypeople, including billionaires, would serve the right-wing hierarchy's positions on homosexuality, contraception, abortion, and other issues in the public square. Weyrich began the critical collaboration, succeeding because he represented a perfect synergy of pious family background, the vision of a Christian nation, extraordinary persistence, and a remarkable talent for networking.

Weyrich and his successors generally (but not always, as in the 1980s) would work in tandem with the goals of the conference of U.S. bishops, which had come together as a group for the first time in 1917 to address great national issues affecting the U.S. Church. The bishops channeled funds, spiritual care, and other kinds of assistance to Catholic service members gone to the First World War, but at a time when Catholics were still outsiders, held in suspicion for their "foreign" ways in an Anglo-Saxon society, the new Catholic "war" council also was intended to show the country that Catholics were as loyal and patriotic as other Americans. (For the same reason, the fraternal organization, the Knights of Columbus, which had been underway since 1882, wrote to President Wilson immediately after war was declared, pledging the 400,000-member order's "determination to protect [the nation's] honor and its ideal of humanity and right.") By the 1920s the bishops had formed the National Catholic Welfare Conference to address concerns such as Catholic schools, immigration, and social action; in 2001 the bishops' welfare arm and its hierarchical secretariat were combined and called the United States Conference of Catholic Bishops (USCCB), which now meets twice a year. National meetings produce debate and voting on statements that present the bishops' vision of the U.S. Church and affairs that can be considered political—such as whether or not politicians who support the right to abortion should receive Holy Communion. In cases where the U.S. bishops' official view collides with the Vatican's—it did on the issue of Communion, which most U.S. bishops wanted to withhold from the offending politicians—the Vatican's view is preeminent; the pope is the ultimate arbiter. (The USCCB stepped back from passing a Communion ban for pro-abortion politicians after receiving a warning letter from the Vatican.)

At home, U.S. bishops oversee one of the biggest national Catholic infrastructures in the world. They run the largest network of private elementary and secondary schools in the country (with a high school graduation rate of 99 percent), open to all faiths (about 19 percent of students are non-Catholic), saving taxpayers who pay for public schools some $20 billion a year. These Catholic schools are good—about 85 percent of their secondary school grads go on to four-year colleges, compared to 44 percent of graduates of public schools. And Catholics run 233 colleges and universities, one out of eight in the world. They are prominent in U.S. health care, with one study showing that Catholic-owned or affiliated hospitals have grown 22 percent since 2001, many due to mergers, so that today one in six acute-care beds is in a hospital connected to the Church, generally beholden to strict USCCB health care directives.

Each bishop is the decision maker for his diocese, or region, answering only to the pope, not directly to the USCCB, which is less a final arbiter with authority per se than the most high-power association of the U.S. Church. Its stands and statements are disseminated among the faithful. For Catholics and, insofar as its influence affects national policy, for non-Catholics, the USCCB matters. It represents the closest thing to a national consensus among Catholic clerical leaders, and serves as the lobbying arm of the U.S. Church in Washington.

RESPONDING TO EFFORTS to legalize abortion in the 1950s and 1960s, the U.S. Catholic bishops oversaw the beginnings of the anti-abortion movement that would be a driving force of Paul Weyrich's early political life. Originally the so-called "pro-life" campaign was carried out almost exclusively by Catholic religious orders and community groups; in 1968 the U.S. conference of bishops formalized their campaign by creating the National Right to Life Committee (NRLC), the first of its kind in modern times. For years, the NRLC provided model legislation to state and national lawmakers on pro-life issues, and eventually grew to have chapters in all fifty states. After the *Roe v. Wade* case guaranteed a constitutional right to abortion, the NRLC became one of the most important national organizations lobbying for its reversal.

Catholics were supportive of the early bishops' campaign, but they were not a majority force in the country, and the abortion cause did not draw broad attention beyond the Church. Weyrich brought the bishops' agenda into the public sphere. He personifies, writ large, what would become a long line of lay-Catholic activists in league with the most conservative Catholic prelates.

Weyrich's master stroke was to unite the political trajectory of Catholic bishops with that of leaders of evangelical Christians, denominations that had long avoided each other when they didn't disdain each other as enemies. One issue at a time over the next fifty years—gay rights, education, "religious freedom," and more—the New Religious Right aimed to impress Christian values as they saw them on everyone in America. Weyrich sparked the powerful union by drawing upon traditional Catholic beliefs and a view that the world was best served by patriarchy, values in which he was steeped from the earliest years of his life.

Born in Racine, Wisconsin in 1942, young Paul grew up in the pious household of a German immigrant father, Ignatius, whose job was firing the boiler at a local Catholic hospital, where he had met Virginia, a nurse's aide, who was to become Paul's mother. Ignatius

Weyrich taught his son to take religion seriously—sometimes he corrected their parish priest after Mass on perceived errors in interpretation of Church doctrine. An only child, Paul once told an interviewer that by the age of five, he knew the names of U.S. cabinet members by heart, because his parents took politics seriously too.

"My father used to say, in America they say that you shouldn't talk religion and politics. But one determines your temporal life, and the other determines your eternal life. What else is there to talk about?"

Paul Weyrich would take his father as a model of the patriarch, a positive exemplar who was not only the indisputable head of the family "but also the conduit through which the family interacts with the rest of society," in the words of the academic Chelsea Ebin, who pored over Weyrich's archives to write of his religious roots. There was plenty of material, Ebin wrote, as Weyrich seemed in a way obsessed by his own history, collecting ephemera, underlining his name every place it was published. The upshot of Weyrich's thought: the family, not government, should have the last word on how children are taught, how health care is managed, whom individuals might associate with—anything else encroaches on the purview of the patriarch, whose authority comes from God. Accepting social welfare from the state was out of the question.

When Paul was just eleven, his father took him by train to visit Washington, D.C., the place for which his mother believed he was destined, "and wanted me to be acquainted with as soon as possible," Weyrich recalled in a 2005 interview with Brian Lamb of C-SPAN. He returned at age seventeen as a member of a Young Republican club, already marked by the diligence and single-mindedness about politics as a tool to achieve the goals he believed were best for the country. The occasion was a series of trainings for aspiring party operatives, and Weyrich has said he was thrilled to meet Vice President Nixon and Barry Goldwater, "my hero." Most of the young Republicans "came for a good time . . . the cocktail parties and things," he told Lamb, but he went to the sparsely attended "seminars on how you get elected." Weyrich was a young man in a hurry. By age twenty-two, he had dropped out of college, started a journalism career managing a radio station, married, and started a family; in 1966, at twenty-four, true to his mother's prediction, he was off to Washington, serving as press secretary for Republican U.S. Senator Gordon Allott of Colorado.

In the 1960s, Weyrich had short, blond hair with a straight side part and wore thick, horn-rimmed glasses as he went about his business on Capitol Hill while the country around him reverberated with demands to implement civil rights, resistance to the U.S. war in Vietnam, and spreading use of the birth control pill, which was giving women the most powerful tool in history to control their own lives, making sexual freedom possible, not to say allowing them to challenge patriarchy—the value Weyrich held in such high esteem—as the ordering principle of society.

FIGHTING THE "FRESH AIR" OF VATICAN II

AT THE SAME time, changes in the Catholic Church were challenging the traditionalist view of the faith that informed everything Weyrich believed. The Second Vatican Council shook him to the core. The term "traditionalist" or "traditional Catholic" would come into use only after the council—before the 1960s Catholics were simply "Catholics," or sometimes "ex-Catholics"—sometimes referring to those who rejected conciliar changes—and Weyrich personified the traditionalist Catholic.

In 1959, Pope John XXIII called the landmark conference of the world's bishops to "open the windows and let in the fresh air," to break down the walls that the two-thousand-year old institution had erected around itself since the time of the Reformation. After Vatican II, popes and bishops would engage with the modern world while abjuring any part in its governing. The Church would no longer aspire to political power, renouncing support for "confessional states" in which citizens were expected or encouraged to abide by a set of principles of a certain religion or confession, namely Catholic. Theocracy was out; rather, said the council document *Gaudium et Spes (Joy and Hope): Pastoral Constitution on the Church in the Modern World*, the Catholic Church would be a moral beacon, unafraid to stand by its principles, to attempt to clarify the important issues of the day as it saw them, but to remain separate from the state. The most traditionalist Catholics, Weyrich among them, resisted the change, believing moral issues should be at the center of politics.

In 1970, Weyrich wrote an open letter chastising Hawaii governor John A. Burns after the governor signed a bill legalizing abortion, attacking a statement by Burns, who said that he "never let his private political and religious convictions unduly influence his judgment as governor of the people." Weyrich made it clear in the letter that he believed the United States was shaped from the beginning by religious faith. "As I read your remarks I could not help but think back to the men who founded America, and those through the years who made her a great nation," Weyrich wrote. "Had these men not been influenced by God's laws, by their religious training and by their personal political convictions, I hesitate to think of reading an American history book today."

Another Vatican II change struck traditionalist Catholics like Weyrich as wrong: the Church would reach out to believers of other faiths with the aim of restoring the unity of all Christians—ecumenism—and recognize that God's "saving design" extended to all, including non-Christians. Religious freedom was a fundamental right—people had a choice of beliefs, indeed "a choice to choose God or not." If this weren't upsetting enough to ultratraditional Catholics, the council fathers decided that the Holy Mass, the central rite of the faith, would no longer be in Latin, an elite and mysterious (to many) tongue, the language of priests and the hierarchy. From then on Mass should be celebrated in the languages of the faithful, wherever they are.

For Weyrich and other traditionalists, Mass in the vernacular was an attack on Catholic sacred identity. For a while, he attended the Traditional Latin Mass (TLM) where it still could be found, but, at age twenty-six, he took his family to join the Byzantine Slavonic Rite, which the Vatican recognizes as a sister church in communion with the pope, although it maintains its liturgy in Greek, which Weyrich found more resonant with his sense of the sacred. He stood against the modern Roman Catholic Church, just as he stood against social changes percolating in U.S. society.

Paul Weyrich and his allies among traditional Catholics would also defy the position of Vatican II against confessional states by aspiring to make America a Christian nation. He doubled down on faith issues as he saw them. Rejecting the ecumenism promoted at the council, Weyrich and other ultraconservative Catholics called for disciplining a Catholic priest who joined an Episcopal church prayer and communion service the night Martin Luther King, Jr., was assassinated, on grounds that praying among non-Catholics was heretical, a "worship of false gods." He opposed busing to desegregate public schools on the grounds it violated parental choice. He joined with presidential advisors Patrick Buchanan and Connaught "Connie" Marshner, both also traditionalist Catholics, to secure President Nixon's veto of a federal day care law that might have taken a burden off working mothers—trusting the formation of young children to strangers was too risky. Nixon said he would not commit "the vast moral authority of the national Government to the side of communal approaches to childrearing over and against the family centered approach."

* * *

KEEPING WOMEN IN their place, especially limiting their reproductive freedom, was fundamental to Weyrich's political development, just as it marks the religious right today. At a time when the birth control pill was newly giving women control over reproduction, separating sex from the risk of pregnancy, he campaigned against contraception, including government support for birth control. At the time he was a spokesperson for Catholics United for the Faith (CUF), founded in 1968, which saw itself as a community of lay defenders of tradition, hierarchy, and the papal teaching that intercourse must be open to procreation. For the CUF and Weyrich, as the scholar Ebin suggests, "'tradition' likely meant social patriarchy, as represented by the nuclear family and traditional gender roles and norms, and 'hierarchy' extended to a husband's dominion over his wife."

Weyrich understood that more was needed to create a serious political force that might change the overall direction of the country toward Christian precepts; he could not proceed piecemeal, one issue at a time. To achieve his vision of a patriarchal Christian state he needed idea factories, wealthy activists, trained operatives, networks of like-minded people with connections in government. All these he achieved in relatively short time in a furious period of founding institutions and networks that affect conservative politics to this day.

In a 1984 book Weyrich edited with Marshner, *Future 21: Directions for America in the 21st Century*, Weyrich gave hints about the parts of his worldview that may have inspired this high-energy spell of organization-building. For one, Weyrich did not see the conservative political movement of which he was a part in conventional terms, as if existing policy entities might not be adequate to answer its demands, but characterized it as "variously called the New Right, the Religious Right, the traditional-values movement." Also, and importantly, he wrote, "Moral problems are at the root of growing dissatisfaction with life in the United States," and he focused on "bureaucracy" as a moral issue, "possibly as important a moral issue as abortion and school prayer, because of the ways it affects the lives of so many of us." If government and industry were riddled with "bureaucracy," as he claimed, forcing people to have short-sighted goals of keeping individual bailiwicks in existence rather than looking at the big picture of the common good, Weyrich, compelled by moral issues as part of his Catholic upbringing, must "cut the federal bureaucracy down to size," which government was not doing, and his groups might address this immoral, bureaucratic "tragedy." The alternative to bureaucracy was allegiance to a "corporative" institution "that helps promote moral instead of immoral behavior," such as, historically, the Catholic Church. Catholic bishops and clergy didn't consider their work as mere "jobs," Weyrich averred, but as "a *calling*" (his italics) in which the "clergyman was expected to accomplish the goals of the Church, to express and further its values, in everything he did." The more that institutions, including government and the military, operated like a "corporative" institution with shared values, the better for all, and Weyrich and his colleagues were just the ones, they believed, to elaborate what these values must be.

So successful was Weyrich's early whirlwind of political activity that another notable conservative, Grover Norquist, founder of Americans for Tax Reform, said, "Most of the successes of the Conservative movement since the 1970s flowed from structures, organizations, and coalitions [Weyrich] started, created or nurtured."

- In 1973, Weyrich established the Heritage Foundation, a think tank charged with producing studies for Congress specifically aimed at influencing members to vote conservative on proposed legislation. He raised the money for this effort from millionaire brewing magnate Joseph Coors, Sr. (also a backer of the far-right John Birch Society), whom Weyrich knew from his days as a newsman in Denver, from Richard Scaife of Mellon family wealth, and from other rich people looking for ways to influence Congress. The foundation also developed lists of recommended cabinet appointees and preferred names for other high offices used by Republican presidents.

- In the same year, Weyrich, working with Henry Hyde of Illinois, who would become a powerful Republican U.S. congressman for thirty-two years (1975–2007) and Republican political activist Lou Barnett, created the American Legislative Exchange Council (ALEC), a corporate bill mill that provides wish lists and model legislation drafted by insiders from oil, mining, finance, big pharmacy, gun manufacturers, and other industries, and presents them to partner members of state legislatures to rubber stamp. ALEC, in a multimillion-dollar operation (companies pay to play), now produces several hundred new bills each year on issues including deregulation of major industries, crimping climate change initiatives, voter ID laws, and methods to limit voting and unions. Many become law.

- In 1973, Weyrich instigated formation of the Republican Study Committee to promote the archconservative voices in the party over moderates among members of the House of Representatives. Today it is the largest ideological faction in Congress, its online brief advising, "We believe that more government is the problem, not the solution."

- In 1974, Weyrich founded the Committee for the Survival of a Free Congress, later called the Free Congress Foundation (FCF) as a counterweight to perceived domination of Congress by liberal groups, especially labor. The FCF produces policy papers and says it trains political activists in "guerrilla tactics to undermine the legitimacy of the dominant regime." The watch-dog Anti-Defamation League identified the FCF as part of an alliance of more than fifty of the most prominent conservative Christian leaders and organizations that threatened the separation of church and state. TheocracyWatch, a nonprofit research group run by the Center for Religion, Ethics and Social Policy at Cornell University, lists the foundation as a "leading example of dominionism," the belief that God desires Christians to rise to power in secular institutions so that their understanding of biblical law might govern the nation.

- In 1981, with conservative fundraiser Richard Viguerie and presidential advisor Morton Blackwell, Weyrich began a secretive group of high-worth individuals that aimed to maximize ultraright influence on the Reagan administration, the Council for National Policy (CNP). Its periodic unpublicized meetings continue at luxurious venues, with principals or representatives of the country's wealthiest companies like Charles Koch, and well-connected activists like Ginni Thomas, wife of the Supreme Court justice Clarence Thomas. A video in 2020 shows CNP executive committee chairman Bill Walton telling attendees before that year's presidential elections that "this is a spiritual battle we are in. This is good versus evil."

- In 1983 Weyrich established what became known as the Weyrich Lunch, a weekly, off-the-record Wednesday meeting of well-connected conservatives to brainstorm new ideas with Republican emissaries from Capitol Hill and the White House. With as many as eighty people at the table, power brokers or those who want to reach them, the lunch has become a Washington institution.

Years after this flurry of organization-building by Weyrich, an organization called the Napa Institute, established in 2011 by businessman Tim Busch in collaboration with right-wing bishops like José Gomez of Los Angeles and former Denver archbishop Charles J. Chaput, would carry the most conservative prelates' agenda to the wealthiest donors, Catholic and non-Catholic. And traditionalist Catholic laypeople like Leonard Leo of the Federalist Society, Domino's pizza king Tom Monaghan, and others would make sure the agenda was present in the courts of the land. But in the beginning, it was Paul Weyrich, with his single-minded vision of what the Christian country should be, who set the course for marriage of the U.S. bishops and the political religious right.

FAITH AND POLITICS: TYING THE KNOT

IN 1967, U.S. bishops held a series of meetings that marked the beginning of abortion as a Catholic political issue. They had always been against abortion, but by the late 1960s some states were liberalizing their laws against the procedure. The bishops became alarmed at the rise of pro-choice sentiment when the American Law Institute, an independent association of eminent lawyers, judges, and academics founded in 1923 to produce scholarly work "to clarify, modernize, and otherwise improve the law," published a revision to its Model Penal Code that called for liberalizing the laws on abortion at the state level. The institute was among the most highly regarded associations of its kind, its counsel often seriously taken into account. The bishops felt compelled to react. They lobbied for a constitutional amendment that might apply everywhere in the country "to protect the unborn."

By election season in 1976 the bishops were issuing statements that

appeared to favor Republican incumbent candidate Gerald Ford for
the presidency over Democrat Jimmy Carter, not because Carter was
an evangelical, born-again Christian, but because Carter, although he
had declared himself strongly opposed to abortion on moral grounds,
did not favor proposals for a constitutional amendment to oppose it.

Voices among the bishops cautioned against giving the impression
that the right to life for which the Church stood was limited to the
highly politicized abortion issue, lest they be identified with a particular political party—Republicans—that added an anti-abortion plank
to their 1976 platform. The bishops' pro-life policy must be seen as
broader than that, dissenters warned, including issues of euthanasia,
capital punishment, peace and disarmament, and fair labor practices.
Chicago cardinal Joseph Bernardin, who opposed abortion, famously
said that nevertheless "the pro-life position of the church must be
developed in terms of a comprehensive and consistent ethic of life."

But a majority, led by Archbishop John O'Connor of New York,
who later would preside over the USCCB from 2010 to 2013, and
Boston archbishop Bernard Law, made abortion the central issue of
their policy agenda. Led by Archbishop Law, New England bishops
referred in a statement to voluntary termination of pregnancy as "the
holocaust of abortion." For the next fifty years, a majority of hierarchs
hewed ever more closely to the path of the ideologues on abortion, so
that U.S. bishops mixed faith and politics until they couldn't tell one
from the other.

Paul Weyrich had no problem with being identified with the
Republican Party, even when he thought it was not bold enough for
his purposes. To move ideological change as far to the right as possible, so the United States might become "again" a Christian nation,
he and ultrarightists set out to capture the party as a vehicle to achieve
their ends.

Two elements were key. Most strategic was an alliance with evangelical Protestants, who commanded large numbers—Weyrich was not above cherry-picking enforcement of his principles for the sake of pragmatism, so where he once abjured ecumenism to protest the murder of Dr. King, he would embrace ecumenism to bring millions of Christians into the religious political movement. And indispensable to party capture by religious rightists was the creation of an atmosphere that portrayed equal rights for women as a threat to the family. Paul Weyrich and ideological allies, led by traditionalist Catholics, would provide the architects, foot soldiers, and money for the anti-feminist campaign, and for the union of Catholics with fundamentalist evangelicals that would be called the Moral Majority.

> *We are talking about Christianizing America. We are talking about the Gospel in a political context.*
> —Paul Weyrich, to a gathering of the Southern Baptist Convention, Dallas,
> August 1980

AFTER THE 1976 elections, which Democrat Jimmy Carter won narrowly over Gerald Ford, hard-core conservatives were ready to leave the Republican Party, deeming it too timid to force the country to shed the New Deal infrastructure that allowed Washington to play a strong role in economic and social affairs. Weyrich and his associates took the long view, however, deciding to make the party an instrument of their movement. Their ranks swelled by veterans of the ill-fated 1964 presidential candidacy of Barry Goldwater, ultraconservatives like Weyrich no longer would fight for a few Republican platform concessions or even a one-time electoral victory. They intended to own the Grand Old Party.

"We are different from previous generations of conservatives,"

Weyrich told William J. Lanouette of the *National Journal* in 1978. "We are no longer working to preserve the status quo. We are radicals of this country." They were the "New Right," he said, focused on social issues, different from the Old Right with its concentration on economics and foreign policy and little to say about the way people led their personal lives. "The Old Right's 'live and let live' idea is not reflective of Christian social teachings," Weyrich wrote in an essay published in 1982. They aimed to build a movement that might reach fruition decades hence, when they expected it to encompass a majority of voters.

Soon, Weyrich's "radicals working to overturn the present power structure" would merge into something he had wanted from the beginning: the New Religious Right.

"Only the truth can make us free, and the truth must be based on the commandments and the moral law," he wrote in a private 1973 memorandum uncovered by Ebin. "So, even though we deal with 'politics and issues,' our real task is a moral one."

Morton Blackwell, who founded in 1979 the Leadership Institute, which trains conservative activists, and was a close friend of Weyrich and a regular at his Wednesday Capitol Hill lunches, has written that one day as they bantered, he told Weyrich that theologically conservative Americans were "the largest tract of virgin timber on the political landscape." Fundamentalist Christians were potentially a giant bloc that might be harnessed for the cause of a new religious right. But there was a problem: they didn't vote.

In 1964, Jerry Falwell, the popular evangelical religious broadcaster whose *Old Time Gospel Hour* had been saving believers since 1956, explained in a sermon, "Preachers are not called to be politicians, but soul winners." Evangelicals ignored elections because they believed that politics was not part of their calling. And they were not particularly exercised about abortion because it was a "Catholic issue" about which evangelical leaders were equivocal: they disagreed about whether abortion was a sin. Billy Graham, the twentieth century's most famous evangelical Christian leader, confidant of presidents, deplored abortion when it became "little more than another means of birth control, practiced for mere personal convenience with no regard for the fate of the infant growing in the womb," as he wrote in his book *Storm Warning*, but he didn't join the crusade against it; Focus on the Family founder James Dobson was saying that abortion didn't appear in the Bible, so an evangelical might believe that "a developing embryo or fetus was not regarded as a full human being."

Instead, the most important Christian evangelical political issue of the time was maintaining racial discrimination under the guise of "religious freedom." Leaders sought to keep white-only Christian schools from being taxed or restricted, to keep the government's hands off the numerous private institutes started by white parents after the 1954 Supreme Court decision in *Brown v. Board of Education*, which mandated integration of public schools.

Paul Weyrich wanted that huge "tract of virgin timber"—millions of evangelical Christians—to undergird the movement toward a nation of Christian principles. His political acumen told him that racism was not an attractive, broad-based mobilizing tool, while abortion might be.

In 1976, Weyrich traveled to Lynchburg, Virginia, to present his thinking to Falwell, sensing the time was right. In March 1965, two weeks after the infamous "Bloody Sunday" in Selma, Alabama, when the late John Lewis led six hundred marchers across a bridge on behalf of voting rights for all, only to be met by beatings from state troopers, Falwell had preached against Martin Luther King, Jr., and civil rights advocates for their political activism. But over the years, the evangelical preacher came to share Weyrich's view of the un-Christian drift of the country.

Before this, according to Morton Blackwell in an account on his institute's website, Weyrich said he had been trying to energize evangelicals over school prayer, abortion, and the proposed Equal Rights Amendment. Finally, he tapped into evangelical rage over government action against Bob Jones University, a Christian college in Greenville, South Carolina, that forbade interracial dating—its founder believed segregation was mandated by the Bible. In 1971, the Internal Revenue Service had created a policy denying tax exemptions to institutions, even religious schools, that practiced racial discrimination. It took away Bob Jones's tax exemption in 1976 and made the decision retroactive to 1970; other Christian schools whose raison d'etre was Jim Crow–style segregation were shaken. Evangelical Christians could no longer assume that they might continue to live isolated from certain laws of the country and teach whatever they pleased. A legal—and cultural—battle was joined. Falwell and other ultraconservative leaders framed the issue as a fight for religious freedom.

Weyrich saw his opening.

By sticking together, Weyrich told Falwell in Lynchburg, fundamentalist Christians and conservative Catholics, along with some individual Jews, could turn the tide on the secularization of society, and fight government intrusion in private lives. "Out there is what one might call a moral majority," Weyrich said when they met. Falwell agreed.

I pledge allegiance to the Christian flag, and to the Savior for whose Kingdom it stands; one Savior, crucified, risen, and coming again with life and liberty to all who believe.

—Pledge of allegiance to the Christian Flag, a white banner with a red cross in the corner on a blue background, which may be flown at Christian schools and events alongside the American flag

THE MORAL MAJORITY took off. Before uniting with evangelicals who looked to Falwell for leadership, Weyrich's movement had lacked foot soldiers and battle-worthy divisions, he told the *Los Angeles Times* in 2007. "It was Falwell who provided us with divisions, with resources and with people."

A longtime Weyrich friend from their days as young activists on Capitol Hill, Richard Viguerie, also a traditionalist Catholic who admired Barry Goldwater, provided a system for financing the incipient movement. Viguerie was a marketing wizard who revolutionized the way conservative political campaigns were financed, skipping over the Republican Party apparatus and reaching out to individual contributors and small, like-minded organizations by means of direct mail, which returned millions of donations. An adamant anti-Communist who had read the books of conservative icon William F. Buckley (an admired Catholic) as a young man, he wholeheartedly supported the anti-communist hearings of Senator Joseph McCarthy (another Catholic he admired) in the 1950s. Viguerie also held the confidence of evangelicals because, early in his career, he had worked for the Christian media evangelist Billy James Hargis, whose *Christian Crusade* aired on 500 radio stations and 250 television stations. Before becoming Hargis's aide, Viguerie marketed the books published by the preacher's company, which carried titles such as *The Negro Question: Communist Civil War Policy*, that called segregation "one of God's natural laws." Richard Viguerie's direct-mail money-raising system assured that the New Religious Right, heavily Republican but outside the reach of party stalwarts, would be well-funded.

The movement now had its religious leaders—Catholic and evangelical—its foot soldiers, and burgeoning financial support, but it is unlikely the New Religious Right would have flowered as quickly and decisively, or perhaps ever, without the anti-feminist atmosphere created by Phyllis Schlafly, founder of the movement that killed the

Equal Rights Amendment (ERA). Schlafly, a lawyer, was also deeply steeped in conservative Catholicism. Alarmed by the rapidity with which states were ratifying the amendment passed by Congress that was aimed at guaranteeing gender equality, she launched a vibrantly written anti-feminist newsletter and the STOP ERA campaign, to head off what she considered a staggering attack on social order. Later called the Eagle Forum, Schlafly's campaign opposing the burgeoning women's movement, amplified by media appearances, led Viguerie to consider her the "first lady of American conservatism." Even liberals admitted her impact. Political scientist Alan Wolfe deplored her ideas as "dangerous and hateful," yet wrote in *The New Republic* in 2005 that, "if political influence consists in transforming this huge and cantankerous country in one's preferred direction, Schlafly has to be regarded as one of the two or three most important Americans of the last half of the 20th century."

Always perfectly appointed with a strand of pearls and an upswept blond hairdo—she had once worked as a model—Schlafly got rid of the visual paraphernalia that customarily had accompanied Catholic anti-abortion campaigns, such as the rosary and images of the Virgin Mary, but kept the religious core of her anti-feminist message: women's equality under the law would upset the order of society created by God. She tailored a call to "protect" the family using universally recognized Bible verses about righteousness and morality that might resonate with equal familiarity among conservative Catholics, evangelical women, and Mormons. Central to the message was the belief that heterosexual sex roles were ordained by God, and women belonged in the home, raising children. (Schlafly was a mother of six who worked continuously outside the home.) She became ubiquitous on television, at rallies, at conferences, spreading trepidation that the traditional heterosexual family was threatened by legal abortion, homosexual marriage, and the specter of female military conscription, successfully mobilizing women who had never before imagined they had a role in politics.

In common with Weyrich, Schlafly regaled traditional Republicans. She authored the book supporting Barry Goldwater that influenced his nomination and became the bible of the Republican candidate's 1964 presidential campaign, *A Choice Not an Echo*. In the bestseller (3 million copies), the first of many texts she wrote or edited on subjects from religion to education and feminism, Schlafly excoriated party moderates—"a small group of secret kingmakers"—and presciently recognized that religious conservatives who were dissatisfied with the status quo could grow into a powerful political movement. In the 1970s and 1980s, with concrete results, she showed how Americans might overcome historical interdenominational enmity by emphasizing a shared moral framework and responsibility to preserve—return to—a Christian nation. Ratification of the ERA floundered, and stopped. Schlafly's traditionalist message about women's place, convenient to men, lived on within the rhetoric of the new religious right, which premises "family values" above all, as embodied in the patriarchal, faith-centered traditional family, a model for the state.

Religious America is awakening.

—Ronald Reagan, Southern Baptist Convention meeting, Dallas, 1980

ALMOST IMMEDIATELY AFTER Weyrich, Viguerie, and Falwell met in 1979 to form the "Moral Majority," they had a champion in a man who would install a New Right ideology at the highest levels of government, Ronald Reagan. At a 1980 gathering in Dallas, which one evangelical outlet, Good Faith Media, calls "the single most important religio-political moment in modern American life," fifteen thousand laypeople and pastors of the Southern Baptist Convention, the largest Protestant denomination in the country, assembled at the brand-new Reunion Arena for what organizers called "The National Affairs Briefing." Schlafly, Weyrich, Viguerie, and James Dobson were on the dais at one moment or another, but Republican presidential candidate Ronald Reagan stole the day, even as he kept to the nonpartisan nature of the gathering. "I know you cannot endorse me, but . . . I want you to know I endorse you and what you are doing," he said. America needed to return to God, Reagan said, and to "that old-time religion," so that the nation might fulfill its destiny of becoming "that shining city upon a hill." As Republican governor of California (1967–1975), Reagan had signed a liberal abortion law, but that fact did not rise to the surface in Dallas. Instead, Reagan now urged the public to recognize that all the problems confronting the country might find their answers in the Bible, and endorsed the teaching of creationism in public schools, a favorite evangelical theme. Those with traditional religious values must not be cowed, but must contribute to public policy, he said.

On all sides of the gathering signs encouraged vo†e! with a cross in place of the T. The *Washington Post* story on the two-day event, headlined "Linking Religion and Politics," reported that "millions of nonvoting Christians were exhorted to 'crawl out from under those padded pews' and take up political arms in the equivalent of a moral war to save America." In 2019's *Shadow Network: Media, Money, and the Secret Hub of the Radical Right*, a history of the Council for National Policy, author Anne Nelson writes, "Weyrich and company offered the Southern Baptists a path to theocracy through the electoral process." Journalist and White House press secretary under Lyndon B. Johnson Bill Moyers, who had once been a Southern Baptist minister, called Dallas "the place where the religious right and the political right formally wed."

* * *

VO✝E!

CONSERVATIVE EVANGELICALS HAD been noncombatants in the political fields of the culture wars in the 1960s and 1970s, but from then on they were being told to participate, indeed told they were sinful if they did not. Evangelical Christians joined conservative Catholics in a battle to "restore" a Christian nation, working so closely on the same path, with the same vocabulary, backing the same issues and candidates, that, forty years later, U.S. bishops and fundamentalist evangelicals would look and sound eerily the same in the public arena.

The Moral Majority had difficulties raising money by 1989, and dissolved as a movement, but the religious right was well entrenched on the national scene by then, and continued to vote in overwhelming numbers for conservative politicians. George W. Bush, John McCain, and Mitt Romney took more than three quarters of the white evangelical vote from 2000–2012, while conservative Catholics and evangelicals together voted decisively for Donald Trump in 2016.

The Catholic vote for Trump—52 percent—came partly because Democrats had a tin ear on abortion; even liberal Catholics unwilling to outlaw the procedure may have been taken aback by often strident pro-abortion Democratic campaigning. In 2020, conservative bishops and their lay allies worked in the trenches to elect the Republican president a second time, despite the fact that the thrice-married Trump modeled none of the pro-family principles exemplified by his opponent, Joe Biden, a life-long Catholic. After fifty years of embedding with an increasingly radical Republican Party to push its Christian nationalism agenda, especially on abortion, the bishops had become a transactional machine: Give us Supreme Court justices (Trump would nominate three) who will expand the role of religion in the public sphere, they effectively said, including rescinding women's right to bodily autonomy, and you get our vote.

"We need you more than ever," gushed Cardinal Timothy Dolan of New York to Trump in a 2020 pre-election phone call with the president and six hundred clergy and laypeople from Catholic institutions. The call had been meant to focus on the importance of Catholic schools, but Trump spent much of the time fishing for praise for his anti-abortion judicial appointments, and patting himself on the back for his efforts on "school choice." He was, Trump said, the "best [president] in the history of the Catholic Church."

Despite the reversal of *Roe* in June 2022, the U.S. bishops are likely to continue their alliance with the radical right because the job of Christianizing America for which Paul Weyrich and others long fought goes on, its working infrastructure now well in place. Justice Clarence Thomas, one of seven Supreme Court justices raised Catholic, said as much in the concurrence to the majority opinion reversing the right to abortion. Thomas cited cases guaranteeing other rights Americans thought they had, including same-sex marriage and contraception, which he considers ripe for review. The U.S. bishops' conference continued the culture war by spurring a battle against 2022 revisions to Title IX, which bans sex-based discrimination in federally funded education programs. Expanding prohibitions to include discrimination based on "sexual orientation" and "gender identity," as the revision would, were fighting words for Cardinal Dolan, Archbishop Salvatore Cordileone of San Francisco, and Bishop Thomas Daly of Spokane, who signed the USCCB-published response. The new provisions on discrimination based on pregnancy or termination of pregnancy "are intended to have implications for abortion, and therefore, life in the womb," they objected. "And by adding self-asserted 'gender identity' to the prohibition against sex discrimination, the rule may foreshadow a threat to . . . the right . . . to speak the truth about the nature of the human person." The rights of religious schools and health care institutions were in play, bishops warned.

FOR THE MOST conservative American bishops, the requirement to moving forward a Christian nationalist agenda is not just vo†e, but vote and coerce. Shortly after Joe Biden's election, only direct intervention from the Vatican kept the USCCB from forbidding the new, Catholic president of the United States to receive Holy Communion until he renounced support for legal abortion. Archbishop Cordileone, already schismatic in his actions by defying the Vatican on adherence to obeying secular authorities on pandemic restrictions and promoting the Traditional Latin Mass, decided unilaterally in May 2022 to deny Communion to Speaker of the House Nancy Pelosi, a resident in his archdiocese, although Pelosi continued to receive the sacrament elsewhere, including at a papal Mass in Rome. One prelate, Cardinal Robert McElroy of San Diego, who often sounds like a voice in the wilderness among his more conservative brethren, has called this practice of forbidding Communion to certain prominent Catholics "weaponization of the Eucharist."

In June 2022, the USCCB launched a three-year National Eucharistic Revival inviting Catholics "to renew the Church by reviving their relationship with Jesus in the Eucharist," a program planned to culminate in a lavish five-day meeting in Indianapolis in 2024. Price tag: $28 million. For Catholics considering Pope Francis's emphasis on care for the poor and leading the simple life for the sake of all creation, the lavish project begs questions about U.S. Catholic leadership. Is it a show of power, to reinforce the bishops' status, even to further make an instrument of the Communion sacrament for political purposes? The questions might only come up decades after U.S. bishops joined the religious far right pioneered by Paul Weyrich, and over concern about where they may go from here.

Much of the answer to concern over which way the bishops are going is found in the increasingly right-wing web over which they sometimes have come to preside, and are certainly now enmeshed:

conservative nonprofits that aspire to influence Catholic youth, education, and politics; ultraconservative Catholic media they use as a
platform; law firms engaged in "religious freedom" issues, by which
is meant keeping and changing laws for the goal of establishing a
"Christian" nation. Strong threads in the web are prominent Catholic
figures backed by huge amounts of money from supportive wealthy
conservatives, including non-Catholics—like Charles Koch—whose
goals can dovetail with those of the bishops, and the new phenomenon
of proliferating conservative "apostolates," nurtured by well-funded
individuals and their vehicles, like the Napa Summer Institute of
Catholic real-estate mogul Tim Busch, and some of the most conservative Catholic bishops in the land.

3

Our Lady of the Grapes

THE SWEET-SMELLING CITRUS groves of Southern California have long ago given way to suburban sprawl in Orange County. But rising from the spread of single-story homes and crisscrossing freeways south of Los Angeles, on an island of green, is a wondrous sight to behold—the all-glass Crystal Cathedral, twelve stories high, made of ten thousand tempered panes, their silvery outside coat reflecting the changing light of day.

Designed by the renowned Phillip Johnson and completed in 1980, the Crystal Cathedral became a regional landmark for its stunning architecture. Today it marks a regional change: in 2012, Protestant megachurch televangelist Robert Schuller, facing bankruptcy, sold the towering edifice to the Roman Catholic Diocese of Orange. Schuller's services, called *The Hour of Power*, had reached a weekly global audience of 20 million, in addition to being the home congregation of 2,700 mostly white evangelicals. Roman Catholic bishop Kevin W. Vann renamed the glassy building Christ Cathedral, and the look of the worshippers changed too. The bishop, who speaks Spanish and some Vietnamese, presides over one of the largest and fastest-growing Catholic dioceses in the country, with many first- and second-generation Latin American and Asian faithful. The thirty-four-acre cathedral grounds are also a locus of another new development: the partnership of conservative U.S. bishops with a powerful web of Catholic nonprofits and media that are creating a magisterium—body of teaching—that harkens back to the days before the Church reforms of the Second Vatican Council.

Kevin Vann is from Springfield, Illinois, where he rose after ordination to become a monsignor at a local parish, which also happened to be the home church of Illinois senator Dick Durbin. The two men agreed on immigration—Dick Durbin cosponsored the 2021 Dream Act, with Republican Senator Lindsey Graham of South Carolina, to provide a citizenship path for children brought illegally into the country, usually by their parents, and Vann defended DACA, a precursor to the act, when it was under threat. But they disagreed on keeping abortion legal.

In 2004 Vann said he would be "reticent" to give Holy Communion to Durbin as long as the second-ranking Democratic Senate leader (and chair of the powerful Judiciary Committee) supported the right to abortion; Springfield bishops went along with Vann, and Durbin was forced to find a Catholic "faith home" in the Chicago archdiocese, several miles away, where the senator's family could fully practice. Vann's marginalization of Durbin has been a continuing source of distress, the senator told *America* magazine in 2021. "I am careful when I go to a church that I have never been to before for any kind of occasion," said Durbin. "You just don't quite know what kind of reaction you're going to get from local clergy," or congregation members. Durbin went to Catholic institutions from kindergarten through law school. His Catholic faith "is a part of my life—I rely on it," Durbin said. Vann and current Springfield bishop Thomas John Paprocki have shown him no mercy, despite the words of Pope Francis that he has "never denied the Eucharist to anyone."

Vann, who was named bishop by Pope Benedict XVI, wrote in protest to the magazine a letter cosigned by Paprocki, who had been elevated by Pope John Paul II, and is also considered conservative. Durbin is guilty of "manifest grave sin," they charged. Despite the senator's "lifelong dedication to public service and his commitment to advancing many policies and programs that recognize the under-privileged and marginalized," as the prelates acknowledged, they said they said he must be "corrected, out of concern for his soul and out of concern for the confusion and scandal his words and actions present to the faithful of the church." Durbin had been warned.

"Asking Senator Durbin not to present himself for Holy Communion . . . is a measure intended to bring about repentance and a restoration of communion," the bishops wrote. "It is not a punish-ment. It is a pastoral measure with the ultimate good of salvation and communion with Christ as its aim . . . If the dignity of defenseless persons in the womb is disregarded [with abortion], there can be no justice or human rights."

FORBIDDING COMMUNION IN the way Vann and Paprocki have done with Senator Durbin is opposed to the attitude of the pope. "If we look at the history of the church, we can see that every time the bishops did not act like shepherds when dealing with a problem, they aligned themselves with political life, on political problems," Francis told reporters aboard the papal plane in September 2021.

Bishop Vann's rigid stand is fine with his billionaire neighbor near the leafy Christ Cathedral campus, Tim Busch, Vann's lead negotia-tor on the $57 million cathedral purchase. Busch, a lawyer, has an office in nearby Irvine, and several conservative Catholic groups have established offices on the Cathedral grounds, all bent upon advocat-ing an alt-right brand of the faith. Busch makes his money handling estate planning, real estate and business transactions, and taxes and litigation for high-net-worth individuals; he has directed over $2 billion to "charities" and foundations for clients. A firm Busch owns, Pacific Hospitality Group, manages eight luxury hotels and a collection of California resorts. Every summer since 2010, Tim Busch has turned one of his properties, the Meritage Resort and Spa, on Bordeaux Way in Napa, into a one-of-a-kind venue for conservative-minded Catholics.

IN VINO VERITAS

AT THE NAPA Institute, over four days and nights every summer, hundreds of Catholics hobnob with bishops and prominent clergy in the wine country venue, receive spiritual guidance from a ranking Opus Dei priest, dine on gourmet meals, sample fine wines, and mix it up at cigar smoking evenings called In Vino Veritas. Amid the vineyards—Busch has his own winery—attendants can attend the Traditional Latin Mass (TLM) in a chapel dedicated to Our Lady of the Grapes. The Latin Mass was intended to disappear in favor of mass in local languages after Vatican II, but the TLM is popular with the traditionalists at Napa. Institute attendees can listen to talks by leading conservative bishops like New York's Timothy Dolan, Paprocki, and Los Angeles's José Gomez, and hear Catholic speakers make presentations with titles like "Key Components in Building a Catholic Portfolio," and "Strange New World: How Thinkers and Activists Redefined Identity and Sparked the Sexual Revolution." And they hear activist conservative priests like Fr. Robert Sirico, cofounder of the Acton Institute for the Study of Religion and Liberty (funded in part by the Koch Foundation and Exxon), who has railed against the environmentalism of Pope Francis in the *Wall Street Journal* and elsewhere, and Fr. Frank Pavone, president of Priests for Life. Both Sirico and Pavone are members of the shadowy Council for National Policy. (During the 2016 presidential election, Pavone placed an aborted fetus on what appeared to be an altar; in 2022, the Vatican removed him from the priesthood.)

The Napa Institute began in 2010 when Busch and Los Angeles archbishop José Gomez decided to create an intellectual bulwark against a nation becoming ever more "secular." Busch saw the country as adrift from its Christian moorings. His inspiration, according to an introductory history on the institute's website, was Archbishop Charles J. Chaput, an archconservative who led the Philadelphia archdiocese until he reached retirement age in 2020. During the 2016 election campaign, Chaput questioned the faith of government officials who supported *Roe v. Wade*, especially Joe Biden and Tim Kaine. They were "prominent Catholics—a sitting vice president, and the next vice-presidential nominee of his party [who] seem to publicly ignore or invent the content of their Catholic faith as they go along," he said. At the 2018 Synod on Youth, the prelate denounced part of its working document, which said that "some LGBT youths" wanted greater closeness with the Church, and "to experience greater care by the Church." Chaput told the young people who had expressed concern, and clergy who supported them, that "'LGBTQ' and similar language should never be used in Church documents." The Church "simply doesn't categorize people that way," he said. Unlike every other prelate who has led the venerable, large, and influential Philadelphia archdiocese in the last hundred years, Chaput was never elevated to cardinal. But his doctrinaire positions and actions have made him a muse for Busch and conservative Catholics, who often are wealthy businessmen who think like him, and consider the Napa Institute their mecca.

Denver archbishop Samuel Aquila is also a big name at Napa. Considered Chaput's ideological mirror, Aquila presides over the

headquarters of well-funded ultraconservative Catholic ministries
with national reach like FOCUS, for college students, patterned partly
on the evangelical Campus Crusade for Christ (now called Crusade)
and the InterVarsity Christian Fellowship; Endow for conservative
Catholic women; Amazing Parish, started by corporate teamwork
expert and bestselling author Patrick Lencioni; and the Augustine
Institute, a school cofounded by Chaput protégé Jonathan Reyes, now
director of the U.S. Conference of Catholic Bishops's Department
of Justice, Peace & Human Development. (Conservative commentators greeted Reyes's 2012 USCCB appointment positively for his
connections and because he "moves easily in conservative circles.")
Two right-of-center news organizations were also born in Denver,
under Chaput, Aquila's predecessor: the Catholic News Agency, and
National Catholic Register, the U.S. bishops' most frequently read religious periodical according to a 2016 survey, with self-identified traditionalist or moderate bishops more likely than progressives ones to
read it. Fordham's Center on Religion and Culture director, David
Gibson, calls the scene in Denver a "Colorado Avignon," a reference to
the French city from which a series of popes reigned in the fourteenth
century instead of from Rome.

IN LITTLE MORE than a decade, with support from conservative bishops like Chaput, Aquila, San Francisco archbishop Salvatore
Cordileone, and at least half a dozen others who have served on its
boards, the Napa Institute has grown into a coast-to-coast network of
Catholic webinars, retreats, and studies abroad. Several thousand men
and a smaller number of women have passed through its various por-
tals. That's a small minority of the population of more than 70 million
Catholics in the United States, but it is a minority influential beyond
its numbers. Laypeople, religious, and seminarians who can swing
the $2,600 entry fee—without lodging (clergy receive a discount and

bishops attend free)—get Catholic teaching with a rigid, conservative stamp, marked by hierarchy and clericalism.

The bishops and laypeople who fill Napa's speaking roster generally do not support Vatican II. Chaput, Busch, and others who flock to the Napa Institute appear to consider Vatican II a mistake. They seem to believe it's time to reverse course to an era before the council, when nuns wore full-body habits and veils, laypeople knew their place in the pews and had few roles in Church administration or policy, and females were never seen on the altar, let alone as acolytes. In those days, hierarchs held out their rings for the faithful to kiss. "I think there was an unfounded optimism that the world would listen to us if we just were friendlier," Chaput told the evangelical Christian leader Albert Mohler, in a 2021 interview. "And it didn't. We got friendlier, we opened the doors of the church to the world, and they didn't come in. But many of us went out."

The message of the Napa Institute contends that waning spirituality in the United States means Catholics face "dwindling relevance," as its website says, but that it doesn't have to be that way. Busch and conservative bishops present at the institute's creation, including Chaput, Vann, and Gomez, offer a "new renaissance for God and his people," a path to renewal of a land where Christian values might rule. In their failure to embrace long-standing Catholic reforms, they are up against Francis, who has said of Vatican II, "The Council is the Magisterium of the Church. Either you are with the Church and therefore you follow the Council, or you interpret it in your own way, according to your desire, you do not stand with the Church."

The Napa Institute and myriad nonprofit Catholic teaching organizations linked to it offer Catholics what amounts to a parallel magisterium, teaching and sacramental formation that is closer to strict and defensive preconciliar norms than it is to the ecumenical, mercy-centered Church led by Francis, which sees itself as sympathetic to the failings of the world, insistently pro-life without considering one failure—abortion—to be greater than many others.

Napa's stand is markedly Christian nationalist in its mix of American exceptionalism and the Catholic faith. Attendees pray the "Patriotic Rosary," which dates from 1995 and includes lines from speeches by Washington and Adams, and rousing text from "The Battle Hymn of the Republic." The fifth decade of the rosary incorporates a prayer from General Robert E. Lee, calling upon God "in the defense of our homes and our liberties, thanking Him for His past blessings, and imploring their continuance upon our cause and our people." Lee wrote the prayer during the Civil War, when the cause was slavery, and defense of Southern homes was a bloody struggle against the North to preserve Southern "liberties." Interweaving the white supremacist cause with the pious practice of saying the Holy Rosary is questionable, at best, at a time when the FBI and Department of Homeland Security report that domestic extremists pose the greatest threat to U.S. security, and white nationalists carried two flags, the Star-Spangled Banner and the flag of the Confederacy, during the January 6, 2021, attack on the Capitol.

THE BATTLE HYMN OF NAPA

CHAPUT AND BUSCH echo Christian evangelical nationalists, and white supremacists, in another way: they look back to a mythical past when all (white) citizens shared presumed common instincts. "In the past, a common Christian culture existed which transcended partisan struggles, giving citizens a shared framework for behavior and belief," says the Napa Institute's public message, quoting the thesis of an article by Archbishop Chaput that he expanded into a 2017 book, *Strangers in a Strange Land: Living the Catholic Faith in a Post-*

Christian World. Institute conferences aim to equip Catholics for "the Next America"—Chaput's phrase coined as a warning to American Catholics of a growing trend toward secularization in U.S. culture, which presumably threatens Catholics' voices in the public square. The crowd that runs the Napa Institute present themselves as underdogs, denigrated and forced to tolerate laws against their beliefs in an ever more secularized society that "sees no need for Christianity but in many cases, views the Christian faith as an obstacle to its ambitions," as Tim Busch's Napa website announces.

If these sound like fighting words, they are. Listen to Napa Institute speeches and you hear a battle plan for a traditionalist, free market body of teaching promoted by Busch and his associated bishops, intended to correct the post–Vatican II practice of the faith. Only if strict, old-fashioned, preconciliar Catholicism survives, the Institute seems to say, will it vanquish what it sees as the evil of a secular society, and replace it with a society of Christian values.

At Napa, the attempt to promote the teaching of the most conservative U.S. bishops undergirds what transpires in conference rooms and tasting rooms, and largely ignores Pope Francis by name. In 2016, for instance, Francis issued his landmark exhortation on the family, *Amoris Laeticia (The Joy of Love)*, but during the Napa Institute summer session of 2018, four bishops on a panel titled "Faith, Family, Love" never once mentioned the document. They spoke only on pronouncements of previous pontiffs, Paul VI and John Paul II, as if the current pope had not written *Amoris Laeticia*, a public teaching document of 255 pages on the subject.

Pope Francis's 2016 exhortation—a papal pronouncement or "encouragement" issued after synods, or meetings, of world bishops—appeared in the wake of two years of meetings with bishops and experts in Rome, and was so grounded in the nitty-gritty reality of ordinary families, that the story on it by the Catholic News Service, the agency owned by the bishops (but editorially independent), carried the sub-heading, "Pope Francis' hymn to love and family life is more like a country song than a Disney tune." In its most controversial section, the pope examined the vexing question of whether divorced and re-married persons may receive Holy Communion. He issued no new law or guideline, but for the first time in a papal document declared that the answer should not automatically be no. Instead, he called for "pastoral discernment" in individual situations, and proposed "the logic of pastoral mercy" in working with remarried persons, a process that might lead to some divorced Catholics receiving the Eucharist. Rightist prelates fumed. Unlike bishops' leadership groups in other countries, the U.S. bishops held no conferences of theologians and other practitioners to explore the message of the exhortation, launched no campaign for its implementation.

The prelates on the Napa panel on the family—Oklahoma City archbishop Paul S. Coakley; Timothy Freyer, auxiliary of the Orange diocese; Madison bishop Robert Morlino; and Bishop Steven Lopes, who oversees seventy-three congregations led by Catholic pastors who were once Anglican or Episcopalian—did not engage *The Joy of Love*, did not even mention its up-to-date teaching on marriage. They fo-cused instead on contraception (not allowed, except for the rhythm method), the beauty of large families, and Church teaching about sex-ual abstinence before marriage. If couples avoid contraception, Freyer assured the audience, "instead of having a one-in-two divorce rate you'll have about one-in-fifty divorce rate." Bishop Lopes admitted that Pope Paul VI's encyclical *Humanae Vitae (Of Human Life)*, which reiterated the Church's prohibition of contraception, sterilization, and abortion, was met with a "tsunami of dissent" from Catholic couples when it appeared in 1968. Pope Francis reiterated the prohibition of artificial contraception but didn't label it as something against the laws of God and nature, as Pope Paul VI did, or "intrinsically evil," as Pope John Paul II did. Neither does Francis say that the marital act must always aim toward procreation, which had been an emphasis of Pope Paul's encyclical. However, instruction from the United States's bishops' group continues to prohibit "interventions" that violate "the inseparable connection, willed by God . . . between the two meanings of the conjugal act: the unitive and procreative meaning."

In *The Joy of Love* Francis wrote, "We need a healthy dose of self-criticism . . . [We] often present marriage in such a way that its unitive meaning, its call to grow in love and its ideal of mutual assistance are overshadowed by an almost exclusive insistence on the duty of procreation." At Napa, the operative papal teaching by Pope Francis that has moved the conversation forward on contraception, with an important, new, and more detailed understanding of marriage, was relegated to a kind of *damnatio memoriae*, as if it never existed.

REACHING OUT FROM ORANGE COUNTY AND THE VINEYARDS OF NAPA

THE SUMMER NAPA Institute is multiplying itself, not only with mini conferences elsewhere, at other times of the year, and online webinars, but also by providing an incubator environment for Catholic nonprofits, and new, like-minded ministries. In a little over ten years, Napa has helped to groom numerous conservative "apostolates" like FOCUS, founded in 1998 by evangelist Curtis Martin, whose members, called "missionaries," recruit fellow students and practice a traditional kind of Catholicism, with Bible study and rosary groups, familiar before Vatican II. Its board of directors is chaired by William Mumma, CEO of the Becket Fund for Religious Liberty, a nonprofit law firm that successfully litigates Supreme Court cases on the basis of "religious freedom," such as a case that permitted a Catholic institution to refuse to place foster children with same-sex couples. Another apostolate connected to Napa is Colorado-based Real Life Catholic, run by the popular (in traditionalist Catholic circles) speaker Chris Stefanick, and which produces videos for the conservative Eternal Word Television Network. Napa events are designed for networking, and a summer conference schedule at the Meritage has slots for preparing development professionals for engaging with participants. Some attendees seeking to develop their own apostolates look for funders among the well-heeled Catholics.

If a start-up nonprofit needs help navigating the shoals of the legal system, the Napa Legal Institute, founded in 2018, supplies Catholic lawyers who provide counsel on corporate, tax, and other non-litigation matters. The help goes to a new crop of "spiritual entrepreneurs," as the institute's director, Josh Holdenried, formerly of the Heritage Foundation, calls them. On the Legal Institute's board are Leonard Leo, the Federalist Society operator; Alan Sears of the Alliance Defending Freedom (ADF), a nonprofit that aims to protect "God's design for marriage and family" and curtail LGBTQ+ rights; and William Mumma.

Conservative Napa sponsors, and the organizations from which other speakers come, are familiar to many Catholics: the Knights of Columbus, the ADF, the Opus Dei–run National Catholic Information Center, and more. Napa's political goals—Christianizing the state—align with those of evangelical Christians, so other names that come up are rooted in the fundamentalist evangelical tradition, like Grove City College, a Christian institute in Pennsylvania, and the $500 million Museum of the Bible in Washington, D.C., created by the Hobby Lobby–founding Green family to convince visitors of the Bible's literal truth.

Because of its support for evangelical Christian causes, the Green family is held in high esteem by free market Catholics such as those who come to Napa Institute events. In 2014, Hobby Lobby won a U.S.

Supreme Court decision that allowed the company to deny health coverage to employees for contraceptives, striking down a key mandate of Obamacare. For the first time, the court held that a "closely-held," for-profit corporation counts as a "person" under the Religious Freedom Restoration Act (1993), because it shares the religious-exercise rights of its owners. "Closely-held" generally refers to companies owned by a family or relatives, but they are not necessarily mom-and-pop operations. Other closely held corporations include Koch Industries ($115 billion in revenue and 60,000 U.S. employees), Dell, and Bechtel. The U.S. bishops filed a friend of the court brief in favor of Hobby Lobby. "Justice has been served," wrote the USCCB president at the time, Archbishop Joseph E. Kurtz of Louisville, when the ruling came down. The decision was seen as a blow on behalf of religious freedom, in the style of a state moving toward Christian nationalism.

"Some good things are happening there," Tim Busch said in an introduction to the 2020 Napa Institute summer session, speaking of the legal arena. He referred to another legal case, *Our Lady of Guadalupe School v. Morrissey-Berru*, in which two female teachers sued the Los Angeles archdiocese for employment discrimination. One woman was fired after she asked for time off for breast cancer treatment; the other was replaced by a younger teacher when she did not comply with a suggestion to retire. The Becket Fund for Religious Liberty represented the Los Angeles archdiocese. The Supreme Court decided 7 to 2 against the women, and in favor of the archdiocese led by Gomez. Justices said the case was about religious liberty; religious institutions could claim an exemption—the "ministerial exemption"—to anti-discrimination laws when they hired employees, deemed "ministers" even though they didn't teach religion.

With an insider's dash, Busch described the course of the momentous decision as if the Napa Institute were part of a high-end tag team. "That case came to Gomez," he said, speaking of the Los Angeles archbishop. "Gomez called me, we put it into the Becket Fund, Becket tried it, and won."

Busch touted connections with a cofounder of the Federalist Society, and two law firms famous for winning controversial "religious liberty" cases before the Supreme Court. "We have Leonard Leo, who's been a big supporter, the guy who has been providing the judges and the justices for our courts to Donald Trump," Busch said. "Becket, Alliance Defending Freedom—they were trying most of those cases. Every one of those cases was involving those guys."

FROM NAPA TO WASHINGTON, D.C.

Oh, we're meetin' at the courthouse at eight o'clock tonight
You just walk in the door and take the first turn to the right
Be careful when you get there, we hate to be bereft
But we're taking down the names of everybody turning left

—Michael Brown
"The John Birch Society," 1962, performed by the Chad Mitchell Trio

IN THE 1920S and 1930s, Fred Koch, a graduate of MIT and owner of a small construction and design firm in Wichita, Kansas, went to the Soviet Union to help Joseph Stalin build fifteen oil refineries. By 1935, Fred Koch had switched his expertise to Adolf Hitler's Third Reich. Hired by Texas oilman William Rhodes Davis, grandfather of the future California governor Gray Davis, and known in his time as "the Mystery Man" for his maneuverings among heads of state during the Second World War, Koch repurposed an oil storage facility in Hamburg to become one of the largest refineries in the world, capable of processing a thousand tons of crude per day, and one of the few in Germany that could manufacture the high-octane gasoline demanded by the fighter planes of the Luftwaffe. The Koch-Davis operation became a key unit of the rearmament campaign that gave the Nazis the wherewithal to launch World War II.

Fred Koch's work for Stalin and Hitler was the origin of the fortune he handed down to his children when he died in 1967. His sons David (d. 2019) and Charles continued to build up the fortune with their own business acumen; the worth of Koch Industries—still based in Wichita—rose to $115 billion in 2022, and Charles Koch became one of the two dozen richest individuals on the planet. The business friendship with Moscow was renewed, with Charles Koch, a chemical engineer who also has a degree from MIT, refusing to bend to pressure to withdraw Koch Industries from Russia when Putin invaded Ukraine. Charles Koch says he is not religious, but family politics is ultraconservative, and the funding priorities of Koch's foundations line up with those of the conservative bishops and Catholic philanthropists like Tim Busch.

Fred Koch, the business empire's paterfamilias, was a founding member of the ultraright-wing John Birch Society, which was founded in 1958, ascendant in the 1970s, and sometimes called "the intellectual seedbed of the right." His son Charles was a Birch Society member until 1968 and has said he believes morality in a person is more important than talent. He hires accordingly. Charles Koch has done a lot of listening to Tim Busch—the two men own a golf course together.

"Tim always said, 'You're a Catholic but just don't know it,'" Koch told *The Wall Street Journal* in 2017.

That was the year Koch donated $10 million to the Catholic University of America's Tim and Steph Busch School of Business and Economics. In books and articles published over several years, *New Yorker* writer Jane Mayer has shown that when the Koch brothers failed at ultra-free market capitalist electoral politics, notably with David's losing Libertarian Party run for the vice presidency in 1980, they started using fortune and friendship to shape the hearts and minds of U.S. voters in their favor. They began to target their money at politicians and policies that would carry out their ideas about what government should do and not do and brought other U.S. billionaires along with them. Together they worked through think tanks, foundations, and political networks like ALEC, the nonprofit that writes corporation-friendly template bills for state legislatures, which are often passed without discussion by Republican lawmakers. They helped bankroll secretive groups of influential conservatives like the Council for National Policy. Eventually, the reasoning went, citizens would choose the kind of men and women who would carry out the vision of the radical conservative world—high on unregulated free markets, contemptuous of taxes, with a view of science as a tool of chicanery used by government to trick the citizenry and put obstacles in the way of decent entrepreneurs trying to create jobs.

In a tightly designed plan started in the 1980s, and meant to be effective in the long run, the Koch brothers began funding academic programs and think tanks to create an intellectual foundation from which "experts" on their ultraconservative vision would emerge, and find the limelight. Through their networks, the Kochs brought in other wealthy conservatives and libertarians who also wanted to degrade or eliminate industrial safety, environmental regulations, or other government oversight that might cut into corporate profits. Twice a year, the brothers hosted secretive, invitation-only "donors' conferences" for top officers of U.S. companies and family foundations at elegant venues. From them they raised donations to favor individual candidates for state and national office, to back conservative judges, and to lobby for friendly legislation, raising money counted not in millions, but in billions. The political "philanthropy" of this small group of wealthy Americans that infests today's electoral process and public opinion-making is divided into such a large number of shadowy foundations, "social welfare" organizations, nonprofits, and donor networks that critics call it the Kochtopus.

One of the newest arms of the Kochtopus is encircling the U.S. Catholic Church. In 2013, Charles Koch gave a kind of starter donation of $1 million to the Catholic University of America (CUA), which set off alarm bells among educators and theologians worried that academics could be suborned by big money that promoted ultra-right-wing politics. Fifty protested in a letter to the president of the university. "You send a confusing message to Catholic students and other faithful Catholics that the Koch brothers' anti-government, Tea Party ideology has the blessing of a university sanctioned by Catholic bishops," the writers said. By this time the Kochs had helped to accrue more than $407 million to develop the Tea Party, a variety of groups and foundations that portrayed right-wing demonstrations and anti-government voices as a political movement coming spontaneously from the grassroots, not the product of careful funding and public relations operators, which it was.

The idea that dirty money might demean the only Catholic university of its kind in the United States, founded by U.S. bishops, was intolerable to the dissenters. The CUA is answerable directly to the Holy See, with a student body that is overwhelmingly Catholic, and a seminary to prepare men for the priesthood. But objectors to Koch money lost. Like funding for other academic and think tank enterprises founded or supported by Koch and his fellow right-wing billionaires, the CUA money came tagged with an anodyne-sounding purpose: "to support research on the role entrepreneurship should play in improving society."

U.S. Catholic bishops do not object to generous donations from Charles Koch, even though he has publicly announced that he is in favor of gay marriage and pro-choice on abortion, both otherwise anathema among the prelates. (Bishops have prohibited schools from inviting openly pro-choice speakers and fired the managing editor of their own Catholic News Service in 2018 for a gay-friendly tweet.) Neither was a peep of episcopal dissent heard in 2015 when Tim Busch put together another $3 million gift to CUA's School of Business, more than half of it from the Charles Koch Foundation.

Busch said, "I am proud to donate to CUA's vision for an educational program that shows how capitalism and Catholicism can work hand in hand." Bishops know that Catholicism doesn't "work hand in hand" with capitalism, especially unfettered capitalism, whose excesses Pope Francis has condemned in his encyclicals, nor does Catholicism work with other ideological "isms." In a *Wall Street Journal* opinion piece, Busch claimed the CUA business school would be educating a future generation of Catholic corporate leaders in Catholic principles. Among these he had the gall to list the "preferential option for the poor," at a time when billionaires like Koch and him contribute to an income gap between the wealthy and the middle class that is growing exponentially. If such a new kind of Catholic business program teaches anything, it is likely to be the preferential option for the superrich.

PARTNERS

U.S. BISHOPS MAY be turning a blind eye to taking big Koch money for their national university because academic institutions that are operating in the prelates' own, individual dioceses often experience part of the same largesse. As of 2019, more than forty Catholic colleges and universities, including Georgetown, College of the Holy Cross, and St. John's, took money from Koch, adding them to his declared "talent pipeline" to feed laissez-faire capitalism, an education network that Koch and fellow billionaires have been building for thirty years with research institutes and funded campus programs.

The pipeline is running increasingly alongside the hallowed histories of Catholic institutions, and today's Catholic bishops appear satisfied to have it that way.

Not everyone is pleased. The *Omaha World-Herald* reported that critics of Creighton University's Institute for Economic Inquiry, founded in 2015 on the Jesuit campus, say the institute is not so much "inquiring" as it is promoting a brand of economics "that contradicts long-established Catholic social thought, endorsed by Pope Francis and his predecessors." The $4.5 million program was funded fifty-fifty by the Charles Koch Foundation and the family of C. L. Werner, an Omaha trucking entrepreneur. A local priest, reported the *Herald*, accused Koch's foundation of pushing its ideas "to the very doorstep of the Vatican."

Students and teachers at Catholic institutions, more conscious every day of the environmental crisis as the earth heats to a perilous point while emissions from fossil fuels keep rising, sometimes object to their campuses being gilded by Koch profits: Koch family foundations have spent more than $160 million since 1987 in direct contributions to groups that question climate change science and attack policy solutions, according to a Greenpeace report, which lists the denial groups by name. In California, when Koch contributed $4 million to the $11 million Ciocca Center for Innovation and Entrepreneurship at Santa Clara University (SCU), named for the family that contributed the rest of the funds, students worried about whether the Koch money had been earned in ways that violated university values—Koch Industries has been fined $935 million for hundreds of violations, most of them environmental crimes. In the early 1980s, the firm took the lead among other oil titans in financing a war against climate science by way of think tanks, cutouts, phony "citizens" groups, publicity campaigns, and ersatz literature like the Koch-founded Cato Institute's *Climate of Fear: Why We Shouldn't Worry about Global Warming*.

"The Koch family is one of the primary forces behind the misinformation campaign to distort science," SCU engineering professor Ed Mauer, who has studied the effect of climate change on water supplies, told *San Jose Inside*. Other SCU faculty worried whether hiring for the academic center would accommodate Koch's wishes; that is what happened at George Mason University, which received $50 million in Koch money, according to private records uncovered in 2018. It happened, too, at Florida State University a decade ago, when Koch first funded its economics department, stipulating that a Koch-appointed advisory committee select professors and conduct annual evaluations. And suspicious students at the University of Kansas filed an open-records request to discover that the director of the school's Center for Applied Economics formerly worked for the lobbying arm of Koch Industries, and a Koch foundation paid his salary, although the director said Koch didn't tell him what to teach. Despite student and faculty objections, administrators typically don't turn down the gifts. Concerned that Koch money would come to the venerable (founded in 1851) Santa Clara University with strings attached, its faculty senate voted to ask the administration to revoke its acceptance of the donation. The administration did not.

Big liberal donors like the Open Society Foundations of George Soros and the Ford Foundation also fund a variety of programs at U.S. universities; yet they do not aim their money as specifically as Koch and his network do, at the politically relevant discipline of free market economics, in order to serve their greater vision of social transformation. That vision, and the steps to its fruition, were succinctly presented in an article written by Richard Fink, the Koch brothers' longtime political advisor, titled "The Structure of Social Change" and published in *Philanthropy Magazine* in 1996. Fink knew the process well, having impressed Charles Koch as a young man in 1976 with a paper with the same title, which treated political change like a product that could be manufactured like any other, following certain steps. With that blueprint, Fink began a lifetime career with the Koch empire. In this section of the *Philanthropy Magazine* article Fink succinctly lays out the strategic framework that Koch's nonprofit ventures have used since the late 1970s to influence policy, aiming at a long-term, three-phase takeover of U.S. politics:

> At the higher stages we have the investment in the intellectual raw materials, that is, the exploration and production of abstract concepts and theories. These still come primarily (though not exclusively) from the research done by scholars at our universities . . .
> In the middle stages, ideas are applied to a relevant context and molded into needed solutions for real-world problems. This is the work of the think tanks and policy institutions . . . But while the think tanks excel at developing new policy and articulating its benefits, they are less able to implement change. Citizen activist or implementation groups are needed in the final stage to take the policy ideas from the think tanks and translate them into proposals that citizens can understand and act upon.

Charles Koch has become one of academia's biggest private patrons, spending more than $450 million between 2005 and 2018 at more than 500 institutions, so that what it calls the "talent pipeline" may flow from the classroom and lecture hall to the cubicles of the think tank to the creation of "citizens'" groups that dovetail with special interests. Together the "citizens'" and special interest groups lobby lawmakers to establish policy that Koch and fellow far-right billionaires desire. The entire process avoids the electoral system, and it is all paid for by fossil fuel and other industries that benefit most from it.

* * *

NOW THAT THE Kochtopus is feeding ultraconservative thought on Catholic campuses, the growing conservative Catholic enterprise of Tim Busch, Archbishops Gomez and Chaput, Bishops Vann and Paprocki, and other prelates makes for an ideal partnership.

At the Napa Conference in the summer of 2021, Busch announced that fifteen families, including that of Leonard Leo, the Federalist Society insider who advised former President Trump on his three Supreme Court nominations, pledged donations totaling $500,000 to expand Busch's programs. The amalgam of right-wing oil money and right-wing Catholicism came together in a big way a few months later at the emblematic Catholic university, Notre Dame. Called the Napa Institute Forum, a series of prominent speakers and events funded by, among others, Busch and the Charles Koch Foundation, the program was established at the university's new Center for Citizenship and Constitutional Government. The center is envisioned as "a bridge" between Notre Dame and Washington, D.C., as the I. A. O'Shaughnessy Dean of the College of Arts and Letters Sarah A. Mustillo said at an October event, welcoming the forum's debut speaker, Justice Clarence Thomas, who was making a rare public appearance.

Like faculty at Santa Clara University, professors at Notre Dame complained of the Koch connection, and now the Napa connection. During the 2021 summer meetings where the new institute was announced, Busch had trashed Black Lives Matter as "neo-Marxist . . . promoting racism, critical race theory, and destroying the nuclear family." One speaker, L. Brent Bozell III, called President Biden a "figurehead" for "elements of Marxism at play in America," and declared that the "Judeo-Christian tradition is being thrown away, as is the very history of the United States." Bozell, a Republican activist, has called Trump the winner of the 2020 election, and signed a letter urging state legislators to ignore certified election results. (In

December, Busch announced the 2023 opening of a Napa Institute office blocks from the U.S. Capitol.)

These were not the kind of bedfellows desired by everyone at Notre Dame. John Duffy, a longtime English professor, told the *National Catholic Reporter* that if Notre Dame took funding from Napa and Koch, the university would look like it was "throwing in our lot with the conspiracy theorists, the race baiters and the climate deniers."

But the show went on. Francis Maier, a longtime advisor to Archbishop Chaput and member of the Napa Institute's board of directors, was named a research scholar at the new Notre Dame center. While on campus, Clarence Thomas taught a one-unit course with the center's director (and Napa Institute speaker), Dr. Vincent Phillip Muñoz, who is also a professor at The Fund for American Studies (TFAS), a partner organization of the Charles Koch Institute whose mission statement says it teaches the principles of limited government and free market economics "to students in America and around the world." The more the connections spiraling out from the Napa–Notre Dame pact are followed, the more they reveal a substructure of supposedly nonpartisan philanthropy undergirding just one corner of Catholic academia that serves the ultraconservative agenda.

Donations can seem purposely hard to track. The Fund for American Studies receives support from DonorsTrust, which has been called by critics a "dark money ATM," a clearinghouse for major contributors who legally—because the trust is a nonprofit—can remain anonymous, while their money is channeled to far-right projects. Rhode Island senator Sheldon Whitehouse, who has followed the path wrought by dark money for years, said in a 2020 speech, "DonorsTrust has a tag-along entity that sends a lot of money into the same places—the Charles Koch Foundation. In fact, it is a little hard to tell where this Koch Foundation ends and where DonorsTrust begins."

Other TFAS money comes from foundations established by brothers Lynde and Harry Bradley, ultraconservatives—Harry avidly supported the John Birch Society—who made their money in the defense industry, and whose bounty has been showered on election fraud conspiracists, and on groups engaged in efforts in the courts to return former president Trump to power. Other lucky recipients of Bradley money include the Public Interest Legal Foundation, which is staffed with lawyers "obsessed" with putative voter fraud, Mayer reported in *The New Yorker* (John Eastman, a former law clerk to Supreme Court Justice Clarence Thomas and author of the White House "coup memo" that promulgated a theory that Vice President Mike Pence had authority to reject certain electors and give the 2020 election to Trump, is one of the foundation's directors) and Turning Point USA, a nonprofit that supplied buses to transport protesters to Washington D.C. and the Capitol on January 6 (Ginni Thomas, the wife of Justice Thomas, once served on its advisory council).

"The [Koch] network is fully integrated, so it's not just work at the universities with the students, but it's also building state-based capabilities and election capabilities and integrating this talent pipeline," said Kevin Gentry, who organized the network's quietly held biannual free-enterprise donor meeting in 2015. The nonpartisan Center for Public Integrity obtained an audio recording of Gentry's speech to the gathering, which focused on higher education strategy, and published excerpts in a report. The Koch network's support for higher education, Gentry said, was an effort to reach young minds first on campus, to develop libertarian-leaning students destined for political power, according to the report. "So you can see how this is useful to each other over time," Gentry said. "No one else has this infrastructure. We're very excited about doing it."

THE TOWER OF HOPE

IN ALLIANCE WITH ultraconservative bishops including Archbishop Gomez, Bishop Paprocki, and Archbishop Chaput, Tim Busch has become one of the most influential Catholics in the country with his targeted philanthropy, high-end summer conference where the Catholic elite rub shoulders, and training for seminarians, priests, and businessmen that espouses a libertarian line. In turn, the bishops benefit from exposure to prosperous Catholics who come to the institute events in Napa, and now elsewhere, and glad-handing activists who run traditionalist apostolates, or aspire to do so, reinforcing the bridge between ultraconservative U.S. Catholic practice and the wealth to keep it in place. Presented as spiritual renewal, the enterprise is politicized religiosity. At the 2021 conference, Archbishop Chaput, accepting a Napa Lifetime Service Award, used the occasion to take a cynical cut at President Biden, who carries a rosary that belonged to his deceased son, Beau.

"An emotional attachment to rosary beads . . . does not exhaust the nature and the demands of a living faith," Chaput declared.

Tim Busch maintains his office, where a daily Mass is said, near the campus of the Orange diocese's crystal Christ Cathedral. Also near the cathedral, but far enough away from other structures (about one hundred yards) that its sleek architecture can be appreciated for itself, is the fourteen-story Tower of Hope, which has become a central command post for divulging messages amenable to U.S. bishops. With vertical elements like columns and upright-oriented windows, the tower looks even taller than it is. Soaring into the Southern California sky, it's topped by a ninety-foot neon-lit cross that can be seen glowing across the county at night.

You can take an elevator to the top of the tower, where the windows of an ecumenical Chapel in the Sky give panoramic views.

On the way down, you can visit the offices of Catholic ministries. Among them is the Magis Center, created by Busch with Jesuit Fr. Robert Spitzer, whose books (*Escape from Evil's Darkness, Christ versus Satan in Our Daily Lives*), videos, YouTube segments, scholarly articles ("Contemporary Scientifically Validated Miracles Associated with Blessed Mary, Saints and the Holy Eucharist"), and online education modules aim to combat the "secularization" of society, giving teachers and ordinary Catholics "answers" to the perceived conflict between science and faith. Spitzer has taken on the thinking of atheists Stephen Hawking and Richard Dawkins on public and commercial television programs, and on his own weekly TV show on EWTN.

Another office is that of the nonprofit Dynamic Catholic, the enterprise of motivational speaker and management consultant Matthew Kelly founded to "re-energize the Catholic Church in America," as Kelly described it to *Orange County Catholic*. Bishop Vann invited him into the Tower of Hope in 2013 when Kelly's mega-publishing operation was only four years old but promised great things. A popular speaker and model of the kind of aspirational ecclesial entrepreneurs that pepper the Napa Institute gatherings—although Kelly himself does not appear there—Kelly has made it big. Perhaps the largest-selling Catholic author of the era, Kelly has published millions of books aiming at the "New Evangelization" introduced by Pope Benedict, "re-proposing the Gospel" where secularization has led to a crisis of faith. The nonprofit Dynamic Catholic is connected to Kelly's for-profit publishing company, and other linked businesses, from which he makes his money. According to an investigation by *National Catholic Reporter* (*NCR*), Dynamic Catholic provided more than $48 million to Kelly's companies in book sales, consulting fees, and rent from 2011 to 2017. There are Dynamic Catholic parish book programs, and thousands of Dynamic

Catholic parish "ambassadors" who donate ten dollars a month to the nonprofit; with gifts and grants, that amounts to a monthly income of nearly a quarter of a million dollars. Of donations, 80 to 100 percent goes to Kelly's companies, according to *NCR*. Kelly has enthusiastic fans across the country for his evangelization, and his books provide the basis for First Communion and Confirmation instruction at parishes, where busy educators value them. He has touched millions of lives, he told *NCR*. "I don't want to be the guy in the Gospel who received one talent and brought back one talent."

The Tower of Hope also houses the West Coast headquarters of EWTN, the ultraconservative network established by the charismatic Mother Angelica in the 1980s, now the largest religious broadcaster in the world. In Orange, EWTN's radio and TV facilities are much closer to the entertainment and information hubs of Hollywood and Los Angeles than its original, one-story, somewhat dowdy-looking home in Irondale, Alabama. That the national Catholic media should move steadily west is logical—in the Southwest, driven partly by Latin immigration, parishes are expanding as quickly as they are shrinking in the old cities of the Midwest and the Northeast.

Cementing its reputation for the place where (Catholic) things happen, the Napa Institute served as the venue for the announcement by EWTN's director Michael Warsaw and Bishop Vann in 2014, just two years after Busch negotiated Vann's purchase of the Crystal Cathedral, that EWTN would install itself on the Orange County campus. Many independent Catholic newspapers and magazines publish a spectrum of views, but the traditionalist EWTN, the behemoth of its kind, is the go-to place to know the position of U.S. bishops. In partnership with Bishop Vann, Tim Busch, and their colleagues, the tower in Orange, with its apostolates and media empire, became a podium for the most conservative U.S. prelates.

So striking is the interior of the Tower of Hope, designed by the Vienna-born modernist Richard Neutra, that it was used as Starfleet command headquarters in the 2013 film *Star Trek into Darkness.* A year after the starship has been saved, Captain Kirk delivers an impassioned dedication to the new *Enterprise* and its crew, standing outside the command center amid the silvery buildings of the Crystal Cathedral campus, remembering "who we once were and who we must be again."

Is it fanciful to hope that a center of rightist Catholic teaching today may someday align itself less with hyper-conservative U.S. bishops, and more with Pope Francis's message of charity, awareness of the earth's fragility, and solidarity with the poor? In the meantime, the sleek and shiny surfaces of the exquisitely designed buildings in Orange may represent the American bishops' megaphone better than any other place.

4

Unholy Trinity

Clarence Thomas, Leonard Leo, Virginia Thomas

AMERICAN CATHOLIC BISHOPS rejoiced at the Supreme Court's June 2022 decision that the Constitution of the United States does not confer a right to abortion. The most ultraconservative prelates, those who want to see their own moral principles become the law of the land, take hope in outlawing abortion even more widely in the future, and seeing the reversal of other laws that have guaranteed rights to contraception and same-sex marriage, for instance, which they consider anathema.

The rightist bishops' hopes are fueled by the concurring majority opinion of Justice Clarence Thomas in *Dobbs v. Jackson Women's Health Organization*, the case that eliminated a woman's right to end her own pregnancy. Thomas, who is among seven of the nine Supreme Court justices raised Catholic, including the six who generally vote as the conservative majority, specifically invited legal challenges to cases that established rights to birth control and same-sex marriage, and the right to intimate sexual conduct between consenting adults regardless of sex in the privacy of the home. Those cases were decided in an era when justices who sat on the bench were less ideologically conservative than those who now serve.

If not a culmination of their efforts, *Dobbs* represents a high point of the work of lawyers and judges like Thomas; activists like Thomas's wife, Virginia Lamp Thomas, known as Ginni; and political operatives like Leonard Leo of the Federalist Society, who played a key role in securing the appointments of the court's conservative majority. Their story reveals how three right-wing lay Catholics helped to bring success to an agenda they share with the most conservative American Catholic bishops.

THE U.S. COURT of Appeals in Washington, just a block from the White House, is a stately building fronted with slender Ionic columns, graced in a forecourt with a statue of Abraham Lincoln caught mid-stride, as if intent upon where he was going. At the court one day in 1990, a judge named Clarence Thomas met a new law school graduate, Leonard Leo, who was clerking for another judge. There was an age gap of seventeen years between Thomas (b. 1948) and the younger Leo (b. 1965), but they had important things in common: both were Catholics, immersed in the law, and both had conservative politics. And like Lincoln striding away from the Court, both were going places.

Beyond similarities in background and politics, there was a chemistry between the men that grew into genuine friendship. They lunched together, visited each other's homes.

Three decades later, the friendship continues. Clarence Thomas is the longest-serving, most conservative justice on the Supreme Court, and Leo is the undisputed architect of the country's conservative legal movement, involved in the process of naming hundreds of federal judges and six of the nine justices on the current Supreme Court, beginning with Thomas. Between the two friends and their allies, including U.S. Catholic bishops, they have politicized the concept of religious liberty, moving the country toward becoming a more Christian—not more democratic—state. Catholic political and legal activists, like Thomas' wife, Ginni, are as essential to the cause as justices like Thomas and the legal über-advisor Leo—they provide the friend of the court briefs considered by judges; organize pressure groups and raise money to finance campaigns like the pro-life movement to support anti-abortion issues; work for candidates who will support a Christian agenda; and develop the cases that will go to the court to establish or reverse U.S. law to suit their ultraconservative social vision.

IT IS DIFFICULT to grasp the force behind the achievements of Leonard Leo and Clarence Thomas without understanding certain mainsprings of family and faith in each man so strong that, combined with a conservative political mindset, their trajectories seem inevitable. Both Leo and Thomas were deeply connected to their Catholic grandfathers, who played important roles in raising them. Leo's grandfather was an Italian immigrant who came to the United States at age fourteen and labored as a tailor, working his way up to the vice presidency of Brooks Brothers, the company's last non–college educated officer, as Leo has it, proof of the American dream. When his father died of cancer while Leonard was still a boy, his mother moved with her two young children into his grandparents' house. Even when she remarried and the family moved, Leo's Italian Catholic elder remained the formative spirit of his youth. "He understood America as being a land of opportunity," Leo told *The New Yorker*'s Jeffrey Toobin in 2017. "He understood the value of capitalism, the value of hard work, personal responsibility." It was his grandfather, Leo said, who made him believe in "American exceptionalism," the idea that the United States is unique among nations in its values and development, destined to lead the world.

Leo's grandparents attended daily Mass, a habit that imprints Catholic practice in the minds of the young in a lasting way that growing up with "Chreaster" Christians, who attend church only on Easter and Christmas, cannot do. If Leo's faith needed reinforcement as he approached middle age, it may have come through the tragic death of his daughter, Margaret. The girl was born with spina bifida, a birth defect that occurs when the spine and spinal cord do not form properly, and she was confined to a wheelchair. Margaret lived with pain, but by all accounts remained cheerful and solicitous of others. On a family vacation in 2007, when she was fourteen, Margaret encouraged her father to go back to attending daily Mass, and he promised he would. The day after they returned from the vacation, as Leo rose early to go to church, he noticed his daughter was having trouble breathing; he called an ambulance, but the shunt that had been placed in her brain to ensure the spinal fluid circulated failed on the way to the hospital, and she died. Leo has gone to daily Mass since. "I will always think that she did her job," he told Toobin. *The Catholic Thing*, a conservative online publication in six languages that describes itself as "a forum for intelligent Catholic commentary," says three miracles have been attributed to the deceased Margaret.

Leo and his wife, Sally, have seven children. To their shock, because the condition rarely appears multiple times in a family, a son born after Margaret died was also afflicted with spina bifida. Leo's profound aversion to the idea of abortion is based not only on Catholic teaching that all life is sacred—he believes life begins at conception—but also likely upon his own fatherly relationship to two children with grievous physical disabilities. Another influence is a belief that the vast majority of abortions are the result of consensual sex, as if pregnancy were, in cases, a problem you create by your own free will. For Leo abortion is "an act of force," he told *The New Yorker*. "It's a threat to human life. It's just that simple."

Leonard Leo would not, could not, support any person for a U.S. judgeship who did not oppose abortion.

Almost three fourths of the American public believe that abortion should be legal if the fetus is expected to be born with serious birth defects, according to a 2020 poll by the Kaiser Family Foundation. In Leo's view, however, public opinion is immaterial to determining what is lawful. Tom Carter, who served as his media relations director when Leo was chairman of the U.S. Commission on International Religious Freedom, described the insight that has shaped Leo's hunt for conservative judicial candidates. "He figured out twenty years ago that conservatives had lost the culture war," Carter said in a 2018 interview with *The Daily Beast*. "Abortion, gay rights, contraception—conservatives didn't have a chance if public opinion prevailed. So they needed to stack the courts."

PIPELINE TO THE CHRISTIAN STATE

THE FEDERALIST SOCIETY, founded as a discussion group for conservative students who felt marginalized at elite, liberal-thinking law schools like Yale and the University of Chicago, has grown in the last forty years to become the single most important right-wing legal institution in the country. It counts seventy thousand lawyers among its members, six of the nine Supreme Court justices, forty-three out of fifty-one of President Trump's nominees to appellate courts, and members of Congress. Leonard Leo, the society's first permanent hire in 1991, has become synonymous with its heft and influence, managing the conservative pipeline to the highest judicial and legislative seats in the land.

Leo is not known as much for brilliance as a lawyer as he is for an extraordinary capacity to strategize, network, and raise money to convince lawmakers, media influencers, and, during the Trump administration, the president himself to support Federalist Society candidates for judgeships. Not tall, but always dressed as his tailor grandfather might have wished, with perfectly cut suits and handkerchief pocket squares, Leo appears to be a calm, almost reverent presence when he presides over the annual National Catholic Prayer Breakfast, which featured an address from President Trump in 2020, or presumably when he attends the secretive meetings of the thousand-year-old, quasi-political Roman Catholic Knights of Malta. At the 2020 prayer breakfast, a "tradition" he founded with a few other ultraconservative Catholics including White House counsel Pat Cipollone, Leonard looked perfectly serene, hands clasped before him, as he presented traditionalist Catholic attorney general William Barr with an award dedicated to "those who have gone to great lengths to advance the teachings and tenets of the Catholic Church." Barr had restarted federal executions a few months before, and was in the midst of breaking a 130-year precedent of pausing federal executions during a presidential transition period, ordering five state killings within a few days after the November elections, including one each on the day before and the day after he received the award. (The Catholic Church condemns capital punishment.) Behind his tranquil demeanor on such occasions, Leonard Leo has the cunning of a political operator, and to judge by the success of his numerous projects, he is utterly convincing as a fundraiser.

"We're going to have to understand that judicial confirmations these days are more like political campaigns," he told the members of the shadowy Council for National Policy, the power group of

Christian right leaders, media, and corporate heads who meet annually to strategize with wealthy patrons and Republican operatives, in 2019. "We're going to have to be smart as a movement."

Leo organized his movement by means of a web of nonprofits with political aims and largely Christian orientations, raising hundreds of millions of dollars over the years from corporations, nonprofits, individuals, and "social welfare" organizations that, by law, do not have to disclose their donors, all of them conservative or libertarian, and in sync with originalism, the term for the Federalist Society's view of the Constitution. Originalism covers a spectrum of thought, and a subset, textualism, generally posits that the Constitution's meaning may only be derived by considering its wording as understood by its eighteenth-century authors, and the public of the time. Broadly speaking, originalists reject the idea that the Constitution is a living document that may be interpreted to meet a changing world. What is not in the Constitution—think abortion, gay marriage—does not demand constitutional protection.

The fathers of the country, originalists may claim, were men of God who founded a shining city on a hill that reflected their Christian values. Conservatives on the court are directed by these understandings. How did these ultrarightist jurists come to be the majority on the highest court in the land? In large part, through the machinations and inspired perseverance of Leonard Leo.

In 1991, when the Federalist Society hired Leo as its first permanent employee, he delayed his start there to help Clarence Thomas through the process of securing a seat on the Supreme Court. With tens of millions of dollars in funding from the Judicial Confirmation Network, a nonprofit "social action" foundation and one of the network of organizations from whose pockets Leo draws, he then led campaigns that resulted in seats on the bench for Samuel Alito and, as chief justice, John Roberts. After Barack Obama was elected president in 2008, the Judicial Confirmation Network changed its name to the Judicial Crisis Network (its president is Carrie Severino, a conservative Catholic, Federalist Society member, and former law clerk for Clarence Thomas), and poured millions of dollars more into blocking the confirmation of Merrick Garland, Obama's nominee to replace Antonin Scalia, an early Federalist Society supporter, who had died in February 2016. A federal judge, Garland had overseen some of the Justice Department's most significant prosecutions of the 1990s—the Oklahoma City bombing, the Unabomber—and was known as a consensus builder at the Court of Appeals where he was serving. Over a period of nine months, with Republican congressional allies, Leo successfully led the campaign to block Garland from even getting a hearing, until Donald Trump was safely elected in November 2016.

The coast was now clear for the new Republican president to name conservative justices, beginning with a replacement for Scalia. But Federalists and ultraconservatives could not take a chance that Trump might name just any candidate. In the past, too many conservatives had moved to the center once they sat on the court, and the constituency for an adamantine rightist justice like Alito or Thomas wanted to make sure it wouldn't happen again. Leo became Trump's judicial advisor, providing him with names of candidates vetted by the Federalist Society. He shepherded the successful confirmations of Neil Gorsuch and Brett Kavanaugh and, when Justice Ruth Bader Ginsburg died in September 2020, the lightning-fast confirmation of Amy Coney Barrett, who took the judicial oath just seven days before Trump lost the election to Joe Biden.

In the meantime, the Federalist Society prospered by means of its connections to conservative Supreme Court justices. Gorsuch, Alito, Kavanaugh, and Thomas have all been featured speakers at the society's annual conferences, with Kavanaugh, Alito, and Thomas advertised as draws at the society's elegant fundraising dinners—donors at the $100,000 tier were seated near the justices.

MONEY TRAIL

WHERE DID THE money come from to tilt the Supreme Court so dramatically to the right, where it now stands? Who paid for media ads, marketing campaigns, briefing sessions for journalists? For lobbying members of Congress, their aides, and other influencers? For placing pundits on the radio and talking heads on TV?

The money trail might be traced back to the 1970s and 1980s, when the fabulously wealthy Koch brothers, David and Charles, created conservative think tanks and study centers to shape public policy in the direction of libertarianism. The brothers were not religious, but their aims and concern for their business's bottom line conveniently aligned with those of evangelical Christians, who were becoming politically active, and conservative Catholics seeking ways to put their radical-right philosophy into the public square.

Besides the Federalist Society and other projects, the Koch brothers funded the pivotal Wellspring Committee, run by Neil and Ann Corkery, members of the traditionalist Catholic organization Opus Dei. Leo raised money for Wellspring, which in turn financed his original advocacy nonprofit, the Judicial Education Project; by 2018, DonorsTrust, the conservative donor-advised fund that facilitates anonymous major giving, backed by the Koch network and other plutocrats, was financing 99 percent of the Judicial Education Project's operations.

As Trump supporters began spreading the lie that U.S. elections were riddled with fraud, Leo rebranded the Judicial Education Project

as the Honest Elections Project, a registered fictitious name of his
Concord Fund, itself a rebrand of the Judicial Crisis Network. At the
same time, he registered the name of a connected "85 Fund," so that,
along with the Judicial Crisis Network, which had funded Leo's campaign to keep President Obama's Supreme Court nomination off the
court, the legal maneuver allowed one pot of money to operate under
multiple names, with little public disclosure that it is all presided over
by Leo. The new Honest Elections Project started off fast, advising
that photo IDs should be necessary to vote, filing Supreme Court and
district court *amicus* briefs favoring restriction on mail-in ballots, and
advocating for state legislature authority in federal elections. Thus the
evolution of just one thread of the Leo network: from confirming
ultraconservative judges to supporting voter suppression.

THE MONEY WEB

THE GRAND PLAN to shift the ship of state toward Christian
nationalism has taken time and enormous amounts of money. In
Leonard Leo's network alone, only depicting a wildly complex grid
showing interconnected foundations and projects might give an idea
of where the funding for the journey comes from, and how the groups
relate to each other. And how that network has moved around hundreds of millions of dollars from a plethora of sources over the last
twenty years, linked to Leo and to one another in aims, finances,
board members, personnel, sometimes even with the same addresses
and phone numbers.

But we can get a hint of points on the grid by looking even briefly at
names of some of the groups of which Leo has been president, the only
employee, or on the board of directors, besides those mentioned above.

- America Engaged. Gave $1 million to the National Rifle Association, which then took out ads supporting the nomination of Neil Gorsuch to the Supreme Court, and funded the Koch-affiliated Freedom Partners organization, which also supported Gorsuch.
- Freedom and Opportunity Fund. Gave $4 million to an advocacy group called Independent Women's Voice, whose president appeared on Fox News to throw doubts on the testimony of Christine Blasey Ford, the Stanford professor who accused Supreme Court nominee Brett Kavanaugh of sexual assault.
- BH Group, LLC. One of the biggest single donors ($1 million) to President Trump's inauguration; received $750,000 million from Wellspring for "public relations," but doesn't have a website.
- BH Fund. Began with an anonymous $24 million donation; gave $20 million to George Mason University to name its law school for late conservative Supreme Court justice and early Federalist Society organizer Antonin Scalia.
- CRC Advisors. A for-profit "public relations" firm that represents high-profile conservative clients, and aims at confirmation of judges at state and local levels and at federal and state deregulation. Leo's partner in CRC Advisors, Greg Mueller, created the "Swift Boat" controversy that maligned 2004 presidential candidate John Kerry.
- Reclaim New York. A self-described nonpartisan group in which Leo partners with former Trump advisor Steve Bannon, and with billionaire heiress Rebekah Mercer, a major contributor to conservative causes. Reclaim encourages small-town residents to file Freedom of Information requests about school board spending, for instance, then sues the often-overwhelmed

boards for noncompliance. A critic quoted in the newspaper of one targeted town said Reclaim aims to "sow distrust" in government.

- Rule of Law Trust. Launched in 2018 with an anonymous donation of $80 million, the trust has no website or online presence, no employees, and Leo is the sole trustee on its tax return, which lists its purpose as "to advance conservative principles." An investigation by Citizens for Responsibility and Ethics in Washington (CREW), a watchdog group, concluded that people who received money from the trust "are either longtime Federalist Society officials-turned-consultants like Leo, or operatives with a long history working behind the scenes on dark money groups tied to Leo."

THE SUMS INVOLVED in Leo's favorite projects have always been staggering. As *The Washington Post* reported in 2019, between 2014 and 2017 alone, Bannon, Mercer, and Leo collected more than $250 million to support conservative policies and judges at all federal and state levels. In the future, Leonard Leo's financial capacity to shape projects and elections will be virtually limitless, underwritten by the largest known political advocacy donation in U.S. history, from Illinois industrialist Barre Seid. During his long—he is ninety—life, Seid has kept a low public profile, although it is known that he has funded right-wing causes such as climate denialism and the fight against Medicaid expansion, and contributed to a group that promotes Islamophobia. In late 2021, Seid donated his company to Leo's Marble Freedom Trust, which had been formed in January of that year, and in a complicated maneuver, Leo's trust then sold the company for an extraordinary sum: $1.6 billion. Leo is now positioned to finance his already sprawling ultraright network with one of the largest pools of political capital in the history of the country.

* * *

LEONARD LEO'S WEB of contacts and advocacy groups may be political, but it is hardly secular. He influences, and presumably is influenced by, a network of rightist Catholic groups to which he belongs. Leo is on the board of the Opus Dei–run Catholic Information Center, a touchstone for fervent Catholics in the capital, which connects him to others who frequent the center, like former White House counsel for President Trump Pat Cipollone and former attorney general William Barr (who are also on the board), former Trump spokeswoman Kellyanne Conway, Catholic members of Congress, and lobbyists. Besides membership in the Knights of Malta, Leo is also a Steward of St. Peter, a fraternity whose members make a $1 million donation to the Papal Foundation in the Vatican "to fund the Holy Father's work." He is on the board of the venerable Catholic Association; of a lobbying group called Catholic Voices, which trains laypeople to speak on television and radio about controversial issues related to the Catholic Church; of the anti-abortion Students for Life of America; and of the Catholic University of America in Washington, D.C., the only pontifical university in the United States, founded by U.S. bishops in 1887.

Tom Carter, the former communications director at the United States Commission on International Religious Freedom, told author Greg Olear about his former boss, "He believes he's on a mission from God."

FROM PIN POINT TO WASHINGTON, D.C.

LEONARD LEO AND Clarence Thomas have in common devotion to their Catholic faith. In a documentary on his life, Thomas said he learned as a child from the Catholic catechism that people were created "to know, love, and serve God in this world, and be with him in the next, and I can't think of a better philosophy."

In the world of law, Thomas may come closest to being the ideal of that other engine of Leo's life, the Federalist Society, because Thomas is the original originalist, the most conservative justice on the court. "When interpreting constitutional text, the goal is to discern the most likely public understanding of a particular provision at the time it was adopted," he wrote in a 2010 decision.

One thing Leo, who so admired his grandfather, would understand about Thomas at an intuitive level is the justice's life debt to his own grandfather, Myers Anderson. Thomas called him "Daddy."

Thomas, too, regards his elder as an embodiment of the American dream, albeit, in Thomas's case, within the racist limits of Jim Crow. Myers Anderson owned several properties and a company that operated out of his house delivering coal and fuel wood. The income allowed him to help relatives or neighbors when a need arose—a model for Thomas's belief that not government but one's own community should provide for the less fortunate.

"He was a deeply religious man who lived by the Christian virtues," Thomas wrote of Myers Anderson in his 2007 memoir, *My Grandfather's Son*. "He was a man who believed in responsibility and self-help. And though this could not bring him freedom in a segregated society, it at least gave him independence from its daily demeaning clutches."

Clarence Thomas was born in Pin Point, Georgia (pop. 250), in a shanty—his word—with no bathroom or electricity except for a single light in the living room. He remembers the town, with its hanging Spanish moss and lazy sun, as idyllic, but describes a harsh reality too. With his mother, younger brother, and older sister—their father had abandoned them when Clarence was two—the family trucked water by foot in lard cans from a nearby faucet through the woods to the house.

When his mother could no longer raise the family while holding on to a full-time job as a house cleaner at ten dollars a week (she refused to go on welfare), she dumped the boys' belongings into paper grocery bags, one for each, and delivered her sons and the bags to the Savannah house of their grandparents, who took them in on the condition that the grandparents alone would do the raising. (Clarence's sister went to live with an aunt.) For Clarence, then age seven, the change to a proper house with built-in plumbing and his own bed was hard to believe, even though it included hard work on his grandfather's farm and helping to deliver fuel oil. But he soon adjusted to the new life and would make good use of the relative advantages it provided over the old.

With the new circumstances came the Catholic faith, which Thomas practices today. Unlike his grandfather's relatives and the rest of the local community, who were Baptist or followers of one of the southern "Holiness" churches, Myers Anderson had admired the orderliness of Catholic ritual and the discipline of priests and nuns. He became Catholic in 1949, and pursued his religion with all the zeal of a convert, sharing his faith with the young Clarence. The boy was soon serving 6:00 a.m. Mass on Sundays, having mastered the responses, which were then in Latin, and attending a Catholic school where nuns taught all-Black classes—for years the state of Georgia would defy the new anti-segregation law decided in 1954 by the Supreme Court, in *Brown v. Board of Education*. Catechism class opened the mornings, and the students said the rosary together each afternoon. Some outsiders called the teachers "the nigger sisters," Thomas recalled, because they showed love for their charges, instructing the children "that God made all men equal, that Blacks were inherently equal to whites, and that segregation was morally wrong."

Whatever the good sisters taught Clarence Thomas as a boy, his later studies and life experience would lead him to believe that equality of Black and white in the United States did not truly exist, and that the condition was unchangeable. "There is nothing you can do to get past Black skin," Thomas told journalist Juan Williams in *The Atlantic*. "I don't care how educated you are, how good you are at what you do—you'll never have the same contacts or opportunities, you'll never be seen as equal to whites."

Thomas attended Catholic high school, and a Catholic seminary, because as a teenager he wanted "nothing more" than to be a priest, although he dropped out after two years in the wake of racist remarks from other seminarians after the murder of Rev. Martin Luther King. He took an undergraduate degree at the College of the Holy Cross, and a law degree at Yale. After graduation however, he peeled a fifteen-cent price sticker from a pack of cigars and affixed it to his Yale diploma, disgusted with the knowledge that no matter how brilliant he might be, the elite-school degree meant one thing for a white person, and another for a Black person. Ineradicable racism would always make people assume he was less capable than a white man. "Conscious and unconscious prejudice persists in our society," Thomas wrote in one of his first Supreme Court opinions (*Georgia v. McCollum*, 1992). "Common sense and common experience confirm this understanding." And Black people should not look to the government for relief, he believed—it only perpetuates the assumption that they are an underclass.

Leonard Leo and Clarence Thomas are not just Republican Catholics; they are ultraconservatives. Thomas comes close to being a libertarian, in his record of rejection of virtually any government regulation. Just as Leonard Leo said of his Italian grandfather, that he "understood the value of capitalism," having worked his way up from the tailor's bench to a top rung of a major corporation, so Clarence Thomas attributes the same understanding of unregulated capitalism to his own grandfather. And he would have "prefer[red] to starve to death" rather than receive government aid, Thomas writes of Anderson, which he perceived as another kind of slavery. His grandfather's faith and worldview—including his economic perspective—were inseparable in the man, and became a model for Clarence. Capitalism made Thomas's grandfather what he was, an independent businessperson, so that attacks on capitalism were personal to Thomas.

In a 1987 speech to the Pacific Legal Foundation, a libertarian think tank in San Francisco, Thomas quoted James Madison in the Federalist Paper Number 10, on the first object of government, the "protection of different and unequal faculties of acquiring property." This, he said, meant "any attack" on wealth, no matter how it was obtained, was "really an attack on the means to acquire wealth." Unregulated capitalism must be protected; it could allow a class of Black businessmen to flourish, liberating the Black entrepreneurs from white supremacy (Thomas leaves out references to Black women in his writing and speeches). "Do you think this man [his grandfather, Myers Anderson] would raise his grandsons to ignore economic freedom as a major part of their lives?" he asked rhetorically in the San Francisco speech.

GINNI

ATOP HIS DESK, under glass, Justice Clarence Thomas keeps two drawings by the young hand of the late Margaret Leo. In the home of Margaret's parents, Leonard and Sally, is a lovely photo of their daughter and Virginia Thomas, Justice Thomas's wife. In the picture, Margaret gazes from her wheelchair at Virginia, known as Ginni, who is looking at her with a smile. Leonard Leo and Clarence Thomas are friends, both pivotal to the Christian conservative movement, but within that movement, Virginia Thomas is more than just a friend of Leo's, or Clarence Thomas's wife. Ginni Thomas is also a Catholic political activist who acts as a kind of bridge connecting prominent fundamentalist evangelicals and Catholics supporting the Christian nationalist agenda. Whether she influences her husband's court decisions, or whether she, Leo, and Clarence Thomas are simply on the same wavelength, is an open question. But Ginni should not be left out of the equation.

Virginia Lamp Thomas (b. 1957) was raised in Nebraska by parents so politically fervent that a neighbor who had grown up across the street described them to *The New Yorker* as "the roots of the modern, crazy Republican Party." Young Ginni, tall and blue-eyed, received a law degree from the Jesuit-run Creighton University, worked in Washington, and, in May 1987, at age thirty, married Clarence Thomas, then chairman of the Equal Employment Opportunity Commission (EEOC), appointed by President Ronald Reagan. "She was a gift from God that I had prayed for," Thomas has said, and still calls her "my bride." Virginia Lamp's white family was surprised that Ginni chose a Black man to marry but welcomed Clarence. The *Omaha World-Herald* quoted her father, Donald Lamp, saying, "If you have any feelings about Black color, you forget about it as soon as you start talking to him."

"The one person [he] really listens to is Virginia," said Thomas's successor at the EEOC, Evan Kemp, also a longtime friend. "He depends on her for advice," Kemp had told *The Washington Post* in the lead-up to Thomas's Supreme Court confirmation hearings.

Ginni Thomas stood by her husband during the tumultuous 1991 congressional approval process in which attorney Anita Hill accused him of sexual harassment, and members of the Judiciary Committee, led by then-senator Joe Biden, questioned him closely. In an emotional closing statement, the nominee said that he was the victim of a "high-tech lynching." Confirmed by a narrow 52–48 margin (Biden voted against him), Thomas speaks bitterly about the experience to this day. In a 2020 documentary about his life broadcast on PBS, *Created Equal: Clarence Thomas in His Own Words*, he says of the hearings: "Do I have like stupid written on the back of my shirt? I mean come on. We know what this is all about. People should just tell the truth: 'This is the wrong Black guy; he has to be destroyed.'" The film is sympathetic to Thomas. Funders included Leonard Leo's advocacy group, the Judicial Education Project; the Charles Koch Foundation; the Federalist Society; the Christian evangelical Psalm 103 Foundation—the last verse of the psalm for which the foundation is named is "Bless the LORD, all his works, in all places of his dominion."

During television coverage of the Thomas confirmation hearings, Ginni Thomas could be seen daily sitting in the second row behind her husband, often glaring at the long panel of white men conducting the interrogation. After the Anita Hill accusations, the process "became something different, [like] spiritual warfare," Ginni told the *National Catholic Register*. She said the couple found strength in "prayer . . . and our own spiritual refocusing." She converted to Catholicism in 2002.

THE COMPANY SHE KEEPS

VIRGINIA THOMAS'S LANGUAGE, sharp lawyer's mind, and open manner—Leo has described her as "extraordinarily vivacious"— appeal to fellow activists in the web of conservative advocacy organizations and "charities" in which she is enmeshed. The groups bring together ultraconservative Catholics and evangelical Christians in the shared quest for a Christian nation. She has presented "Impact Awards" to honor "courageous cultural warriors" such as Fox News commentator Sean Hannity, Islamophobe Frank Gaffney, Jr., Leonard Leo, and others on behalf of United in Purpose, an organization at the heart of the Christian nationalist power movement. United in

Purpose cosponsored the 2018 Values Voter Summit with the fundamentalist evangelical Family Research Council and the Faith and
Freedom Coalition to mobilize white evangelical Christians to elect
Republicans; in 2020 the organization pledged to mobilize "dormant
evangelical and conservative Catholic voters," using religious affiliation to stir up nonwhite voters who had been weak on supporting
Trump. Both Ginni Thomas and Leonard Leo have occupied leading
positions in the power-broking Council for National Policy and its
political action affiliate.

In 2010 Virginia Thomas founded Liberty Consulting (listed as an
asset on her husband's Supreme Court disclosures) to offer "strategic
advice, build coalitions [and] connect people and projects," according
to her LinkedIn profile reported on by CNBC.

The businesess's site appears to have been taken down some time
after news broke of her email exchanges with presidential chief of
staff Mark Meadows during the Capitol takeover. But on LinkedIn,
Ginni Thomas reportedly described the firm's purpose was to assist
"citizen activists, leaders and nonprofits to succeed and have impact
in defending the principles that have made America an exceptional
nation." She has said she is not a lobbyist, although the business was
once called Liberty Lobby.

Many of the advocacy groups to which Ginni Thomas is connected
produce *amici curiae*, or friend of the court briefs, to the Supreme
Court. Justices may read and consider these legal arguments and
observations, from conservative and liberal entities, that are not direct parties to a case, but have an interest in its outcome, and want
to influence the judges in their favor. Sometimes the briefs are so
cogent, or friendly to a justice's thinking, they are quoted in final
decisions. Yet they can be submitted by groups funded by anonymous
donors, allowing special interests to influence the law without public
accountability. As courts are increasingly seen as vehicles for social

change, the number of briefs is increasing—decades ago they were rare, but today it's a rare case that doesn't have them. Sometimes a dozen or more are attached to cases important for adherents of Christian nationalism, such as those that treat abortion, freedom of speech, freedom of religion, or incarnations of "freedom" issues like COVID vaccinations, masking, and mandates. (More than 140 *amicus* briefs were filed in *Dobbs v. Jackson Women's Health Organization*, the case that reversed *Roe v. Wade*.) Conservative briefs may reinforce the aims and political thinking of Leonard Leo's Federalist Society, which is not surprising, as its members often craft them.

Supreme Court spouses like Virginia Thomas customarily avoid activities, sometimes even careers, that might conflict with the work of the justices to whom they are married. Martin D. Ginsburg, a successful tax lawyer, went into teaching when his wife, Ruth, was nominated to the Supreme Court. But that is not Ginni Thomas's way.

In 2009, she openly declared war on the Obama administration's "hard left agenda" by establishing a conservative nonprofit organization aligned with the Tea Party, Liberty Central, which became a clearinghouse for right-wing political donations. Thanks to *Citizens United v. FEC*, the landmark 2010 Supreme Court case in which her husband voted with the 5-4 majority, a century of campaign finance precedent was thrown out, and wealthy corporations were allowed to funnel unlimited amounts of donated money through "social welfare" nonprofits like Liberty Central, where Leonard Leo was a member of the board. Liberty Central campaigned against the signature Obama-era issue, the Affordable Care Act, lobbying lawmakers to repeal it while promoting falsehoods, such as calling Obamacare a "disaster" for small businesses. Ginni Thomas announced grandly to the public that she "felt called to the front lines with you, with my fellow citizens, to preserve what made America great."

Congress tried to resist the Ginni Thomas onslaught. In 2011, seventy-four Democratic members sent a letter to Justice Thomas. "The line between your impartiality and you and your wife's financial stake in the overturn of healthcare [sic] reform is blurred," they wrote. "Your spouse is advertising herself as a lobbyist who has 'experience and connections' and appeals to clients who want a particular decision—they want to overturn health care reform."

The Congress members who signed the letter also wrote that Justice Thomas had failed "to disclose Ginny [sic] Thomas's receipt of $686,589 from the Heritage Foundation, a prominent opponent of healthcare [sic] reform." They asked him to recuse himself from cases on the Affordable Care Act. He did not do so. Future decisions on cases involving the act would favor plaintiffs with religious claims, with Clarence Thomas in the majority, further restricting the reach of government-supported medical care.

Virginia Lamp Thomas was a political activist before she met Clarence Thomas, didn't stop when he was nominated to the Supreme Court, and continues today, despite appearances of conflict of interest. When Donald Trump lost the 2020 presidential election, she sent emails to twenty-nine Arizona lawmakers telling them to name a list of electors who would cast their ballots for Trump in the Electoral College, despite Biden's victory in the state—the responsibility was "yours and yours alone," she wrote. She sent twenty-nine post-election texts to President Trump's chief of staff, Mark Meadows, urging him to work on overturning the election. On January 6, 2021, she sent rousing texts to others supporting the crowd that was with her listening to President Trump's provocative speech in person, before a mob stormed the Capitol. In March 2022, it was discovered that she exchanged text messages with Meadows while the Capitol was under siege, telling him, "Do not concede. It takes time for the army who is gathering for his back."

Ginni Thomas has said she was elsewhere during the Capitol

violence, but it was not her first acquaintance with members of the mob. In 2010, she cohosted a banquet with the president of Moms for America, at a symposium described as the "largest conservative training event in history," where a featured guest was Stewart Rhodes, a Yale Law School graduate who founded the extremist militia group the Oath Keepers, which claims more than thirty thousand members including law enforcement officers, soldiers, and military service personnel—some were accused of planning the Capitol attacks, holding trainings in the weeks before January 6. In 2022 a federal court jury in Washington D.C. convicted Rhodes of seditious conspiracy against the United States and other crimes related to the Capitol breach and attempt to block the legal transition of presidential power. Ginni Thomas also served on the advisory board of a group of young activists called Turning Point USA, whose leaders bragged of renting buses that brought hundreds to the capital that day. The group, begun in 2012 and now on 1,300 college and high school campuses, it claims, is funded by right-wing mega-donors "with a history of flooding the political process with money," as the watchdog Center for Media and Democracy describes them, including the Lynde and Harry Bradley Foundation, the Ed Uihlein Family Foundation, Foster Friess, Michael Leven, and Koch brothers–affiliated groups including DonorsTrust. In 2021, Turning Point CEO and cofounder Charlie Kirk, also a member of the Council for National Policy and spokesman for its political arm, CNP Action, sought $43 million from donors for a nonprofit called Turning Point Faith to recruit pastors and other church leaders to become active on local and national issues aimed to "win the American Culture War and to inspire our kids [to] love America again."

In April 2021, after her husband spoke from the bench against Twitter and Facebook, which had just banned Donald Trump, Ginni Thomas sent out an email blast inviting associates to an "influence

network," to fight "corporate tyranny over free speech." By this time
Leonard Leo had shifted away from his long-held position as executive vice president of the Federalist Society, to devote time to the for-profit CRC Advisors, where, according to *The Washington Times*, he
will "build public policy projects, coalitions, and groups that connect
nonprofits, philanthropists, and prominent lawyers in pursuit of the
conservative movement's agenda." In other words, just what he has
been doing for the last thirty years.

One year after the attack on the Capitol, in January 2022, the
Supreme Court rejected a request by former president Trump to block
the release of presidential records wanted by the congressional committee investigating who was responsible for the violence. The records
contained text messages, like those sent by Ginni Thomas, to and
from White House chief of staff Mark Meadows during the Capitol
siege. The court's decision was nearly unanimous.

Only Clarence Thomas disagreed with the decision. No legal reasoning for his dissent was given.

In September, Ginni Thomas gave three hours of testimony to
the United States House Select Committee on the January 6 Attack,
which was investigating the Capitol riot and probing the "fake electors" scheme in which she was involved. She told the committee that
she still believed the false claim that the 2020 election was stolen.

The web of nonprofits Leonard Leo has created or energized over
the years is transferring its clout from shaping laws and judicial rosters
to placing limits on voting and redesigning the electoral process in
other ways to serve its ends. With the colossal $1.6 billion donation
to his nonprofit Marble Freedom Trust, the best-financed political
operative in U.S. history will have unprecedented means to pursue his
mission, which dovetails with that of his good friends Clarence and
Ginni Thomas, moving the country to run ever more closely upon
Christian principles as they see them.

5

The Pizza King and the Princes of the Church

ON JULY 1, 2021, the United States Supreme Court invalidated California's donor disclosure law, allowing charities and nonprofit organizations to use "dark money," a term for funds from sources that the organizations are not required to identify. The decision was a victory for leaders of dozens of conservative nonprofits that use politics and the courts to install their version of Christiandom in the United States.

For U.S. bishops, the Republican-dominated Supreme Court proved again to be the answer to their prayers. And for one eighty-four-year-old Florida resident, Domino's Pizza founder Thomas Monaghan, among the most important laypeople pushing the Christian nationalism agenda, the decision surely brought the kind of satisfaction he may have envisioned when he took "a rich man's vow of poverty" more than two decades ago. That was when Monaghan, a multimillionaire and lifelong daily Mass goer, decided to divert his wealth into an audacious project: creating the kingdom of God on earth.

"I try to remember that my main job is to become a saint," Monaghan told biographer Joseph Pearce.

One of Thomas Monaghan's most important tools in the quest, the Thomas More Law Center (TMLC), launched with his millions in 1998, challenged the California donor disclosure law along with another nonprofit, the libertarian Americans for Prosperity, founded by billionaire brothers Charles and David Koch in 2004. Public interest law groups, which marshal legal tactics in support of policy goals, were once identified mostly with the American Civil Liberties Union and the NAACP Legal Defense Fund. In the 1980s, however, the evangelical preacher and former Republican presidential candidate Pat Robertson and other televangelists including James Dobson and Jerry Falwell founded or lent their support to some early Christian conservative legal organizations—sometimes called CCLOs. Today there is a boom in these Christian-oriented legal advocacy firms, including the Alliance Defending Freedom, American Center for Law and Justice, Center for Law and Religious Freedom, Liberty Counsel, and several others. The Becket Fund for Religious Liberty, one of the most active, isn't called a CCLO because it takes cases involving non-Christian religions, but its cases, and friend of the court legal briefs, overlap with the others. What Becket says of itself might be said of all, that they "reside at the crossroads of church and state."

Monaghan's Thomas More Law Center, one of the few CCLOs with explicitly Catholic foundations, exulted in its 2021 Supreme Court victory in the dark money case *Americans for Prosperity v. Bonta*, which split the justices 6–3. Dark money donors to certain causes like to remain hidden, making them virtually untraceable by journalists, investigators, or political opponents. Their funds destroy transparency during political campaigns and efforts to pass laws on social issues, such as gay rights. Who is giving the money for, or against? What interests do they have? Lack of disclosure also means that the wealthy can direct money to nonprofits that act like clearinghouses, like DonorsTrust, which are then able to direct the donations wherever they want, including disbursing them during political campaigns, as long as they don't endorse a particular candidate and politics is not their main activity—guidelines so loose that they are honored in the breach. The donors, often wealthy corporations, do their best to remain secret.

The TMLC and the Koch organization chose to challenge donor disclosure law in California, where nearly a quarter of the country's charitable assets are held—$851 billion in 2018—which gave the state a particularly compelling reason to exercise oversight on the sector. Charitable organizations that wished to solicit tax-deductible contributions from California residents had to maintain membership in a registry managed confidentially by the state's attorney general, for which it was necessary to submit a tax form that listed the organizations' biggest donors. The Thomas More Law Center and the Koch foundation claimed the donor disclosure requirement was against the law, and the conservatives on the Supreme Court agreed. Writing for the majority, Chief Justice John Roberts said every request for information "that might chill association" is unconstitutional. The California rule violated the First Amendment, he said, by deterring donors from making contributions.

Writing in dissent, Justice Sonia Sotomayor said no "chill" had been demonstrated; rather, the kind of donors in question were "only too happy to publicize their names across the websites and walls of the organizations they support."

"Today, the Court abandons the requirement that plaintiffs demonstrate that they are chilled, much less that they are reasonably chilled," Sotomayor wrote. Instead, she said, the ruling meant tax-exempt "charitable" organizations "who wish to avoid their obligations can do so by vaguely waving toward First Amendment 'privacy concerns,'" even if "not a single individual" who donates risks reprisals. That is "'all irrelevant'" to the majority's decision," said Sotomayor's dissent, which was joined by Justices Breyer and Kagan. "Neither precedent nor common sense supports such a result . . . The evidence shows that California's confidential reporting requirement imposes trivial burdens" on rights of association, but did play "a meaningful role in the ability to identify and prosecute charities engaged in malfeasance," and the requirement, she insisted, was indeed constitutional.

Nevertheless, the court conservatives carried the day, allowing the money behind elections to recede more deeply into the shadows under the cover of law. Warning of its effect on political campaigns, Sotomayor said the court's decision marked "reporting and disclosure requirements with a bull's-eye."

PAVING THE ROAD TO THE COURTS WITH GOLD

FROM ITS BEGINNINGS, Monaghan's Thomas More Law Center declared itself "The Sword and the Shield for People of Faith." Its lawyers lost a 2010 case, *Miles Christi v. Northville Township, Michigan*, in which a Catholic religious order holding services for others in a single-family residence ran afoul of local zoning laws, and invoked the free exercise protections of the First and Fourteenth Amendments. A judge decided that the good fathers had alternatives they should have tried before the lawsuit, and the case went nowhere. From then until the 2021 victory against the California donor disclosure law, Tom Monaghan's center had litigated and sometimes won more than two dozen cases that involve core interests of the bishops: abortion; public prayer; speech about God in the classroom; "culture wars"; and intelligent design—the notion that some things in the universe are so complex they are best explained by a supernatural intelligence, like God, not evolution. With its choice of cases, and the legal talent it can command, the TMLC rises as an example of what a good, rich Catholic can accomplish for the bishops' brief. The status of the legal center that Tom Monaghan founded may be heady for a man who spent years of his life in an orphanage, was kicked out of seminary, and dropped out of college, but Monaghan has written that he always knew he was destined for great things.

TO LOOK AT the arc of his life, it is difficult not to admire Monaghan the man, who came up from poverty and bad luck. Tom's beloved father died when he was a boy of four, and his jobless mother could not handle two young boys and nursing school, so she sent them to a nearby orphanage run by strict Polish nuns. Sometimes the sisters resorted to the whip for discipline. In a 1986 autobiographical account, Monaghan describes the place as a "prison" where he felt himself an "inmate." The single golden memory from those years, it seems, during which he often took refuge to pray in a small chapel, was the kind attention of one Sister Bernarda, who "always encouraged me, even when my ideas were far-fetched." As a teenager on his own, "the clockwork of ritual I had grown accustomed to . . . religion was the one thread of continuity in my life."

The young Monaghan held on to that thread in the U.S. Marines (he had mistakenly thought he was signing up for the Army), and on discharge when he lost almost all his money by trusting scammers, and finally when he invested borrowed cash in a pizzeria in Ypsilanti, Michigan, despite having so little business sense at age twenty-three that he advertised "Call-In and Delivery" before a phone was installed. By dint of round-the-clock work and some luck, however, Monaghan grew his Domino's Pizza until it was one of the biggest companies of its kind in the country. By age fifty, he wore on the same finger two rings "symbolic of me and my life": a twelve-dollar band he bought when he married his wife, Marjorie, in 1962, and the 1984 ring from the World Series won by the Detroit Tigers, the team that Monaghan had bought the year before for $53 million.

The law center is not Monaghan's only legacy. In 1987 he founded an influential club of extremely wealthy Catholic businesspeople, Legatus, described by EWTN, the international religious media conglomerate, as "a sort of spiritual home-base for those Catholics who stand at the helm of America's entrepreneurial ship." He has created—there is no other word for it—an entire Catholic-inspired town in southwestern Florida, called Ave Maria. Another biographer, James Leonard, implies that Monaghan's ego drove the orientation of the town's street grid so that on March 25, which happens to be Tom's birthday, the sunlight streams down the eastward-facing streets and rests on the holy oratory. But more important to the town and the university, and Monaghan's Ave Maria Foundation, March 25 is the Feast of the Annunciation, on which the angel appeared to Mary and she gave her yes to God, her "*fiat*," agreeing to bring Jesus into the world. The town has neat houses, shops, a café, a university, and an accredited law school, spread over four thousand acres, all surrounding the imposing oratory first designed by Monaghan on a napkin and inspired by the architecture of Frank Lloyd Wright. As his wealth grew, Monaghan, who once aspired to be an architect, has owned a Wright house, and designed his corporate headquarters in Michigan in Wright's visionary "prairie style."

Tom Monaghan wants to imbue everything he touches with his own fundamentalist Christian version of the world. He once described development plans for the Ave Maria University town in draconian terms: "We're going to control all the commercial real estate, so there's not going to be any pornography sold in this town. We're controlling the cable system. The pharmacies are not going to be able to sell condoms or dispense contraceptives."

Monaghan's high-end Legatus association of wealthy corporate

Catholics has been called "the most influential lay organization in the Church" by Cardinal Anthony Bevilacqua (d. 2012), a former archbishop of Philadelphia. But besides Legatus, and the Catholic-centered university town, the Thomas More Law Center ranks among Monaghan's most significant legacies because its lawyers aim to change the face of American democracy, toward becoming a Christian nationalist state. The enterprise is named for the sixteenth-century saint who coined the word "utopia."

In the words of Cardinal Raymond L. Burke, formerly the archbishop of St. Louis and now serving in Rome, the Thomas More Law Center is a bulwark against the steady slip away from the authority of religion in U.S. national life.

"During these difficult times in which we are living, in which secularization has ravaged the culture of our homeland," the center's work on abortion, religious liberty, and the family provides a pivotal service "for the restoration of Christian culture," said Burke in an endorsement on the TMLC website.

The center's lawyers have argued, so far without success, that Common Core Standards limit education to a utilitarian "readiness for work" mentality, and "crowd out" Catholic identity in parochial education. They replace "great literature" with objectionable readings, impose an unacceptable burden on homeschoolers, and impinge upon Catholics' control of their own schools, they say.

TMLC lawyers argue other cases involving gay rights (against), and contending violations of freedom of religion and freedom of speech. When Pope Benedict XVI named former San Francisco archbishop William Levada to the pope's former position of prefect of the Congregation for the Doctrine of the Faith in Rome (once known as the Inquisition), Levada ordered his San Francisco successor to forbid Catholic agencies from placing children for adoption with same-sex couples. In the face of an angry public response from the city,

Monaghan's lawyers sued. They charged that a resolution condemning the decision by the board of supervisors was a "state sponsored message of disapproval of religion." (The case was dismissed on grounds the plaintiffs lacked standing to sue.) The center also argued that the Matthew Shepard and James Byrd, Jr., Hate Crimes Prevention Act, named for a gay student beaten to death in Wyoming and an African American man murdered by white supremacists in Texas, was unconstitutional, because it singled out gays for extra protection. The Monaghan lawyers lost that case, but they successfully argued that a seventh grader was within her First Amendment rights in wearing to school a pro-life T-shirt bearing pictures of a growing fetus and a black square representing an aborted fetus.

While incidents of litigation such as these fall within four of the center's declared interests—abortion, family values, religious liberty, national security—a review of its legal efforts over the last twenty years shows more cases than any other belong to a fifth of its categories: "Confronting the threat of radical Islam."

ISLAMOPHOBIA: CHRISTIAN NATIONALIST TOOL

ISLAM IS THE third-largest religion in the United States, after Christianity and Judaism, but the number of Muslims in the country is small, 3.5 million, or 1 percent of the population. And there is no indication Muslims or Islamic organizations aim to take over the country, as the TMLC hysterically warns. Yet Monaghan's lawyers want the public to be afraid: Muslims "have already infiltrated the highest levels of our government, the media, our military, both major political parties, public schools, universities, financial institutions and the cultural elite," a message on their public-facing site declares.

Bowing to "political correctness," it says, our "national leaders refuse to identify Radical Islam as the enemy."

The center's anti-Muslim crusade reflects a bedrock characteristic of Christian nationalism—Islamophobia, a mix of religion, nationalism, and militarism shaped by an irrepressible presumed clash of civilizations that regards the West, represented by Christianity, as pitted against Islam in an existential battle for souls. The perceived struggle goes back 1,400 years to the time when Mohammed, born among polytheistic desert tribes in the deserts of the Arabian Peninsula, began to preach about his revelations that there was only one God, not many, and to spread the teachings of the monotheistic prophets, including Abraham, Job, and, according to Islam, Jesus. Mohammed was supposed to be the last in the line of these prophets to appear. Like Christianity and other religions, Islam historically sometimes spread with the sword. Only after the September 11, 2001, attack on New York by nineteen radical Islamists, however, and especially with the U.S. "war on terror" that followed, often targeting Muslims, did sectors of modern American Christians viscerally connect themselves to the putative clash. Among them, traditionalist Catholics could say they followed their leaders.

During his first visit, in 2006, to his native state, Bavaria, after being elected pope, Benedict XVI gave an address at the University of Regensburg in which he quoted a fourteenth-century Christian emperor who said to an "educated Persian," perhaps himself an emperor, "Show me just what Muhammad brought that was new and there you will find things only evil and inhuman, such as his command to spread by the sword the faith he preached." Later, the Vatican was forced to declare that the pope was quoting from a seven-hundred-year-old document, and the views were not his. But the words took on a life of their own, and both Muslim leaders and ordinary believers reacted with outrage.

Nationalist Islamophobia fed the "birther" calumny used against President Obama, the lie that he was not born in the United States, and was secretly a Muslim. As candidate Donald Trump, who promoted the deception, surged ahead in the race for the Republican presidential nomination, a 2015 survey by the Public Policy Polling organization found that 66 percent of Trump supporters believed the lie that Obama was a Muslim. As soon as Trump became president (having garnered the majority of the Catholic vote), he signed the "Muslim ban," locking out travelers from six countries with majority Muslim populations. The executive order was called "Protecting the Nation from Foreign Terrorist Entry into the United States."

"To resist large-scale Muslim immigration in my judgment is to be responsible," said American traditionalist Cardinal Burke. At a 2019 conference in Rome, Burke said Islam "believes itself to be destined to rule the world . . . You don't have to be a rocket scientist to see what has happened in Europe," citing Muslim immigration to France, Germany, and Italy.

In Burke's case, no spokesman came along later, as the Vatican secretary of state had done after Benedict's Regensburg address, to insist that the cardinal didn't really mean what he seemed to say. In fact, Burke referred to a controversial book to prop up his argument that Muslim immigration is harming the United States: *No Go Zones: How Sharia Law Is Coming to a Neighborhood Near You.* The author, Raheem Kassam, was an editor at the Breitbart News Network, the former home of Trump's one-time chief strategist Steve Bannon, a traditionalist Catholic.

In U.S. courts, Thomas Monaghan's "sword and shield for people of faith" is on the front lines of the Christian Islamophobic crusade. Pat Buchanan, an advisor to Presidents Nixon, Ford, and Reagan, called the center "a cutting edge agency in the culture war for the soul of America," an endorsement that the TMLC displays on its website.

Buchanan, a traditionalist Catholic, suggested that "Christians need warriors in the courts where the culture war is being fought, and the Thomas More Law Center is a crucial element on the crucial front of that culture war." Another admirer, former Florida Republican congressman Allen West, said the TMLC "has initiated and funded more cases challenging the Stealth Jihad being waged against our Nation than any other public interest law firm in America."

THE CASE OF DEARBORN

IN THE MID-NINETEENTH century, French entrepreneurs looking for a way to meet the demand for silk thread sent cocoons and weaving trainers to villages in the Mount Lebanon region of Lebanon, where young women for the first time left their homes to go out and work in the new enterprise. Cheap transport from Marseilles to Beirut, and cheaper labor in Lebanon than could be found in France, led to a local industry for creating fine silk thread for French fabric, a business so lively it led, in turn, to establishing the first Lebanese banks, and constructing the port of Beirut as a major trade hub. In the 1880s fashion changed, and China started exporting cheap synthetic fabrics; the silk thread–weaving industry in Mount Lebanon crashed. Beirut's population was growing fast, and the possibility of military conscription was in the air. For the people of Mount Lebanon, it was a good time to look elsewhere for a living.

So it was that the first Arab immigrants, most of them Christian, came to Dearborn, Michigan. The population of descendants of the silk thread weavers grew, swelled in more recent decades by refugees from conflicts in the Middle East, until today the birthplace of Henry Ford has become home to the country's largest per capita population of residents of Arab descent, now mostly Muslim, in the United States.

Sometimes the city known most for its importance in the history of the automotive industry is also called the heart of Arab America.

Other white ethnic immigrant groups eventually merged smoothly into cities they came to call home, like Poles in Chicago, Sicilians in Brooklyn. But Arabs, especially Arab Muslims, have faced obstacles, particularly since the burst of suspicion and venom directed at Muslim Americans after 9/11. In Dearborn, Thomas Monaghan's law center has pursued cases that add fuel to the fire, involving the Islamophobic alt-right network that intersects with the religious right.

Take the case of *Acts 17 Apologetics v. City of Dearborn*, brought before the federal Nineteenth District Court in 2011 by TMLC attorneys on behalf of an evangelical organization that sought to convert Muslims to Christianity. Speaking for the plaintiffs was cocounsel David Yerushalmi, an attorney known for controversial statements about race, immigration, and Islam. Arguing a case that straddled religion and politics, Yerushalmi was in his element. He also served as counsel for the Center for Security Policy, a think tank founded in 1988 by Frank Gaffney, Jr. After leaving his position as assistant secretary of defense for international security affairs, Gaffney had taken to heart the words of President Reagan's assistant secretary of defense Richard Perle, to whom Gaffney had been a top aide: "What we need is the Domino's Pizza of the policy business . . . If you don't get your policy analysis in 30 minutes, you get your money back." Gaffney was an instigator of the lie that Barack Obama was secretly a Muslim. At least one of his Center for Security Policy think tank's annual reports quotes Perle on the need for a political strategy group on the model of Domino's Pizza.

The incident that sparked *Acts 17 Apologetics* took place at the 2010 Dearborn Arab International Festival, an annual event featuring foods from various countries, art, book sales, information booths, and entertainment. Four Christian evangelical missionaries from a group called Acts 17 Apologetics proselytized among the crowd. When security monitors asked the men to stop distributing gospel tracts and video-taping, a ruckus began and the monitors called on police, who arrested the missionaries on a charge of breaching the peace. They spent the night in jail.

The TMLC brought a federal civil rights action against the Dearborn police and the local Arab American Chamber of Commerce for violations of the missionaries' rights under four amendments: the First (freedom of speech and freedom of religion); Fourth (freedom from arbitrary arrest); Sixth (right to a speedy trial); and Fourteenth (equal protection under the law). In remarks to local press, Richard Thompson, TMLC's president and chief counsel, charged that Dearborn's politics and law enforcement process were "dominated" by Muslims.

"This is a classic example of stealth Jihad being waged right here in America," Thompson said. "And it should be a wake-up call for all patriotic Americans."

In 2013 the City of Dearborn lost the case in a unanimous jury verdict, was required to issue a public apology, and paid the missionaries a confidential settlement, reportedly $300,000. The *Dearborn Free Press* called the trial one of the top stories of the year.

A closer look at the *Acts 17* case suggests the aim of its protagonists was to create a loudspeaker to amplify their radical view of Islam. Other Christian groups give out information at the festival without problems; unlike them, Acts 17 missionaries repeatedly tried to videotape encounters, despite requests to desist and their own publicly expressed purpose to "convert Muslims to Christianity through discussion, debate and dialogue." Even other Christian evangelists were incensed.

"I think [Acts 17] was fishing for somebody to come attack them," pastor Haytham Abi-Haydar of Dearborn's Arabic Fellowship Alliance Church told *Christianity Today*, the flagship publication of evangelical Christians.

"They do ministry with a camera, they're about as abrasive as they can be," said another local pastor. This made it more difficult, he said, for others to evangelize.

In 2009, the Acts 17 missionaries had been expelled from the same event for videotaping interviews at a Muslim booth, so there can be little doubt they went to the 2010 festival knowing how participants would react to their camera. They posted a YouTube video calling the 2009 expulsion an example of "Sharia Law in the U.S."

Reaction to the missionaries' behavior and the court case gave them a wider public platform than they might ordinarily find for expressing their anti-Islamic beliefs. The message from Michigan was clear: the Muslims are taking over. As news spread, voices far from Dearborn rang with fear and condemnation of "sharia." Running for a U.S. Senate seat from Nevada, candidate Sharron Angle, endorsed by talk show host Mark Levin, Sarah Palin, and other ultraconservatives, drew applause at a Tea Party rally when she said, "We're talking about a militant terrorist situation . . . And I don't know how that happened in the United States. It seems to me there is something fundamentally wrong with allowing a foreign system of law to even take hold in any municipality or government situation in our United States."

In 2010 Newt Gingrich told the conservative American Enterprise Institute, "I believe sharia is a mortal threat to the survival of freedom in the United States and in the world as we know it." (By 2016 Gingrich was calling for a "test [of] every person" in the United States "who is of a Muslim background," and for deportation—it wasn't clear to where—of any who "believed in" sharia.) In the wake of the Dearborn incident, Texas Republican state representative Leo Berman of Tyler falsely told the Texas House Committee on Judiciary and Civil Jurisprudence that "the judges in Dearborn are using, and allowing to be used, Shariah law," thereby winning approval of a proposal that would prohibit Texas courts from making legal decisions based on "foreign laws."

No need exists for anti-sharia legislation because if an aspect of sharia law violates a constitutional provision, the Supremacy Clause of the Constitution voids it.

Not only politicians or activist attorneys have cited sharia as menacing. Chief Justice John Roberts referred to it negatively during oral arguments in a case (*Abbott v. Abbott*, 2010) that had nothing to do with Islam or Muslims.

When Anderson Cooper asked Dearborn's mayor John O'Reilly to tell a national television audience whether sharia had been instituted in his city, the mayor answered no. "This is an invention of the people who believe the Muslim faith is a false faith," he said. "They really believe . . . that if Muslims won't convert they should be removed from America."

In targeting sharia, Islamophobes target Islam. Between 2010 and 2012 alone, lawmakers in at least thirty-two states introduced almost one hundred bills to restrict the use of "foreign or religious laws"—the word *sharia* was taken out of early versions when they were deemed unconstitutional, but no one was fooled. Such bills continue to be introduced every year. Their language is intentionally vague, and appears innocuous, with neutral wording to withstand constitutional scrutiny while still limiting the way courts handle cases involving Muslims. Even Richard Thompson, president of Thomas Monaghan's law center, admitted that "Sharia law is the thing people think about" when it came to the bans.

The template for almost all the anti-sharia bills in state legislatures was a piece of model legislation drafted by David Yerushalmi, cocounsel in the TMLC *Acts 17* case. The model is promoted by the American Public Policy Alliance (APPA), an advocacy organization funded by Koch organizations that approaches state legislators through its program American Laws for American Courts (ALAC). The motive of APPA is not hidden. "American Laws for

American Courts was crafted to protect American citizens' constitutional rights against the infiltration and incursion of foreign laws and foreign legal doctrines, especially Islamic Shariah Law," its website says.

Besides his law work, Yerushalmi heads an organization called the Society of Americans for National Existence (SANE), whose charter turns on American exceptionalism, calling the United States a "unique people" bound by a commitment to "America's Judeo-Christian moral foundation." SANE suggests that democracy was the farthest thing from the minds of the founding fathers.

"America was the handiwork of faithful Christians, mostly men, and almost entirely white, who ventured from Europe to create a nation in their image of a country existing as free men under G-d," its charter states. "The founding fathers understood that party-led parliaments and democracy were the worse form of government and sought to resist the movement that was soon to find fertile ground in France with the French Revolution."

No U.S. court has been known to make a decision based on sharia. Proponents of the "foreign law" antipathy bills in statehouses say the action is preemptive, to erect a defense against a problem that might arise. But the spread of anti-sharia legislation and anti-sharia rallies, and the fallout from cases like *Acts 17* and others handled by the TMLC and other Christian law groups, were not so much about the facts or even about laws as they were about the campaign to marginalize Muslims for the sake of a putative Judeo-Christian American nation.

"If this thing passed in every state without any friction, it would have not served its purpose," Yerushalmi told *The New York Times* in 2011, suggesting the bills themselves are a secondary goal. "The purpose was heuristic—to get people asking this question, 'What is shariah?'"

Sharia in Arabic means "the way" or "the path," as in, the path to right conduct. It is not a body of law as such but a philosophical code derived from Islamic scripture, meant to guide the behavior of observant Muslims. By demonizing the term, Islamophobes throw American Muslims to the edge of national society, if not off a cliff. American Muslims are a multitude: African Americans who are Muslim converts or descendants of Muslim Black African slaves; immigrants (most have become U.S. citizens); or descendants of the silk thread weavers of Mount Lebanon who came to Dearborn more than 130 years ago.

> *An immense secularization of the West . . . converges with something we have to face, and it's a very unpleasant topic, but we are in an outright war against jihadist Islamic fascism.*
>
> —Traditionalist Catholic Steve Bannon,
> former presidential strategist who helped design Trump's executive
> order banning citizens from seven Muslim-majority countries

JORDAN DENARI DUFFNER, a scholar of Muslim-Christian relations at Georgetown University, is a former associate of the university's Bridge Initiative, which researches Islamophobia and tracks its expression in the news, in academic studies, and among well-known figures such as Donald Trump, Fox News commentator Tucker Carlson, and former secretary of state and director of the CIA Mike Pompeo, whose anti-Muslim screeds pepper his speeches and commentaries. From her position at the Catholic university, as a practicing Catholic, and as an author of two books on Islamophobia, Duffner said she laments the lack of engagement from most Catholic bishops on public hate of Muslims.

"There has been a good amount of silence from them," Duffner told me in an interview. "They are not very strong on criticizing Catholics who are contributing to it."

Duffner cites George Weigel, distinguished senior fellow of the Ethics and Public Policy Center, a darling of the conservative Catholic press, and the author of a monumental biography of Pope John Paul II, as one of those who "helped normalize Islamophobic ideas in the church and beyond" with a 2009 book, *Faith, Reason, and the War Against Jihadism*. Weigel expresses himself in cutting, sardonic fashion, but others write more stridently, like *New York Times* bestselling Catholic author Robert Spencer, who cofounded, in 2010, a group called Stop Islamization of America (also known as the American Freedom Defense Initiative) with blogger Pamela Geller. Spencer and Geller campaigned against the construction of an Islamic community center near the site of the 9/11 attack, bringing the issue to national prominence as a rallying cry against Muslims. They placed advertisements on the buses and in the subways of American cities that ran a message alongside a picture of a woman wearing an Islamic-style head covering: "IN ANY WAR BETWEEN THE CIVILIZED MAN AND THE SAVAGE, SUPPORT THE CIVILIZED MAN. SUPPORT ISRAEL DEFEAT JIHAD." Spencer and Geller were funded by the Shillman Foundation, which also supports former Boston College professor William Kilpatrick, whose Turning Point Project is "dedicated to educating Catholics about the threat from Islam by arming them with the information . . . necessary to meet the challenge." Just as the writings of Spencer appear in Catholic media, so too do Kilpatrick's, in outlets like *Catholic World Report*, *National Catholic Register*, *Aleteia*, *St. Austin Review*, and *First Things*.

Other ultraconservative Catholic writers and media personalities repeat the anti-Muslim positions, especially those of Spencer, including radio host Al Kresta, who was recruited by Tom Monaghan in the 1990s to run Monaghan's media apostolate, Ave Maria Communications. Kresta eventually became president and CEO, and now hosts his own popular program on Ave Maria Radio. The commentators and apologists cross-tweet, cross-reference, cite, and endorse one another, creating a network that feeds fear of Islam and misinformation about Muslims to Catholics, who may be ready to believe what they hear and read from fellow Catholics and Catholic outlets—especially in the absence of strong guidance from their bishops.

TRUTH AND CONSEQUENCES

Any university worthy of the name is committed to searching for truth and, as far as possible, to finding it.
> —Philosophy of the Curriculum, Ave Maria University

[A] hostile and aggressive religion
> —Description of Islam by Ave Maria University founding president
> Nicholas J. Healy, in the campus newspaper

YEARS AGO, THOMAS Monaghan gave up his multimillion-dollar classic car collection, private plane, and many other trappings of the ultrarich. For all the wealth he accumulated with his hard work, with non-collapsible pizza boxes and promises of thirty-minute delivery, Monaghan has said he believes "there's something in life that's a lot bigger and more important than Domino's."

"I have faith that God will help me find it," he wrote in a 1986 memoir, *Pizza Tiger*, "and that He'll show me the way to my ultimate goal, which is to go to heaven and take as many people as possible with me."

Monaghan's creations, like the Thomas More Law Center and Ave Maria University, appear to operate under the assumption that salvation belongs to a chosen few, and since Muslims are not going to heaven with the likes of their founder, and endanger Christian values, it is permissible—obligatory, perhaps—to treat them as the enemy in this world.

In its advocacy for Islamophobic clients, the TMLC harkens back to a centuries-old attitude among fundamentalist Christian believers: that the very presence of Muslims, by definition heretics, taints a community and makes the City of God on earth further out of reach. Sometimes the noise created by the cases appears to be the point.

The TMLC took on two cases for Robert Spencer and Pamela Geller against a suburban Dearborn transit authority that wanted to keep their anti-Muslim messages off its buses; the authority argued that the content was against their rules because it subjected a group to scorn, and won its case against Spencer and Geller. Other cities, including New York and San Francisco, that claimed the ads could lead to violence were unsuccessful in blocking them.

What might the kind of provocative messaging promoted by these flamboyant fringe Islamophobes lead to? Critics point out that Anders Breivik, the Norwegian spree killer behind the 2011 Norway terrorist attacks that killed seventy-seven people, wrote of his admiration of Geller and Spencer, citing Spencer sixty-four times in his manifesto. (Spencer has condemned Breivik.) At a conference center outside Dallas in May 2015, Geller sponsored a $10,000 prize contest for the best cartoon depicting the Prophet Mohammed—physical depictions of the Prophet are considered blasphemous, and an insult to Muslims, and satirical drawings have engendered violence around the world. Two gunmen opened fire outside the Dallas center at Geller's contest and were shot dead by police.

It may not seem fair to link the work of intellectual or media-savvy Islamophobes, the kind of clients TMLC takes, to such deadly acts. They do not pull the trigger. But their constant negative messaging is like the repetition and recycling of lies about unproven voter fraud by certain politicians: the endless insistence leads some to believe that votes are stolen; huge sums are spent on unnecessary audits; election officials leave long careers in the face of threats of bodily harm; and the very democratic election system is put at risk. Just as a certain level of sound is harmful to humans, persistent public prevarication can erode private judgment. Or act like a tonic to invigorate prejudice. It's fair to ask whether TMLC bears responsibility for assessing the pattern of cases its lawyers represent. Of eighteen cases featured on its website, eight involve clients who take actions knowingly hateful, and virulently opposed, toward Muslims or Islam.

One of the most outrageous Islamophobes defended by the law center founded by Monaghan was the Florida pastor of a tiny Gainesville congregation (fewer than fifty members) who sparked outrage in 2010 when he called for commemorating an anniversary of the September 11 attacks with a "Burn the Koran Day." Protests broke out at the news in Afghanistan, where four were killed, but in the United States supporters jumped on the bandwagon of the idea in social media. President Barack Obama asked Pastor Terry Jones to reconsider his call, and General David Petraeus, then commanding allied forces in Afghanistan, angrily warned that the stunt would jeopardize U.S. troops. Jones stood down, but in March 2011, he burned a Koran on a grill outside his Dove World Outreach Center church, and streamed the event on social media. Another Afghanistan protest cost eleven lives, including those of seven United Nations peacekeepers. "It actually burns very good," Jones can be heard saying on a videotape of the destruction on the grill.

Stand Up America Now, a religious organization formed by Jones and his assistant pastor in Gainesville, Wayne Sapp, to preach the Bible to Muslims and educate about the "threat" of sharia law, sued the City of Dearborn in 2011 when police forbade Jones from burning a Koran in front of the Islamic Center of America, the largest mosque in the country. The TMLC took the case for Jones. As it moved through the courts, the evangelical Christian pastor promoted a fourteen-minute video on YouTube called "The Innocence of Muslims," which portrays the Prophet as a philanderer. Muslims globally were incensed. On September 11, 2012, a protest that began outside the U.S. State Department Special Mission Facility in Benghazi erupted into violence that left more than fifty dead, including four Americans, among them the well-liked U.S. ambassador to Libya, Chris Stevens. The Muhammad trailer, as it's sometimes called, is so poorly produced, risibly written, and woodenly acted—a real effort to sit through—that a viewer wonders what the fuss was about. But for many, the film was an assault on the Prophet at a time when Muslims were feeling under siege from several sides, at war in the Middle East, targets of increased suspicion since 9/11. The film was a spark fallen on tinder ready to burst into flame, made from resentment and frustration, exploited by local organized Islamist groups.

In late August 2013, a federal court ruled in favor of Terry Jones in the Dearborn case, saying police had violated his First Amendment rights when they arrested him at the Islamic center. Days later, on September 11, sheriff's deputies in Polk County, Florida, pulled Jones over for an unlicensed trailer and found almost three thousand Korans soaked in kerosene. They arrested him on charges of unlawfully transporting fuel and unlawfully carrying a firearm. A book burning at a local park was canceled.

The point of laying out the history of the infamous Pastor Jones is not that Monaghan's law center took him as a client—even the ACLU supported Jones's right to free speech in the Dearborn case, an irony because the Thomas More Law Center proudly features a website description of itself by TV host Bill O'Reilly as "the antidote to the ACLU." Instead, reviewing the trajectories of TMLC clients like Jones, Geller, and Spencer reflects the depth of Monaghan's law center's commitment to one of its principal aims, far-fetched though it may seem: to prevent the United States from becoming "a Muslim nation."

The trope, a version of white supremacist replacement theory, which warns that white people are being outnumbered, is meant to spark fear of Muslims as the perennial "other," and places the TMLC in opposition to issues that Pope Francis champions: immigration, human equality, the brotherhood of believers. Francis is noted for his outreach to the Islamic world. He is the first pope to take the name of the famous saint who walked in sandaled feet from Assisi to Egypt during the crusades to meet in peace with the emir—Pope Francis referenced the visit when he traveled to Abu Dhabi in 2019 on its eight hundredth anniversary. In Cairo, Francis signed a declaration of human fraternity with Sheikh Ahmed el-Tayeb, the grand imam of al-Azhar, considered the highest authority in Sunni Muslim jurisprudence. On the first visit by any pope to Iraq, in March 2021, he met with Grand Ayatollah Ali al-Sistani, Iraq's most prominent Shiite leader, in Najaf, a holy city to Shia Muslims, the first time a Roman prelate has met with such a prominent Shia representative. The pope described al-Sistani as "humble," with "wisdom and prudence," adding that "it was good for my soul to encounter him." Francis called the historic meeting a "duty" in his "pilgrimage of faith" to promote human fraternity among religions.

For his efforts Pope Francis has been branded a heretic by 1,500 signatories to an "Open Letter to the Bishops of the Catholic Church, Easter Week, 2019," written by twenty priests and lay scholars. They cited the Document on Human Fraternity cosigned in Abu Dhabi. The pluralism and the diversity of religions, color, sex, race, and language are "willed by God in His wisdom," the document says, but the letter writers branded this "a denial of the truth of the Catholic faith," because "God positively wills the existence only of the Catholic religion."

Former papal nuncio to the United States Carlo Maria Viganò, who remains influential among conservative U.S. bishops, called the Abu Dhabi document "apostasy." He publicly warned against following Europe, which has been "invaded by waves of Muslims who demand rights."

Islamophobia is a weapon in the arsenal of enemies of Pope Francis, like Burke and Viganò. Monaghan has not publicly criticized the pope, but when Viganò demanded the pope's resignation over a false accusation that he let sexual abuse charges against a ranking cleric slide, Monaghan wrote a public letter advising that Legatus, his high-end businessman's salon, which had always tithed to the papacy, was no longer sending its designated offering, but putting the money in escrow until Viganò's contentions against Francis "became clearer."

MEANWHILE, THE LAW school at the university that Monaghan established in Florida is turning out foot soldiers for the causes championed by the Thomas More Law Center. The curriculum at Ave Maria Law School was partly designed by the late ultraconservative Supreme Court justice Antonin Scalia. Its faculty has included Robert Bork, the Supreme Court nominee rejected partly because he said he would roll back civil rights legislation. The school's inaugural Ave Maria lecture was given by Clarence Thomas. The governing board has included Charles Chaput, an admirer of Viganò and former archbishop of Philadelphia, who asked his pastors not to give Holy Communion to those who violated Church teaching on marriage and homosexuality—a rebuke to Francis's outreach to gay people and the divorced. In 2021 Chaput contradicted the pope—virtually calling him a liar—when Francis criticized Eternal Word Television Network, the conservative Catholic operation, for its slanted coverage of the papacy. A current Ave Maria School of Law board member is Cardinal Adam Joseph Maida, retired from the Green Bay diocese, who is also an attorney and episcopal advisor to Ave Maria Mutual Funds (Monaghan is on the board), which describes itself as "America's largest family of Catholic mutual funds built on Pro-Life beliefs." Monaghan has bragged of Ave Maria that, of twenty-seven Catholic law schools in the United States, "we're the only one that's genuinely Catholic."

In Thomas Monaghan the righteous, the alt-right bishops have an ally and a friend. The metaphor of the sword and shield that the TMLC uses to describe itself reprises the Christian militancy within which ultraconservative Catholic laypeople like Monaghan live.

Why do Christians need a "shield" like the TMLC, the biographer James Leonard asked Monaghan. "They need a shield as a defensive thing to protect themselves from the onslaught, taking God out of everything, all the worldliness and the pornography that's getting into the media against society," Monaghan replied.

And the sword? "Probably the sword to take back what's been taken away."

6

The Ministry
of Propaganda

THE MEETING IN a spacious office of the papal nuncio in Bratislava began with a joke. After watching fifty-three Jesuits enter the room, Pope Francis said he had had no idea so many Jesuits were in the country. "The plague has begun," he said to laughter—the pope is a Jesuit. But the session quickly turned serious.

An older priest said he was one of several in the room who had been clandestinely ordained during the Cold War, when the Church operated underground in countries under Moscow's control. "Some . . . said that a Jesuit could not be formed during communism, but others disagreed and we are here," volunteered another.

The visit to Slovakia in 2021 came at a time when traditionalist prelates and their followers, especially in the United States, were promulgating a return to the pre–Vatican II Latin Mass, which Francis has warned against. The pope called it part of a "going backward" movement, which he said was "an ideology that colonizes minds." This was not a universal problem, he said tactfully, without mentioning the United States, but "specific to the churches of certain countries."

"How are you?" asked another priest. The pope had recently undergone colon surgery.

He had pulled through well, he said. But he added that some people had wanted him dead. Certain prelates were already meeting to discuss his successor, champing at the bit for change, he said, "preparing for the conclave," the meeting of bishops that elects the next pope. The shocking words continued. The pope spoke in deep frustration over Catholic media for U.S. audiences that served as a platform for the ultraconservative U.S. bishops, and the most right-wing Catholic advocacy groups that support them.

"There is, for example, a large Catholic television channel that has no hesitation in continually speaking ill of the pope," he said, clearly aiming at the Eternal Word Television Network (EWTN). EWTN reaches a self-reported 240 million viewers in 140 countries and runs 25,000 videos on its website. It covers the Vatican with a staff of thirty, more than any other English language outlet by far. The network's conservative commentators would be at home on the Fox network; in fact, the host of EWTN's flagship program, Raymond Arroyo, sometimes fills in for Fox's Laura Ingraham. EWTN broadcasts Mass and recitation of the rosary, but also provides a regular platform for critics of the pope—both in its star personality, Arroyo, and among bishops who appear as guests.

"I personally deserve attacks and insults because I am a sinner," said Pope Francis. "But the Church does not deserve them. They are the work of the devil."

To call a media organization's operations the "work of the devil" doesn't sit right with Americans steeped in the importance of a free press, and freedom of speech. What could have pushed the usually mild-mannered pontiff to such a judgment, such language?

* * *

BEGUN IN THE early 1980s in an Irondale, Alabama garage studio by the nun Mother Angelica of the Poor Clares of Perpetual Adoration, EWTN soon attracted the attention of wealthy conservative Catholics who believed the U.S. bishops of the time were placing too much emphasis on Catholic social teaching, and on the mandates of the modernizing Second Vatican Council of the 1960s. Traditional in spirit, Mother Angelica, with her round face set behind spectacles and a demeanor of personally knowing her viewers, drew an audience of millions with her talks (*Mother Angelica Live*), delivered like a folksy aunt, or with the no-nonsense authority of a schoolmarm. Money flowed in. In the early 1990s, Mother Angelica decided that U.S. bishops were becoming too liberal. She and the other nuns in her monastery went back to wearing full-black habits and veils and white wimples, religious dress that had been disappearing during the previous several decades. She berated clergy who followed the tenets of Vatican II—such as increased roles for the laity, Mass in the local language. Daily televised Masses went Latin. Talk on church doctrine replaced talk of social justice.

Beyond the TV network, EWTN radio now broadcasts on hundreds of domestic and international affiliates. In 2011, the television network bought the *National Catholic Register* newspaper, which leans ultraconservative. In 2011 EWTN bought the Catholic News Service (CNS), a wire agency; as part of the deal it acquired a CNS partner, the Lima-based ACI Prensa, the world's largest Spanish-language Catholic news service. (A majority of U.S. Hispanics—55 percent—identify as Catholic.) In 2020, for a White House interview with President Trump as he ran for reelection, EWTN centerpiece host Raymond Arroyo was sycophantic enough to bring on cringing, more the work of a courtier than a journalist.

Sniffing the wind of the success of the late Mother Angelica, who died in 2016, other traditionalist-minded entrepreneurs began what has become a slew of Catholic right-wing outlets.

Catholic columnist Michael Sean Winters calls the EWTN empire a "gateway drug" to these more radical expressions of Catholic media. In 2017, two prominent intellectuals, Jesuit Antonio Spadaro of Rome's *La Civiltà Cattolica* and Presbyterian pastor Marcelo Figueroa, editor of the Argentine edition of *L'Osservatore Romano*, wrote a blockbuster essay in Spadaro's journal, which is subject to review by Vatican authorities before publication. The authors— Spadaro is a friend of Pope Francis—asserted that the most militant rightist Catholic press exemplifies the "surprising ecumenism" in the United States between evangelical fundamentalism and "integralism," a school of Catholic social thought that holds the political order ought to be more firmly united with the spiritual realm (think Franco's Spain). The essay caused a storm in Catholic opinion circles for the significance of what it said, who said it, and where it appeared. Believers from both traditions are marked by a shared desire for religious influence in the political sphere, the authors asserted, and are connected by shared visions of Armaggedon, the final fight between Good and Evil, God and Satan, so that efforts at peace and dialogue over any issue "collapse before the needs of the end— a final battle against the enemy—and the community of believers (faith) becomes a community of combatants (fight)." Villanova University theologian Massimo Faggioli, commenting on the essay to *Vanity Fair*, said it marked the drift of American Catholicism away from the global Church. "I think it's the beginning of a trajectory that is likely, unfortunately, to make the Catholic Church in the U.S. what happened to white evangelicals over the last 40, 50 years—placing the deep feeling of their theological tradition at the service of nationalism and now ethnic-racial nationalism."

Interviews with the most conservative U.S. bishops can appear in the kind of rightist Catholic publications and blogs cited in the historic Spadaro and Figueroa essay, or the prelates write for those publications, or show up on their radio programs and YouTube segments. In this way the conservative bishops lend respectability to the ultrarightist media that are among the most powerful arms of propaganda advocating Christian nationalism.

Two extreme examples of the type, *Church Militant*, a homophobic news site based in Detroit that calls Islam "an ideology that spreads by murder and coercion," and *LifeSiteNews* which is based in Canada with a U.S. edition and big following, racked up 10 million views in the days before the attack on the Capitol. *Church Militant* invited readers to "sign up for the resistance," and to "get ready for war—donate today." *LifeSite* instructed readers to show up "to support the president's re-election," even though Donald Trump had lost to Joe Biden. Both news organizations covered the violence on January 6 as if it were the advent of a Christian state. *Church Militant* tweeted a photo of Trump supporters erecting a tall wooden cross alongside the iconic Joe Rosenthal photo of U.S. Marines raising the flag at Iwo Jima. A *LifeSite* reporter on the ground stated, "What I saw was a lot of people who love God and love their country."

LETTERS

THE RIGHTIST CATHOLIC propaganda platform began in the 1980s when Catholic neoconservatives, who believed in free markets and big military, came upon the political scene, even as the bishops of the time were taking positions that contrasted with those of the Republican Ronald Reagan administration. The bishops argued against the use of nuclear weapons in a 1983 pastoral letter, "The Challenge of Peace: God's Promise and Our Response," even though the issue was hugely controversial in an atmosphere of the global Cold War arms buildup. But the letter made its mark.

George Kennan, the U.S. diplomat who successfully advocated the post–World War II policy of "containment" toward Soviet expansionism, called the bishops' letter "the most profound and searching inquiry [into nuclear ethics] yet conducted by any responsible collective body." Andrew Greeley, the Catholic priest, sociologist, and popular author, declared the U.S. bishops' stand to be "the most successful intervention to change attitudes ever measured by social science."

In 1986, the bishops issued another extraordinary missive, on Catholic social teaching and the U.S. economy. They argued that the measure of the economy is not only what it produces, but how it protects or demeans individuals, and whether it promotes the common good. But this time the bishops' letter triggered an opposing "Lay Letter" from the Church's powerful neoconservatives, Catholics from the world of finance, business, and government, who denounced the prelates' criticism of capitalism—it was morally and factually incorrect, they said. The two missives marked the beginnings of a rightist Catholic media, not all as fringe-leaning as *Church Militant* and *LifeSite*, but many of them trashing a pope, subtly or overtly, who challenges the global status quo, and impugning Catholics who accept the reforms of Vatican II.

In their 1986 letter "Economic Justice for All," U.S. Catholic bishops used straightforward language, Scripture, and quotations from Pope John Paul II, then the head of the Church, and from previous popes, to make a case for a national economy that would eliminate a serious gap in wealth between the very rich and millions who struggled for the basics of a dignified life. Using the country's surfeit of natural resources and human talent, they said, it was possible, indeed morally imperative, to engender a refreshed system that guaranteed the economic well-being of all, with a particular focus on the poor and most vulnerable. The bishops said they were not proposing any particular policy, or embracing any particular theory of how the economy works, but insisted that an ethical framework "faithful to the Gospel" was essential when considering economic decisions. That meant full employment; structuring work to take the family into account; taxes based on assessment according to ability to pay; and other changes.

The poor were central in Scripture, the bishops reminded the faithful, and warned the prosperous against blindness to poverty, including its outcomes like bad health and the indignity of being jobless. "That so many people are poor in a nation as rich as ours is a social and moral scandal that we cannot ignore," they wrote. Government policy and business decisions have moral dimensions and human consequences, while free markets "have both advantages and clear limits." Importantly, they insisted, the state has a role to play by instituting just economic policies to raise up people on the margins—not to bring about equal wealth for all, but to bring about chances for all to participate in the economy.

The letter stirred a hornets' nest among the conservative Catholics who were some of the wealthiest people in the country. Many took it as an indictment of a system in which they flourished.

WILLIAM SIMON, NEOCONSERVATIVE

LEADING THE CHARGE against the bishops was William Simon, a fervent Catholic and wealthy businessman, who had served as secretary of the treasury in the Nixon and Ford administrations. Politically, Simon was a neoconservative, part of an evolving group of intellectuals who differed from traditional conservatives by placing even more emphasis on individualism and free markets; championed aggressive militarism and big budgets to back it; unflaggingly supported Israel; and vocally disdained the liberal political activism and mores of the 1960s. Many—although not Simon—had once been politically liberal.

In his origins and trajectory, Simon epitomized the kind of figure who might be taken aback by the bishops' public stand.

Born in 1927, William Edward Simon, Jr., was the son of "a couple right out of *The Great Gatsby*," he wrote in an autobiography, *A Time for Reflection*. His father was a bon vivant, his mother strikingly beautiful. Young Billy, as he was called, was chauffeured in style to his Catholic grammar school "in a 16-cylinder Cadillac," and lived among three grand family houses in New Jersey, including a Victorian mansion "with a staff of seven to attend to our every need." After his mother died, when he was just eight years old, his father began to fritter away the (inherited) family fortune; yet comfort with wealth was already imprinted on the boy, and as he grew, young Simon drifted inexorably toward Wall Street, which he took to like a fish to water. Before he reached the age of forty, youthful looking, with dark, slick-backed hair and ever-present round glasses, Bill Simon was a partner at Salomon Brothers, a millionaire bond trader with seven children, building the first of a series of dream homes, with the presidency of the U.S. Olympic Committee and a 125-foot yacht in his future.

Bill Simon believed his own bishops had it all wrong. They were attacking aspects of capitalism he held sacred. The prelates had taken a "gargantuan leap," he wrote, from solid biblical principles to a false conclusion "that the American economic system is in direct conflict with morally responsible behavior—a conclusion that flies in the face of history and common sense." Simon championed the philosophy behind what would come to be called the Reagan "revolution": shrink government (except for the military), giving it fewer responsibilities. Today, neoconservatism has merged with the Republican right, but much of the opposition to Pope Francis is rooted in the same resistance to criticism of unregulated capitalism that William Simon and his fellow conservatives expounded forty years ago. Indeed, so closely does that 1986 U.S. bishops' letter reflect Francis's thinking today, he might have written it himself.

Unlike the populist New Right, which focuses its religious rhetoric on "family values," sexual preferences, and abortion, and is generally funded by direct mail, the neocons—Catholics among them sometimes called "theocons"—may focus on the same issues but are funded by corporate-backed foundations and think tanks aiming to build a base within churches for unregulated capitalism and militant anti-communism and to affirm U.S. military hegemony. Most people in the country belong to Christian denominations, or at least respect them, and they would be key to spreading the neoconservative ethic. The obstacle: churches often hold strong positions against U.S. force abroad, and hold stances on other political issues considered liberal.

During the time of U.S. involvement in Vietnam, faith-based activists were at the forefront of opposition to the war and militarism; by the 1980s, Christian groups were opposing apartheid in South Africa, and demanding attention to human rights in El Salvador and Guatemala, where U.S.-backed troops committed massacres and assassinated political, church, and social leaders with impunity. At home, Christian groups generally favored social welfare programs that aimed to feed and educate the poor. If neoconservatives were going to bring Americans around to their way of thinking, they had to bring Christians into the tent. As the country's largest denomination, Catholics were essential.

Bill Simon wrangled together a Lay Commission on Catholic Social Teaching and the U.S. Economy, made up of thirty-one prominent Catholics, to push back against the 1980s bishops. The roster was illustrious, mostly household names, including four-star general Alexander Haig, chief of staff under presidents Nixon and Ford and President Reagan's first secretary of state; Clare Boothe Luce, an author, playwright, journalist, ambassador, and member of Congress who was also the widow of the founder of the Time Life publishing empire; and multimillionaire industrialist J. Peter Grace, a member of the elite Knights of Malta, the ancient (founded 1048) global Catholic order to which Simon also belonged. Knowing that the episcopal letter was coming, the laypeople produced their tract, called "Toward The Future: Catholic Social Thought and The U.S. Economy," while the bishops were still working on the draft of theirs.

In presenting themselves as "*the* Lay Commission," Simon and his collaborators implied that everyday Catholics thought alike in opposition to the bishops' stand on the economy, which was not true.

To read the documents side by side is to see a huge difference of thought between the Catholic bishops of the time and Simon and his colleagues.

For the self-appointed lay commission, freedom and liberty meant freedom from government regulation that might impose limits or conditions on businesses and manufacturing. For the bishops, the same word, *freedom*, meant the shared capacity to participate in the economy. For the Simon neocons, dignity meant self-reliance, the "responsibility of every person for his own well-being"; the bishops underscored the word's communal sense, considering that "how we organize our society—in economics and politics, in law and policy—directly affects human dignity and the capacity of individuals to grow in community." U.S. prelates used a particularly significant phrase, "the preferential option for the poor," nine times in their ninety-nine-page missive, referring to the social teaching that mandates Catholics to follow the example of Jesus, who took the side of those most in need, physically and spiritually. The "preferential option" demands an assessment of "lifestyle, policies, and social institutions" in light of their impact on society's most vulnerable members.

The neocons' "Lay Letter," in 120 pages, does not mention the "preferential option for the poor" at all. It suggests a cause of poverty is "cultural," and attempts to diminish its effect on society by quoting a contemporary survey (*Statistical Abstract of the United States: 1984*) that suggests the poor are relatively few. "Almost 24 million whites and 10 million blacks [sic] are poor," the laypeople said. "Looked at another way, almost 90 percent of whites and two thirds of blacks are *not* poor."

The phrase key for the bishops, "the preferential option for the poor," was associated with the powerful liberation theology movement of Latin America, which was spreading the world over in the 1970s and 1980s, just as Black Liberation Theology was spreading in the United States, most prominently in the work of Rev. James H. Cone. Liberation theologies believe that Jesus came to free the oppressed to lead full lives, and suggest that unfettered capitalism, which rigs markets for the elites, is part of the reason the poor are kept down. The Catholic bishops used the concept wittingly because they, unlike most who opposed them, actually knew the situation on the ground in inner cities of the United States, but also in Latin America. They talked with brother bishops; they sent missionaries to Latin America who came back with firsthand information, or in some cases didn't come back at all—several U.S. clergy and religious women were murdered by rightist forces; bishops took it upon themselves to visit Latin countries including Nicaragua, Cuba, and El Salvador, where the country's prelate, Óscar Arnulfo Romero, had been assassinated in 1982. When they stood against President Reagan's militarized, pro-autocrat Latin America policy, angering neoconservative Catholics, the bishops of the 1980s did so with the understanding that grinding poverty in unjust systems

was behind rebellion in the region, not "communist aggression."
Neoconservatives, for their part, could not get out of the Cold War
box, and saw the tumult in Latin America as if it were a reflection
of a Soviet threat in what had historically been the U.S. "backyard,"
and they associated liberation theology with Marxist thinking. It
was another break between bishops and Catholics on the far right.

Milwaukee archbishop Rembert Weakland, chairman of the committee that produced the bishops' letter on the economy, which was
approved by a vote of 225 to 9, called the product of Simon's commission "libertarian," whereas the bishops preferred a more "communitar-
ian" ethic. Simon released his letter along with the commission's vice
chair, Michael Novak, who has been called "capitalism's theologian."
A former seminarian, and prolific author of fifty books who once
wrote speeches for President John F. Kennedy, Novak became a major
voice for rightist Catholics and neoconservatism. He contributed to
the heft of the document's argument, and so cogent did he believe it
to be, that he presumed to ask the bishops to append it to their own.
(They did not.)

The Reagan years (1981–1989) began the heyday of Catholic neoconservatives, when they filled government positions in Washington
and shaped policy. Meanwhile, U.S. bishops were challenging the
president's policies from Central America to Star Wars—in 1988,
when Reagan wanted to stretch the meaning of a 1970s treaty limiting missile testing and deployment by testing extensively in space, the
bishops unanimously voted to update their 1983 anti–nuclear weapons
letter, questioning the idea's morality. Catholic neoconservatives were
not exactly in schism with their own bishops then, but if the American
Church totters close to schism with Rome today, it may be said to have
begun in the tumultuous 1980s.

William Simon named three experiences that made him "a more
truly committed Christian and Catholic," especially toward the end

of his life: pilgrimages to Lourdes and Medjugorje; his time as a Eucharistic minister, frequenting a hospital where he gave Holy Communion to patients afflicted with AIDS; and volunteering for years at, as well as monetarily supporting, an international network of crisis centers for runaway and abandoned youth called Covenant House. In his first inaugural speech, President Reagan praised the project by name as an ideal example of privatization of social services. When Simon met the founder of Covenant House, Father Bruce Ritter, to whom he was introduced by J. Peter Grace, he said the Franciscan "immediately impressed me with his commitment, genuine love, and respect for runaway and abandoned children." Ritter founded his first refuge in New York in 1972; by 1990, Covenant House had grown into a $90 million international operation, when the charismatic priest resigned in the face of accusations of sexual misconduct with boys and young men, and of financial irregularities. Ritter denied the allegations, and was never convicted of a crime; an independent investigation for Covenant House of fifteen cases of alleged improper sexual contact by Ritter reported that no single case could be proven beyond question, but that the "cumulative evidence" suggested that, if Ritter hadn't resigned, "the termination of the relationship" between him and the refuge network "would have been required."

Bill Simon and others stuck by the priest, Simon remaining on the Covenant House national board. And he never lost his conviction that outreach to the disadvantaged was best done by private entities, individuals, churches, community groups, and volunteers, and that government should have no part of it, a key concept of the neoconservative "Lay Letter." Simon put his money where his personal convictions were, donating $80 million to charity in his lifetime.

PLATFORM PROLIFERATION

[Business must fund] intellectual refuges for the non-egalitarian schol-
ars and writers in our society who today work largely alone in the face
of overwhelming indifference or hostility. They must be given grants,
grants, and more grants in exchange for books, books, and more books.
                              —William Simon, *A Time for Truth*

WILLIAM SIMON DIDN'T just battle the bishops of his day, but
took on what he saw as the serial crucifixion of Catholics in mainstream media, and what he considered its denigration of religion in
general—when they covered it at all. By raising awareness that conservative Catholics had little voice in the way they were portrayed,
he planted seeds about the pivotal role of public communication in a
political fight for hearts and minds that led, as a consequence unin-
tended or not, to the archconservative Catholic media that spreads the
bishops' message—and sometimes toxic rightist commentary—today.
It was up to big business, Simon believed, to finance opinion makers
friendly to the Catholic neoconservative cause.

In a 1994 article in *Crisis*, a magazine started by Michael Novak,
Simon said that U.S. newspapers, radio, and TV only gave the pope a
fair shake when he sounded like a Democrat. Reporters were all open
or closet liberals, which affected their reporting. They rarely presented
the Catholic pro-life position in an objective or fair-minded way.
Plenty of ink was spilled, however, on the pro-choice movement, or
when pro-choice individuals were harassed, or, in the case of abortion
provider Dr. David Gunn, murdered. The unbalanced coverage, he
wrote, "simply underscores an ugly but inescapable reality in America
today: prejudice is still condoned as part of our national conversation,
especially if it is directed against the Catholic Church." Journalists

were "hostile" toward religion because most don't believe in God or attend religious services, "and only 2 percent are practicing Catholics," he said, quoting surveys. What the underdog needed was a soapbox of its own.

More than anyone, William Simon was responsible for the new tsunami of corporate money that began to flow to influential conservatives in the 1970s and 1980s, which in turn produced reporters and commentators who carry the neocon line. The corporate-supported think tanks, such as the Heritage Foundation, cofounded by ultra-Catholic Republican strategist Paul Weyrich, and the American Enterprise Institute (AEI), founded by industrialist Lewis Herold Brown (chairman of Johns-Manville, the planet's largest manufacturer of asbestos), profited. They provided the apologetics for the New Right. They churned out policy plans ready-made for Republican administrations, and entire slates of personnel recommendations accepted by Republican presidents, from bureaucrats to cabinet members. Business needed to shape national thinking in various ways, believed Simon, for the good of the country. Corporations must not just donate money "mindlessly," but in a targeted manner, to mobilize politically. Later, wealthy Republican funders like the Koch brothers, Charles and David, and the Mercer and DeVos families would hone the process to perfection, but in the 1970s, it was William Simon who started the ball rolling.

Simon "played as great a role as any in eliciting and coordinating the [corporate] contributions," wrote Jerome L. Himmelstein, Andrew Mellon professor of sociology at Amherst College, in a political history of the era, *To the Right: The Transformation of American Conservatism.* "After arguing at considerable length how government spending, taxes, and regulation threatened capitalism and economic liberty, Simon issued a clarion call for business to fight back."

SIMON TOLD THE nation's biggest companies—he was on a first-name basis with many of their CEOs—that it was less important to promote specific laws or candidates, but rather, citing the writing of his neoconservative colleague Irving Kristol, to square off against the entire "New Class" of journalists, intellectuals, foundation heads, and bureaucrats who were less than 100 percent convinced about unregulated free markets. What business must do was create a neoconservative "counterintelligensia," Simon famously said, to regain ideological dominance. Since then, tens of millions of dollars have gone into grooming and supporting communicators who express the neoconservative—and theocon—cast of mind.

After 1977, when Simon took over the Olin Foundation from his East Hampton neighbor, the wealthy industrialist John Merrill Olin, he helped to create what is considered conservative-movement philanthropy, a network of foundations relatively few in number but fabulously wealthy and focused that brought the fringe ultraconservatism of the 1970s into the political mainstream. They began to do it by supporting neocons in academia and helping to funnel others into government, and also, importantly, by funding neoconservatives in the public square of media and books.

Three major conservative foundations, Scaife (the Mellon banking family), Smith Richardson (the family of over-the-counter drug giant Vick Chemical Company), and Olin, funded what would become a new generation of college newspapers, aiming at bringing in the young to the neoconservative way of thinking. Their Institute for Educational Affairs (IEA), a brainchild of Simon and Kristol, acted as a clearinghouse for channeling money from the country's biggest corporations into conservative ideas, immediately, in 1979, setting up an enterprise called the Collegiate Network that, to date, has underwritten more than one hundred conservative and libertarian college newspapers and magazines, with an estimated readership of

some two million. Funding the campus press was a way "to gener-
ate a network of young conservative writers and editors who might,
at some point, go into journalism, and thus bring some balance to
that profession," Simon wrote. Their role was to challenge what the
Collegiate Network called "political correctness."

The first of the network's subsidized papers, *The Dartmouth Review*,
published a stolen list of members of a gay club, thus exposing many
individuals for the first time to family and friends, and once hosted a
lobster and champagne spread to mock a student fast against global
hunger. The paper nurtured Fox News celebrity Laura Ingraham, and
author and filmmaker Dinesh D'Souza, who calls the mainstream media "the propaganda arm of the Democratic party." In the 1990s, the
network gave a financial start to *The Stanford Review* of libertarian
student Peter Thiel, who wrote a book criticizing multiculturalism in
higher education, and, as the Silicon Valley billionaire he became, now
funds right-wing causes and ultraright candidates, including Trump
followers, with his fortune.

Under William Simon, Olin generously underwrote a panoply of
other culture warriors who made their mark on American thinking,
like Allan Bloom (*The Closing of the American Mind: How Higher
Education Has Failed Democracy and Impoverished the Souls of Today's
Students*), and David Brock, author of a teardown of Anita Hill,
the lawyer who accused Supreme Court justice Clarence Thomas
of sexual misconduct. *The Real Anita Hill* was a tract full of lies for
which the author later apologized, and candidly described as "char-
acter assassination." With the right kind of politics, the Olin grants
were not hard to get, Brock told the *Observer* in 2005. "There was
a lot of money available for an awful lot of conservative-oriented
projects . . . and that helped develop a kind of farm team of people
who would later become quite influential."

The list of intellectuals and journalists who earned their keep with support from Simon and conservative-movement philanthropy goes beyond Catholic readership. With Kristol as advisor, Olin supported hawkish policy journals like *Commentary*, which calls itself the "flagship of neoconservatism," and Kristol's *The National Interest*. Support to the AEI still buoys prominent conservative Catholics, like its president emeritus Arthur Brooks, author of *The Conservative Heart: How to Build a Fairer, Happier, and More Prosperous America*, and current fellow Ross Douthat, who writes a regular column for the *New York Times*. Unlike leaders of many foundations, who concentrate on funding projects, Simon promoted *ideas*, supporting individuals who would write books that carried the neoconservative flag, and reached a large popular audience. *The Clash of Civilizations and the Remaking of the New World Order* by political scientist Samuel P. Huntington is an example. In a reading of his political theory, which posits that future wars will no longer be between nations, but cultures, or "civilizations," Huntington provided intellectual underpinning for Islamophobia and the Christian nationalist desire to marginalize Muslims in American life.

THE THEOCON TRINITY

WILLIAM SIMON DIED in 2000 at the age of seventy-two, having channeled his personal fortune, accumulated largely as a pioneer of leveraged buyouts, into his own William E. Simon Foundation to support the usual conservative money recipients like the Federalist Society and the Knights of Columbus. He also funded the Ethics and Public Policy Center, founded in 1976 "to apply the riches of the Judeo-Christian tradition to contemporary questions of law, culture and politics." Money to the center was specifically earmarked for the work of the ubiquitous Catholic commentator George Weigel, author of more than two dozen books, including a biography of Pope John

Paul II that verges on hagiography, and whose columns and articles run in outlets from diocesan papers to *The Wall Street Journal*. Weigel is the last survivor of the theocon "triumvirate," as it has been called, which included Novak, who died in 2017, and Richard John Neuhaus (d. 2009), a Lutheran minister who became a Catholic priest.

George Weigel has opposed Pope Francis at various turns. A typical example is over the landmark Pan-Amazon Synod of 2019, an event close to the heart of the Latin American pope, which Francis called to address the needs of the region's indigenous peoples and new urban populations, and to protect their rain forests, which were being destroyed by big agricultural enterprises, logging, and international mining. Preceding the synod, eighty-seven thousand ordinary residents of the nine countries of the Amazon region had met over a period of two years to examine problems and solutions, and provide their views to the bishops meeting in Rome. Weigel dismissed the synod as "nothing less than the creation of a New Model Catholicism, in which the Church is conceived primarily as an international non-governmental organization advancing the progressive agenda globally." He slammed liberation theology, which he saw as an influence on the synod, and cautioned against "privileging" undeveloped places of the world when considering the environment, even though much of the earth's remaining natural creation exists in developing countries.

The theocon trinity—Weigel, Novak, and Neuhaus—created the ecumenical Institute on Religion and Democracy (IRD) in 1981 as an intellectual bulwark against bishops and clergy who, in a 2006 mission statement, they said, "have thrown themselves into multiple often leftist crusades—radical forms of feminism, environmentalism, pacifism, multiculturalism, revolutionary socialism, sexual liberation, and so forth." The IRD was so influential it was sometimes tagged "the official seminary of the White House." The intellectual trinity wove its understanding of Catholic social doctrine into ultraconservative politics, as Weigel continues to do, managing to subsume Catholic anti-war teaching into militarism. Richard Neuhaus strongly supported the invasion of Iraq, and the war in Afghanistan, often in the pages of his magazine, *First Things*, a figurehead for the anti-Francis media.

For forty years, neoconservatives and their media platforms got along fine with the anti-communist Pope John Paul II and the ultra-traditionalist Benedict XVI, who were conservative enough that theocons could drown the papal statements against war, for the environment, and for the poor in their own sea of words. And the popes never publicly corrected them. Theocons helped to bring along ever-better U.S. relations with the Vatican. In 1984, Ronald Reagan, to whom Michael Novak was an advisor, established formal diplomatic ties with the Holy See.

Much of the Catholic neoconservative movement in which William Simon was an emblematic figure changed, chameleonlike, after the attacks of September 11, 2001. Conservative Catholic media began to emit a startling mix of theology and right-wing politics, especially Islamophobia. By the Trump years they were mixing theology and conspiracy theories, a path that has led, in alliance with like-minded white evangelical Protestants, to the embrace of Christian nationalism.

It was the 2013 election of the outsider candidate Jorge Mario Bergoglio as pope, however, that propelled the rightist Catholic media, acting as an amplifier for U.S. bishops, to the edge of schism.

ENTER FRANCIS

CARDINAL BERGOGLIO OF Argentina disdained the traditional baroque trappings of office, criticized the unregulated free market as "inhumane," and insisted upon attention to the environment, as well as to the social "peripheries" of the world. The first non-European pontiff in more than 1,200 years, Bergoglio took the name *Francis* after the saint sometimes called "the Poor Man of Assisi," and made his first papal trip outside Rome to the island of Lampedusa to embrace "illegal" refugees, swept up on the shores of the Mediterranean. The new pope's first apostolic exhortation, in 2013, *Evangelii Gaudium*, threw Catholic neocons into shock. The document promoted evangelization and unity, but spoke most memorably about attention to economic structures ("No to a financial system which rules rather than serves"), and condemned the "new idolatry of money." For ultraconservatives, great wealth was not a potential occasion of sin, but a signifier of correct behavior, a creative use of "liberty." But this new pope saw it as something of which to be wary.

"The dignity of the human person and the common good rank higher than the comfort of those who refuse to renounce their privileges," Francis said in the exhortation, a teaching document. "How can it be that it is not a news item when an elderly homeless person dies of exposure, but it is news when the stock market loses two points?" Business was a "noble" vocation, he said, but the goods of the world produced by business and technological innovation must be more "accessible" to all.

The pope struck another blow to the Islamophobic ultraconservative worldview when he wrote, "Authentic Islam . . . is opposed to every form of violence."

Francis's programmatic manifesto "cast sharp doubt on the Catholic neoconservative agenda and criticized its assumptions plainly," wrote Massimo Borghesi, an Italian professor of moral philosophy, in *Catholic Discordance: Neoconservatism vs. the Field Hospital Church of Pope Francis*, in 2021. "After thirty years spent weaving a web of institutional relationships and exercising hegemony within the church, first in the United States and then throughout the West, the shining lights of a Catholic neoconservatism were experiencing an unexpected backlash."

But they fought back.

Rightist Catholic media, tweeters, bloggers, and YouTubers began to promote *sedevacantism*, a word from the Latin for "vacant seat," that is, the Seat of Peter, the first pope, meaning that they promoted the idea that Pope Francis was illegitimate because of his views. By now, most U.S. prelates have been elevated by the two popes that preceded Francis, having replaced the group of prophetic bishops of the 1980s, and they have been aligning themselves with Republican neocons for years. The views of the new pope did not align with either the Democratic or the Republican Party. Dominating the USCCB, the conservative bishops failed to wholeheartedly promulgate *Evangelii Gaudium*. Cardinal Raymond Burke, the conservative Catholic thought leader, spoke out against its authority. The apostolic exhortation was merely "the Pope's [personal] thinking," Burke said, that does not teach "an official doctrine." The late Bishop Robert Morlino of Madison, who once criticized the University of Wisconsin city as existing below a "moral minimum," partly for supporting a gay and lesbian theater group, followed with echoes of Burke's opinion in an interview on EWTN and a column for his diocesan newspaper.

In his own Catholic newspaper in Philadelphia, Archbishop Charles J. Chaput reprinted emails complaining about the pope. (Chaput has also supported papal nemesis Carlo Maria Viganò.) Cardinal Timothy Dolan of New York and San Francisco's Archbishop Salvatore Cordileone have gone to Catholic media platforms and the mainstream press to express conservative stances out of sync with papal insistence on a political middle ground. By way of Catholic media, millions hear, watch, or read their viewpoints: on Relevant Radio, with 169 stations and affiliates in English, and seven

more in Spanish, run by a priest who belongs to the ultraconservative Opus Dei order; on Ave Maria Radio, founded in 1997 by pizza
king Thomas Monaghan, now grown to more than 150 markets; on
EWTN, both radio and TV. *Rorate Caeli* ("Drop down, ye heav-
ens"), a blog, posted Cardinal Burke's dismissal of the exhortation.
(*Rorate Caeli* has been described by Catholic columnist Michael Sean
Winters as having "a kind of cult following" that acts as a conduit
"for a crimped, theologically unsophisticated form of Catholicism,
combined with right-wing political agitprop.")

As the tone of public discourse in the country has become more
shrill, so too have the alt-right Catholic platforms. "Is Pope Francis a
Heretic?" asked *First Things* in a headline. (Its answer: he can speak
so ambiguously it's hard to tell.) The longtime (founded 1967) traditionalist newspaper *The Remnant* ran a feature article by former *First
Things* blogger Ann Barnhardt, taken from *Ethika Politika*, an online
magazine that says it endeavors "to form consciences by exploring
the intellectual and moral traditions of the Catholic Church," calling
upon "those bishops remaining who still hold the Catholic faith" to
unseat Francis, a "Diabolical Narcissist Peronist-Fascist" who she says
is responsible for the loss of human souls with his (false) presenta-
tion of Catholic teaching. He must be "deposed and anathematized,"
Barnhardt wrote. "Satan . . . has the See of Peter."

The body of U.S. Catholic bishops do not come to the pope's defense when attacks on him circulate, or speak out on the particularly
American scandal of an ever more poisonous war against the pope's
teaching, much of it carried out on media that calls itself Catholic. The
pope, of course, can speak for himself.

On a papal flight to Mozambique in 2019, Francis accepted a book
from a longtime Vatican reporter, the French writer Nicolas Senèze,
who argued that Americans want a different pope, and the pontiff
told him, "It's an honor when Americans attack me." The pope handed

the book to an aide, saying, "a bomb." Shortly, the papal spokesman delivered a tamped-down statement to reporters on the plane: "In an informal context, the pope wanted to say that he always considers criticisms an honor, particularly when they come from authoritative thinkers—in this case from an important nation."

"Some people wanted me dead," the pope had said after his 2019 operation, on the Slovakia visit, before assuring the Jesuit who asked after his health, "I'm still alive."

CONFLICT OF INTEREST, UNRESOLVED CONFLICT

IT'S NOT CLEAR what U.S. Catholics will hear about the pope as time goes on, or about other national and world issues, from their own press. In May 2022, the U.S. bishops unexpectedly closed the domestic bureaus of the Catholic News Service (CNS), the editorially independent news organization with a reputation for unbiased reporting, that the bishops' conference has owned for more than a century (it left the Rome bureau intact). CNS articles were a mainstay of diocesan newspapers. Malea Hargett, the editor of *Arkansas Catholic*, told *America* that a "gap" would now exist for her readers. "We can't cover what's going on at the Supreme Court or what's going on at the U.S.C.C.B. We just don't have the staff," she said.

Eliminating CNS coverage in the United States allows conservative and evangelical media to expand to fill the void of Catholic news and commentary. It also raises questions about the transparency of the bishops' decision.

At his Christ Cathedral complex in California, Bishop Kevin Vann, a member of the USCCB Committee on Communications that made the decision on CNS, hosts the West Coast operations of EWTN, owner of CNS competitor, the Catholic News Agency. The EWTN service skews to the right, in keeping with Vann's conservative ideology, and is distributed free, making it attractive to diocesan papers usually strapped for funds.

The bishops' decision may also help the publisher of a growing, aggressively marketed network of glossy diocesan magazines, FAITH Catholic, by hampering its print competition—diocesan newspapers that relied on CNS stories. Elizabeth Solsburg, FAITH Catholic's president and CEO, is a consultant to the bishops' communications committee. (Solsburg and the bishops denied she was involved in the CNS decision.) One in five Americans who receives a diocesan periodical, some 24 million according to FAITH Catholic's website, now gets one of its publications, which run profiles of saints and feel-good stories about inspirational Catholics and model parishes, a sort of Catholic news lite. (Diocesan bishops make the decisions to replace their newspapers with the magazines.) FAITH Catholic publishes the quarterly magazine for the Archdiocese of Detroit, whose archbishop, Allen Vigneron, serves as USCCB vice president and oversees the Lansing diocese where the publisher has its headquarters. The nonprofit also publishes products for three members of the bishops' committee who made the CNS decision, including its chairman, Boston auxiliary bishop Robert Reed, who is also chairman and president of the CatholicTV Network, founded in 1955. Kelsey Cronin, CatholicTV's director of social media and marketing, is another consultant to the committee.

By hobbling CNS in its surprise decision, the USCCB shot itself in the foot, at a time when it is already under fire for lacking transparency and for the "Communion Wars" against prominent politicians, and when individual bishops still receive criticism for

mishandling incidents of sex abuse. David Gibson, a veteran journalist and head of Fordham University's Center on Religion and
Culture, warned in a *National Catholic Reporter* commentary that
closing the CNS domestic operations eliminated "a rare source of
credibility for the hierarchy." Gibson called the independent news
organization a "counter-witness" to the proliferation of "ideologically
driven Catholic media platforms that are driving the church apart,
and regular Catholics around the bend."

FIFTY YEARS AGO William Simon began supporting a wave of
neoconservative Catholic influencers that fed the development of a
rightist Catholic media. Now partisan Catholic publications, radio,
websites, and TV have multiplied. They are propaganda disguised as
journalism. And in a move that symbolizes the trajectory of Catholic
media, U.S. bishops themselves killed off one of its domestic voices.
The sad truth may be that the majority of conservative U.S. prelates
do not care about ensuring an unvarnished reportorial take on the
Church as it is. Or they do not want a counter-witness to the platforms that support their particular take on what the American Church
should be.

7

The Bishops and
Black Catholics

SPEAKING TO A global meeting of grassroots activists in October 2021, Pope Francis addressed the extraordinary outpouring of anger and solidarity that had spread around the world in response to the brutal murder of an unarmed forty-six-year-old Black man, George Floyd, by a white policeman in Minneapolis in 2020. "In that protest against this death, there was the Collective Samaritan who is no fool!" the pope told the fourth World Meeting of Popular Movements, a papal initiative to discuss problems of land rights, housing, and labor. The pope's comparison of protesters against Floyd's death to the Samaritan who stopped to help a traveler who had been robbed, beaten, and left to die—after two religious authorities had ignored him—was a clear endorsement of action in the face of injustice.

"This movement did not pass by on the other side of the road when it saw the injury to human dignity caused by an abuse of power," Francis said.

No words could be further from those spoken two weeks later by the president of the U.S. Conference of Catholic Bishops (USCCB), Archbishop José Gomez of Los Angeles. For Gomez, activist solidarity movements like Black Lives Matter (BLM) are an expression of "secularization . . . which means de-Christianization," he told the fourth Congress of Catholics and Public Life, meeting in Madrid, speaking in a video address he immediately posted to Twitter in English. Such movements are "pseudo-religions," according to the archbishop, aiming to replace Christianity in the heart of America.

"For years now, there has been a deliberate effort . . . to erase the Christian roots of society and to suppress any remaining Christian influences," Gomez said. "I want to offer a 'spiritual interpretation' of the new social justice and political identity movements," he continued, describing them in terms of stealth and mayhem, and alleging they originated in the "Marxist cultural vision." Using an anti-intellectual trope, Gomez claimed that the contemporary social movements had been "seeded and prepared for many years in our universities and cultural institutions." With tension and fear caused by the pandemic and social isolation, he said, "and with the killing of an unarmed black man by a white policeman and the protests that followed in our cities, these movements were fully unleashed in our society."

These contrasting messages from the pope and the archbishop show a yawning gap between the papal view of social justice and that of the leader of U.S. bishops. Gomez's pronouncements were laced with terms commonly heard in the rhetoric of the political right, such as disparagingly equating "social justice" with "wokeness." Pope Francis called the grassroots social movement organizers "social poets" for "the ability and the courage to create hope where there appears to be only waste and exclusion." Gomez slurred people who were involved in social and "political identity movements" as followers of would-be anti-religions, "rivals to traditional Christian beliefs." For the archbishop, the death of George Floyd was "a tragedy," as he said in a

USCCB statement seven days after the murder, and a reminder that "racism has been tolerated for far too long in our way of life," not a call for massive, committed social action.

U.S. Catholic bishops do not all speak as Gomez did in his talk to the Madrid conference. Seven bishops who were chairmen of USCCB committees said in a statement at the time of Floyd's death that they "stand in passionate support of communities that are understandably outraged." But José Gomez will remain one of the most prominent U.S. prelates, heading the largest archdiocese in the country, with 4.3 million believers. And his position will continue to be embraced by the most rightist bishops: defensive of Christianity, blaming "elites" for corrupting the national soul. The stand has implications not only for Catholics, but for white Christian nationalists.

Fordham University professor Rev. Bryan Massingale was among the few voices raised against the Gomez speech. Massingale is also one of the few African American theologians in the U.S. Church.

"White nationalism is the real idolatrous pseudo-religion that poses a grave threat to both national unity and authentic Christian faith," Massingale told the *National Catholic Reporter* (*NCR*). "Yet, the archbishop suggests that the forces that oppose this movement are the real threats to genuine religion."

José H. Gomez was born in Monterrey, Mexico, in 1951, schooled in Spain at a university of the conservative Opus Dei movement, and naturalized in the United States, becoming a bishop in 2011. He is a close advisor to the Napa Institute. In the months before the prelate's controversial address, speakers at the Napa Institute's annual meeting in California's wine country condemned Black Lives Matter as "dangerous" and "Marxist inspired."

Gomez's stand made him notorious to liberal Catholics—*NCR* gave him its Newsmaker of the Year award as a "failed culture warrior." But he reinforced his position as a darling of ultraconservatives.

Breitbart News, the alt-right network aligned with Steve Bannon, a Catholic traditionalist and former Trump strategist, ran the story under a breathless headline: "L.A. Archbishop Decries Rise of Globalism, Anti-Christian 'Elite Leadership Class.'" CatholicVote, a nonprofit whose political action committee supports Republican candidates, named Gomez one of the year's Courage Award winners. Others included San Francisco archbishop Salvatore Cordileone, for challenging House Speaker Nancy Pelosi's description of herself as a "devout Catholic," and launching a "national campaign of prayer for her conversion and salvation"; Florida governor Ron DeSantis, for his "aggressive push against wokeism"; and Mississippi attorney general Lynn Fitch, who worked to take her state's abortion restrictions to the Supreme Court in the case that would overturn *Roe v. Wade*, *Dobbs v. Jackson Women's Health Organization*, "truly a chosen case by God," she told the *Pro-Life Weekly* program on EWTN in December, adding that the case was an issue of "states' rights."

WHITE NATIONALISTS ARE fighting back as they watch their worst fears materialize: a vice president who not only is a woman, but a woman of color, and a U.S. president who, for the first time, condemns racism using the term "white supremacy," as Joe Biden did in his inaugural address. The USCCB as a group, meanwhile—not only Gomez—fails to confront white Christian nationalism as a threat to the country and the Church.

In the void, a few theologians, often people of color, like Massingale, take it upon themselves to decry the scourge. "White nationalism is the existential, visceral conviction that this country—its public spaces, its history, its culture—belong to white people in a way that they do not and should not belong to 'others,'" Massingale told an audience of members of Pax Christi USA, a peace organization, in 2021. White nationalists believe that "America is, was meant to be, and always should remain, a white Christian nation," he said. The "existential threat" to white nationalism is "multiracial democracy."

When a white supremacist gunman targeting Latinos killed twenty-three people at an El Paso Walmart in 2019, Archbishop Gomez said, "If 'white nationalism' is on the rise, it is a sign of how far we have fallen from the Christian universalism of our nation's founding ideals."

But the prelate is inconsistent, denying the legitimacy of the very people fighting against white nationalism by branding them anti-Christian. And why did Gomez accept the honor from CatholicVote, a partisan organization that waged a $9.7 million campaign against Joe Biden in 2020, identifying potential Trump voters at Catholic and evangelical Christian churches without their knowledge, using "geo-fencing" to scrape cell phone data? In a 2022 move that smacked of intimidating humanitarian workers on the border, CatholicVote sued to review communications between the U.S. government and Sister Norma Pimentel, one of *TIME* magazine's one hundred "most influential people in 2020," and known as "the pope's favorite nun" for tending to undocumented migrants and children. Judicial Watch, a legal nonprofit connected to Republican activist Ginni Thomas, Justice Clarence Thomas's wife, is partnering with CatholicVote in the lawsuit, and advocates for a border wall. On its website, Judicial Watch refers to CatholicVote as "a community of patriotic Americans who believe that the timeless truths of the Catholic faith are good for America."

A NEW RELIGION, OR INSPIRED BY FAITH?

FAR FROM DESIRING to establish "pseudo-religions," as Archbishop Gomez would have it, immigration activists and campaigners against white supremacy say they have been inspired by their

Christianity. M. Shawn Copeland, professor emerita of theology at Boston College, a Jesuit university, has said that Black Lives Matter exemplifies Christian teaching, and serves as "public theology," that is, the study of God as it pertains to issues in the public sphere. Speaking of BLM to a meeting at Notre Dame of the Black Catholic Theological Symposium in 2021 "in theological terms," she said of the movement that "each one sees the other as an icon of the divine transcendent one, as another human made in the likeness and image of God."

Copeland, a former Catholic nun, has been speaking about BLM since its founding in 2013 by three African American women, Alicia Garza, Patrisse Cullors, and Ayọ (formerly known as Opal) Tometi, who were responding to the rage that ignited after the acquittal of a white man, George Zimmerman, in the Florida killing of Trayvon Martin, an unarmed Black teenager. When Michael Brown of Missouri, and Eric Garner of New York, both Black, and unarmed, were killed by police in 2014, the movement spread nationally, calling on the public to recognize police brutality and the systematic racism that pervaded U.S. institutions from schools to courtrooms. BLM caught on. From suburban house lawns to city apartment windows and outside shops of all sizes, signs announced BLACK LIVES MATTER. Between 2013 and 2018, people shared the hashtag #BLM more than 30 million times on Twitter alone, according to a report by the Pew Research Center.

Then came 2020, when police killed 164 Black men and women in the first eight months of the year. Among them, Breonna Taylor, a twenty-six-year-old emergency room technician, was shot dead in her bed in a no-knock raid gone amok. George Floyd, arrested on suspicion of passing a counterfeit twenty-dollar bill, died after Derek Chauvin, a white policeman, kept a knee on Floyd's neck for more than nine minutes, until he stopped breathing; a cell phone video of the incident, taken by a brave and composed seventeen-year-old girl, went viral and led to what *The New York Times* has called the country's most massive social protest movement in its history. As many as 26 million persons around the United States took to the streets to decry racial inequity; 20 million more messages appeared on social media using the hashtag #BLM.

But U.S. Catholic bishops as a group remained silent. Gomez in particular appeared tone deaf to the reality of Black people's experiences. To dismiss this welling up of rage—and, in cases, of new consciousness—as part of "broad patterns of aggressive secularization" that threaten contemporary Christianity, as he said in the most famous speech of his life, was to miss a profoundly teachable moment about how racism affects all institutions, including the Church. It also ignored the yearning of 3 million Black Catholics, most of whom (77 percent) consider that opposing racism is essential to their faith, according to polling by the Pew Research Center in 2021.

For the BLM founders, as recounted by journalist Olga M. Segura in her 2021 book, *Birth of a Movement: Black Lives Matter and the Catholic Church*, the BLM movement is about community, supporting women, "centering" the most marginalized, such as transgender people, for instance, and it includes other people of color who suffer discrimination, not just Black people. And it is "spiritual." Tometi, for one, told Segura she is influenced by liberation theology, which calls upon the faithful to study Jesus's teachings through the experience of the world's most marginalized people. During the Cold War, liberation theology was controversial because some followers used Marxist economic analysis to examine the effects of capitalism on social development. The analytic tool became a negative for many who believed unregulated capitalism was the only acceptable economic structure.

"No doubt that we can recognize in these movements certain elements of liberation theology," Gomez said in his "de-Christianization" speech. "They seem to be coming from the same Marxist cultural vision." Yet, since the 1960s, some of the most renowned theologians have been liberation theologians, including the late James Cone, known as the founder of Black Liberation Theology, which Cone described as "mainly a theology that sees God as concerned with the poor and the weak."

For Copeland, the Catholic theologian, Black Lives Matter "imagines and forms a new public space . . . for conversation and interchange." It also exemplified "creative public action . . . rooted in the ideas about public theology shared by, among others, Reinhold Niebuhr and the Rev. Martin Luther King Jr." Dallas auxiliary bishop Mark J. Seitz wrote in an opinion piece for the *National Catholic Reporter* "that black lives matter is just another way of repeating something we in the United States seem to so often forget, that God has a special love for the forgotten and oppressed."

MISS THE MOMENT—FUEL WHITE SUPREMACY

UNLIKE SEITZ OF Dallas, few in the U.S. hierarchy make the connections between BLM and Catholic teaching against racism and prejudice. Few bring up the Church's own dismal history of slaveholding, segregated congregations, or discouraging Black people in seminaries and women's convents. A priest in Indiana called the BLM protesters "maggots and parasites" (he was suspended), and another in Michigan compared them to al-Qaeda "terrorists," splitting the parish between those who supported the priest and those who did not. Disparaging the anti-racist activism, Rev. Paul Graney of the Church of the Divine Child in Dearborn said in a homily that Americans are "wanting to remake America into something else by destroying what it is today."

Remaking America, of course, is precisely the aim of BLM, albeit peacefully. Of 10,330 BLM-linked demonstrations in 2020 tracked by the Princeton University–cosponsored U.S. Crisis Monitor in all fifty states and Washington, D.C., the vast majority—94 percent— "involved no violent or destructive activity" (although authorities responding to them used force more than 51 percent of the time). Whether U.S. bishops regard BLM as an ideological movement with an extremist agenda or a secular version of Catholic social teaching, they do not appear to have placed racism, let alone white supremacy, at the top of their agendas of concern. Part of the problem may be that bishops, who are overwhelmingly white, do not want to roil their white congregations.

From the time massive immigration began to swell the population of the United States in the mid-nineteenth century, each wave of new-comers—German, Irish, Italian, Polish, and other Europeans—found defenders in Catholic bishops, who spoke up in favor of their coreli-gionists in the face of rejection by members of the country's Protestant Anglo-Saxon majority. Anti-immigration politicians and activists fa-vored quotas or denying admission altogether to "papists," and those they reckoned were not completely "white," like the Irish and Italians. But bishops insisted that the (Catholic) new arrivals brought skills and enriched the American way of life. The prelates established parishes where people could speak their own languages; the parishes became the heart of ethnic enclaves, offering comfort and mutual support in a new land. Catholic bishops supported ethnic fraternal organizations like the Sons of Italy and the Ancient Order of Hibernians, which in turn fought discriminatory treatment and eased the path to assimila-tion for the groups they represented. So effective in placing themselves in the mainstream of U.S. history were Italian Americans, with the Knights of Columbus, for instance, that Christopher Columbus of

Genoa was installed in the pantheon of founding fathers as America's "discoverer," his birthday celebrated as a national holiday.

Even as U.S. Catholic bishops have done little to lift up the descendants of African slaves brought to the country against their will, with the prelates' help yesterday's European immigrants have become the heart of today's middle class. In cases, the oppressed have become oppressors.

"It is obvious that the church has always perceived . . . its primary constituency as the white, European immigrant community," Brother Joseph Davis, then executive director of the National Office for Black Catholics, told a regional gathering that was preparing for a Catholic bicentennial conference in Detroit in 1976. In an assessment that Davis said was based on "analyzing the church's own documents," he stated that "on several significant occasions, when the Catholic Church had the opportunity to depart from the structures of racism so rigidly imposed by the dominant society [and] to affirm the humanity and dignity of black people . . . it has invariably backed off in deference to the sensitivities of the white Catholic community." Anything said about race "always has the comfort of white Catholics in mind," Massingale told Segura. "That white comfort sets the terms of Catholic engagement with the issue of race."

BISHOPS' WORDS

IN MAY 2022 an eighteen-year-old man aiming to kill Black people, lest they "replace" white people, gunned down thirteen Saturday afternoon shoppers at a grocery market in Buffalo, New York, killing ten, most of them Black. Local Black religious leaders begged fellow white religious to preach in acknowledgment "that there are still people who hate Black people," as Bishop Darius Pridgen of the

True Bethel Baptist Church in Buffalo said to *The New York Times*. Yet, following a pattern of many other U.S. Catholic bishops in the face of egregious racist killings, Buffalo's Bishop Michael W. Fisher managed only to produce a milquetoast public statement condemning "what unfortunately has become an all too common occurrence in this country," without once mentioning Black people or racism, let alone white supremacy, or white nationalism.

Letters emerging from the USCCB and its predecessors, speaking as a group, carry more weight than those of individual bishops. They are most likely to be read to the faithful at Mass, spark discussion and coverage in the media, comments by the clergy. Not only did the USCCB fail to opine on the Buffalo massacre (although it retweeted Fisher's statement), it did not instruct priests to bring up racism and white supremacy in its aftermath.

Only four times in the last seventy years has the body of U.S. bishops delivered a major teaching document on racism. Their 1958 offering, "Discrimination and Christian Conscience," might not have been released at all, had not Pope Pius XII, the day before he died, sent a cable "ordering the American bishops to issue the statement at once," wrote a priest involved in the letter. The timid prelates had been stalling, "fearing it might cause division among the bishops." Even then, most U.S. bishops tried to sweep the declaration under the rug. But Archbishop (later Cardinal) Patrick O'Boyle, who had racially integrated Catholic schools in his diocese, Washington, D.C., six years before the 1954 Supreme Court (*Brown v. Board of Education*) decision integrating schools, managed to prevail over the obstructers, and made sure the letter went out. It repeated the reasoning against enforced segregation found in *Brown*: Separate is not equal.

Action for change must be tempered by prudence, however, said the bishops as a group, with an excess of caution. They "pray[ed] that responsible and sober-minded Americans of all religious faiths . . .

will seize the mantle of leadership from the agitator and the racist." Catholics must act quietly, courageously, and prayerfully "before it is too late," they said.

In 1968, the bishops were forced to address the race issue when civil disturbances in major cities stoked dread of a national racial insurrection. They called their joint pastoral letter "Statement on National Race Crisis," reflecting the urgency and trepidation of the moment. Dr. Martin Luther King had been murdered. And a devastating government-ordered investigation called the Kerner Report concluded that "our nation is moving toward two societies, one black, one white—separate and unequal." The bishops could not *not* emit a document.

But in their letter the U.S. prelates only came close to recognizing how deeply ingrained in its institutions and way of life was the racism tearing the country apart. Referring to the Kerner Report, they said they agreed "it would be futile to deny . . . that a white segregationist mentality is largely responsible for the present crisis . . . We must recognize that racist attitudes and consequent discrimination exist not only in the hearts of men but in the fabric of their institutions."

The solution was to "build bridges of justice, compassion, and understanding." In a tone of fear, they advised the faithful to act, but gave no doctrinal justification or reasoned articulation of their position. When they tried again to address the crisis in 1979, the bishops called their letter "Brothers and Sisters to Us," its very title demonstrating how little they had internalized the problem of racism toward people who were not white.

"Racism is not merely one sin among many, it is a radical evil dividing the human family and denying the new creation of a redeemed world," they wrote. "To struggle against it demands an equally radical transformation in our own minds and hearts as well as in the structure of our society."

Despite such passages, the bishops' overall tone on racism was devoid of the more passionate kind of language they use as a group when treating what the conference calls the "pre-eminent" issue of abortion. In an era of de facto segregation that saw the rise of hate groups, the bishops' 1979 letter seemed to emphasize what white Catholics might cede to Black people, about how "attitudes" (mentioned six times) should change. Racism, the bishops continued to suggest, can be eliminated with goodwill, education, and dialogue—counsel more naive than realistic.

Nevertheless, the occasion of "Brothers and Sisters to Us," its principal author the African American bishop Joseph Francis, was the first time U.S. Catholic bishops went on record as a national conference calling racism a "sin." The letter noted the persistence of overt and covert racism despite legal changes after the civil rights movement linked racism to economic injustice, and said that insofar as social structures "reflect the values which society upholds . . . each of us, in varying degrees, is responsible." It gave concrete suggestions for parishes and dioceses that would amount to an affirmative action program even stronger than that of secular society. But parishes and dioceses dropped the ball on the recommendations, and bishops didn't push them.

Indeed, so little were the positive elements of the letter promoted that five years after "Brothers and Sisters to Us" appeared, Rev. Edward Braxton, an African American theologian who later served as bishop of Belleville, Illinois, wrote that the pastoral letter "is not implemented, preached, studied or even printed in many places."

Thus, even when the words in Catholic teaching documents are unequivocal in their condemnation of racism, the U.S. Church's prevailing tendency toward right-wing leadership, overwhelmingly white, hollows out their message, making it ineffectual, let alone prophetic. A 2004 anniversary bishops' report on "Brothers and Sisters to Us" notes that "white Catholics over the last twenty-five years exhibit diminished—rather than increased—support for government policies aimed at reducing racial inequality."

ON OCCASION, BLACK clergy and the few Black Catholic bishops speaking outside the USCCB as a conference have been the Church's clearest voices on racism. In one dramatic moment, right after the murder of Dr. Martin Luther King in 1968, a caucus of Black priests attending a national clergy conference, including the only Black Catholic bishop of the time, Harold Robert Perry of New Orleans, described the Church as a "primarily white racist institution."

"The same principles on which we justify legitimate self-defense and just warfare must be applied to violence when it represents black response to white violence," they wrote in a prepared statement signed by fifty Black clergymen—130 Black priests served at the time in the United States, out of a total of 58,000. "Black people are fully aware that violence has been consciously and purposely used by America from its fight for Independence to its maintenance of white supremacy," they wrote. "Black people are encouraged to fight abroad for white America's freedom and liberty. We are now asking why it is not moral to fight for liberty at home." They demanded more Black deacons and more Black priests in leadership positions.

Again in 1976, at the bicentennial conference in Detroit, a coalition of Black, Hispanic, Native American, and white clergy represented by Auxiliary Bishop Eugene Marino of Washington, D.C., one of only four Black members of the hierarchy at the time, elaborated a resolution passed by the assembly that called once more for more racial and ethnic minority bishops. The resolution also called for a national pastoral letter—it would produce "Brothers and Sisters to Us"—that recognized "the sin of racism in both its personal and social dimensions." Church teaching on racial equality was clear, the group said, yet the American Catholic community's response "is in fact a mockery of this teaching."

But this kind of full-throated cry for equality in the Church and society has been rare, perhaps at least partly because Black clergy and bishops are so few.

In 1965, Archbishop Phillip Matthew Hannan of New Orleans introduced Perry, his new auxiliary, who recently had been elevated to the episcopacy by Pope Paul VI, as "the first American-born Negro bishop." Hannan, like most Catholics, may have been unaware of Bishop James Augustine Healy, a slave at birth, the eldest of ten children born to a wealthy Georgia plantation owner, Michael Morris Healy, and an enslaved woman he owned whom he called his wife, Eliza Healy. James Augustine Healy became bishop of Portland, Maine, in 1875 and served until his death in 1900. (Bishop Healy's brother Patrick Francis, a Jesuit, served as president of Georgetown University.) Bishop Perry's appointment more than half a century later was not taken well by racist Catholics, some of whom argued, as one demonstrator at Perry's episcopal ordination proclaimed on a placard, JESUS DID NOT CHOOSE NONWHITE APOSTLES.

In 1984, Perry of New Orleans joined nine other Black U.S. bishops who had been appointed by then to issue a pastoral letter on evangelism called "What We Have Seen and Heard." Perry and the others said their Blackness and Catholic faith were gifts meant to be shared "within the Black community at large and within the Church," and that Black spirituality, based on Scripture, carries a message of liberation and hope, expressed in appreciation of freedom, which should never be taken for granted. In the "Black tradition," they explained, prayer is at once contemplative, spontaneous, and pervasive, and Black spirituality is "joyful," rooted in community, and ever conscious of "social concern and social justice." Being Black Catholics, who belong to "a reality called 'The Black Church,'" in which Black

Christians feel at ease in joining in prayer with one another, places them "in a special position to serve as a bridge with our brothers and sisters of other Christian traditions," they wrote. Much of "What We Have Seen and Heard" focuses on how Black Catholics can bring others to the faith, although the bishops recognized what they only called "subtle racism" within the institutional Church, which failed to develop leadership among minorities and closed inner-city parochial schools that serve Black people. The Gospel message calls for forgiveness and reconciliation, they wrote, values that come "from our Black heritage," but "true reconciliation arises only where there is equality."

THE YEARS AFTER the election of Donald Trump called for concern and leadership from Catholic bishops. Rates of hate crimes went up, building a wall to prevent Latin American migrants was a political meme, white supremacist groups were boldly holding demonstrations, and the Black Lives Matter movement had been underway for years. In 2018, the first USCCB teaching document on race in nearly forty years, *Open Wide Our Hearts: The Enduring Call to Love*, landed with a thud, too weak for what the times demanded.

"Racist acts are sinful because they violate justice," the bishops wrote. "They reveal a failure to acknowledge the human dignity of the persons offended, to recognize them as the neighbors Christ calls us to love." Hispanics and African Americans "all too often" faced discrimination in hiring, housing, educational opportunities, and incarceration, the hierarchy informed us. "Despite the great blessings of liberty that this country offers, we must admit the plain truth that for many of our fellow citizens, who have done nothing wrong, interactions with the police are often fraught with fear and even danger. At the same time, we reject harsh rhetoric that belittles and dehumanizes law enforcement personnel who labor to keep our communities safe. We also condemn violent attacks against police."

There was no challenging white Catholics to consider themselves part of the problem as a people who were privileged along with other white Americans over their brothers and sisters of color. Daniel Horan, a Franciscan friar who teaches at the Catholic Theological Union in Chicago, has suggested that the bishops stop writing their heralded public epistles that nevertheless fail to recognize how racism "has been and remains a white problem." Everyone knows racism is a sin—we don't need another pastoral letter from the bishops to repeat what they have said before. In the thirty-two pages of the most recent USCCB teaching document on race, the words "supremacy" and "privilege" never come up, as if the abysmal state of the nation's institutionalized racism could be explained without them, and the word "white" only appears when referring to past eras, such as that of the coming of "white European immigrants." Nowhere do the bishops say racism is a *white* problem in a country where white people continue to set social norms and overwhelmingly hold the levers of institutions and government.

In a column in the *National Catholic Reporter* assessing *Open Wide Our Hearts*, the bishops' message on the consequences of what has been called the country's original sin, slavery, and the white supremacy that enabled it, Horan wrote that "nothing will change as long as those who benefit from an unjust system remain vincibly ignorant. It is not enough for the American church to decry the sin of racism; we must dare to name the sinner too."

IGNORING THE SHADOW
OVER THE BALLOT BOX

AT A TIME when civil rights gains are being reversed, the U.S. bishops do not examine white privilege or white supremacy in detail, or offer an action plan for Catholics to use. Absent has been any powerful, unequivocal condemnation of the rock-hard exclusionary system that began with slavery, continued through Jim Crow, and today proceeds with gerrymandering, voter suppression, and toxic fallout from the pivotal 2013 Supreme Court decision *Shelby County v. Holder*, which took away federal oversight of voting laws in those states with a record of disenfranchising Black voters. After record turnout of voters in the 2020 election, Republican lawmakers in forty-nine states introduced more than four hundred bills to limit voting, often aiming at communities of color, according to the Brennan Center for Justice, a nonprofit institute at New York University.

The USCCB failed to comment upon, let alone prophetically denounce, the new wave of voter suppression laws. "The silence is very noticeable, and it's sad and disappointing," said Sister Anita Baird, a member of the board of directors for the National Black Sisters' Conference, to *National Catholic Reporter*. Archbishop Gomez of Los Angeles was quiet.

Gomez's predecessor in the archdiocese, however, Cardinal Roger Mahony, who left office in 2011 upon reaching the mandatory retirement age of seventy-five, wrote a spirited cry exhorting the U.S. bishops to take a firm public stand. Published by the Catholic News Service, owned by the USCCB, Mahony quoted Pope Francis describing racism as a "virus" that mutates and, instead of disappearing, "lurks in waiting."

"Framing voting suppression laws as racially neutral preservations of voting integrity embodies this racism in waiting," Mahony wrote. The Church must throw its weight behind legal challenges to the unjust laws, he said, and bishops needed to inform the faithful of "these insidious threats . . . Time is of the essence." A disclaimer at the bottom of Mahony's commentary dutifully noted that his words "do not necessarily represent the views of . . . the U.S. Conference of Catholic Bishops."

In view of the history of American bishops' longtime dereliction of duty to lead strongly against racism, Archbishop Gomez's 2021 attack on movements that challenge racial injustice is only a different kind of failure, what Catholics might call a "sin of commission," rather than the "sin of omission" committed historically by the USCCB. Failing to call out racism in a definitive way, the USCCB helps keep the door open to white supremacy, and to Christian nationalism. In this it continues to share a path with the most fundamentalist evangelicals, whose politics were seeded in 1960s resistance to civil rights gains for Black Americans.

U.S. bishops also share another path with the white evangelicals, which comes along with the (white) male hegemony that marks Christian nationalism: denial of higher religious office to women.

8

Catholic Women, Catholic Girls

WHEN I WAS a girl attending Immaculate Conception Catholic grammar school in Monrovia, California, excitement grew over several months one year—I was probably age ten or eleven—as the parish church planned to reopen its doors to an expanded space for the fast-growing congregation. Rumor had it that the new interior was beautiful, but we students were not allowed inside until official opening day. So I was thrilled when a teacher, a Sister of Loretto, discreetly invited me to accompany her across the playground to the building and through the locked doors—for some reason she had a key—and have a look inside before any of my classmates, even the altar boys.

Indeed, the place was stunning, bigger and grander than the old stone-walled church to which I was accustomed. Empty of people, it looked vast. As we approached the altar rail and Sister stepped beyond it into the sacred precinct, I held back in surprise. She motioned for me to follow her into the sanctuary, the area around the altar where the priest said Mass. "It's all right, dear," she said about entering the space. "It's not consecrated yet."

In the years before the changes wrought by Vatican II, it was forbidden for females, except for cleaning ladies, to be inside the (consecrated) sanctuary of a Catholic Church. As a daily Mass attendant, I knew the Latin responses in the Mass as well as any of the boys—my St. Joseph's Missal rendered the celebration in Latin with an English translation. I led classmates in processions on special days, and my behavior was acceptable enough for me to be considered as an altar server—had I only been a boy. (Even now where bishops and priests celebrate the Traditional Latin Mass girls and women are not seen around the altar.) Today a ten-year-old Catholic girl might not be reluctant to enter sacred space that should be open to all who embrace the faith—or such fear should be gone—but females remain second-class members of the Church.

While this discrimination is a fault that runs through the Catholic institution, American bishops with their power and financial clout have failed to be a prophetic voice urging the Church toward the direction of greater leadership and the ordained participation desired by millions of Catholic women. Instead, the prelates ignore the consternation of female Catholics, or they attempt to hoodwink women young and older into staying in their place. That was what Archbishop José Gomez appeared to be doing when he invited teenagers to share a stage and tell him what concerns of theirs he might take to the Vatican for the Youth Synod of 2018, the year Gomez was elected by his peers to the presidency of the U.S. Conference of Catholic Bishops.

A CRASH *WILL* OCCUR

"I WAS WONDERING what type of leadership roles the women can obtain in the Church in the upcoming years," asked a girl on the stage, in a video clip posted to the archbishop's Facebook page. "As a woman I was wondering for me and for future young ladies, what we can do to become more of a leader within the Church?"

The archbishop chuckled. "So you want me to tell the pope that, no?" he said, begging laughter from the audience. "Why not, huh?" he continued. He shrugged his shoulders and grinned.

The girl, wearing a school uniform and Oxford shoes, looked down briefly at the microphone in her hand, biting her lip. The role of women in the Church has been "essential," the archbishop assured her, naming Mary, the mother of Jesus, and female saints, like Mother Teresa. "Obviously the most important thing . . . is that we need women that are saints," he said.

If the young lady was aspiring to something less daunting than canonization, she might have been disappointed. With his titter-provoking response to the student's serious question, Gomez ignored what has become one of the most vexing issues in the Roman Catholic Church: women's increasing demands for greater roles in leadership, and in the hierarchy that is central to the institution, including ordination as deacons and priests. Bishops respond that the original twelve apostles were male, suggesting that this fact means females cannot succeed them as priests, for instance. And Jesus was male, so a woman cannot "image" him, they say, cannot mirror him, even as a deacon, as the man he was on earth. (A similar argument was once made by U.S. Catholics who said a bishop could not be Black because Christ's apostles were white.) The theological response held by women who aspire to the diaconate and the priesthood, and their male and female allies, is that such thinking is heretical, because the Church teaches that the resurrected Christ is God and, as every Catholic schoolchild learns, he or she, male or female, disabled or in any other way limited in life, is made in the "image of God."

For their part, Christian evangelical fundamentalists typically do not permit women to teach men, or hold positions of authority over men. A woman's role is holiest not as a church leader, but as a mother and homemaker. The greatest threat to America is that "gender lines could become blurred, and the family fundamentally redefined," said Rafael Cruz, a fundamentalist evangelical preacher, on the campaign trail in 2016 for his son, Senator Ted Cruz, who was vying for the Republican presidential nomination. "When the ship of righteousness departs from the proven route established by Scripture, a crash *will* occur," warned the elder Cruz.

> *Christian nationalism is intimately intertwined with Americans' defini-*
> *tions of the family and the proper roles for men and women within the*
> *family. The stakes are high, in this view, because having families that*
> *conform to God's ideal standard are a vital step toward having a country*
> *that he will bless with prosperity.*
>
> —Andrew L. Whitehead and Samuel L. Perry, *Taking America Back*
> *for God: Christian Nationalism in the United States*

RIGHTIST CATHOLIC BISHOPS and evangelical leaders make common cause not out of a desire for the kind of ecumenism promoted by the teachings of Vatican II, but because they share a Christian nationalist cultural vision of how the world should be, including idealizing "traditional"—that is, patriarchal—social arrangements. They also share a point of view that these values are under attack, and that only a return to norms of the founding fathers, which they assume to be their own, will keep the state from crumbling underfoot.

As a member of Opus Dei, an ultraconservative, elite Catholic movement founded in Spain in 1928, Archbishop Gomez would have held a version of this point of view since the time he was a young man. Gomez took degrees at the University of Navarra, the largest of fifteen international Opus Dei universities, regarded as the cornerstone of the order's "corporate," or public-facing, works, which also include primary and secondary schools, business schools, hospitals, and agricultural institutes.

Women are equal in Opus Dei, say members, with the same religious education as men, although they receive it separately. The expectations of men and women are the same in what the movement, numbering about eighty thousand members worldwide, calls the "Work," which involves a "universal call to holiness," the belief that ordinary people in society can achieve Christian perfection. Women can hold positions in Opus Dei institutions like its schools. John Allen, a veteran Catholic journalist who has written an exhaustive, and ultimately friendly, book about the movement, says "there is no taboo against men and women interacting" at Opus Dei congresses and symposia, for instance, and at any rate, the majority of members are married, raising families in environments where women naturally come into contact with men.

But women are considered so fundamentally separate from men by Opus Dei that attempts to keep the sexes apart (except for the married couples) look fanatic seen from the outside.

In his 2005 book, *Opus Dei: An Objective Look Behind the Myths and Reality of the Most Controversial Force in the Catholic Church*, Allen recounts a 2004 conversation with Rev. James Martin, S.J., who reported on the movement for the Jesuit magazine *America* in 1995. Martin, Allen wrote, "tells a story about how far the emphasis on separation" went while building the seventeen-story U.S. Opus Dei headquarters in downtown Manhattan during the 1990s, when Martin had a friend who worked on the information systems in the building. He quotes the priest: "The Opus Dei people told him, 'We want separate phone systems, and we want separate computer systems, and we want separate everything.' And he said, 'Why would you want that?' And they said, 'We want to treat it like two separate buildings.'

And he said, 'That doesn't make any sense. You're going to be talking to each other.' They said that was okay. And he said, 'It'll cost you twice as much money.' Their response? 'No problem.'"

Members who clean and cook at Opus Dei centers are female; they number about four thousand, or about 10 percent of female Opus Dei members. Allen gives two reasons for why the domestic work of the organization falls only to women, according to members: (1) It has always been that way, and (2) "Women have an instinctive aptitude for creating and maintaining a homelike environment that most men lack."

To Christian nationalists, society itself is undermined to the extent that the patriarchal family structure is undermined, with civil rights laws like those allowing same-sex couples to marry or to adopt children, and so must be reinforced by the ultraconservatives' own "fundamental" values. Opus Dei families contribute to the patriarchal paradigm by having more children than the average U.S. family, sometimes eight, nine, or ten, even though the mother may have a professional career. The home, wrote Opus Dei founder Josemaría Escrivá, who was canonized a saint in 2002, "is a particularly suitable place for the growth of [a woman's] personality . . . [S]he can achieve her personal perfection there."

The official archdiocesan biography of Archbishop Gomez describes him as "instrumental in promoting the leadership of . . . women in the Church and in American society." It refers to Gomez's cofounding, in 2003, with Archbishop Charles J. Chaput of Denver and three politically conservative Denver women, of Endow, which is an acronym for Educating on the Nature and Dignity of Women and counts 40,000 participants from 130 parishes in a network of women's discussion and study groups. The chairman of Endow's board is cofounder Marilyn Coors, of the Colorado brewing family, a bioethicist and mother of six who, with her husband, Peter, is a major donor to the traditionalist Catholic student group the Fellowship of Catholic University Students (FOCUS), which recruits and ministers generally on non-Catholic campuses. Joseph Coors, Marilyn Coors's father-in-law, funded the Heritage Foundation founded by Paul Weyrich, among the most important conservative think tanks in the country; the Coors family remains a major donor to ultraright political and legal causes.

In Endow's publications for sale, webinars, podcasts, and retreats, the group echoes the Opus Dei females' concentration on thinking about, and praying over, what Pope John Paul II called the "feminine genius," that is, the fact that woman is born different from man, by her very essence born to be a mother, if not physically then in behavior and soul ("spiritual motherhood"), receptive, encouraging, nurturing, affirming to every person she meets. Endow describes itself as bringing "women together to discover their God-given dignity and to understand their role in humanizing and transforming society" by way of this "feminine genius." A person expressing interest in the group is soon bombarded with email invitations to talks and to buy products. Endow speakers and endorsed literature propose the "feminine genius" in opposition to secular feminism, which they may refer to as "radical feminism," conventional though it may be, perceiving it to be anti-maternal, or, in cases, anti-male.

Supreme Court justice Amy Coney Barrett, a Catholic working mother of seven, is just the sort of model of the "feminine genius" to which Endow members and other devout women might aspire rather than looking to the secular model of feminism, with its emphasis on social and economic equality for men and women. Barrett belongs to a small, ultraconservative, charismatic Christian group called People of Praise, which maintains a male-dominated hierarchy and view of gender roles. She has served as one of the group's "handmaids"—now called "women leaders"—who give advice to other women, under an all-male board of governors; married women acknowledge the "head-ship" of their husbands in spiritual and economic matters. In 2006 Barrett signed her name to a newspaper ad that defended "the right to life from fertilization to natural death," a stand worth remember-ing in the post-*Roe* climate when model legislation for states is be-ing drawn up—including by the National Right to Life Committee, founded fifty years ago by Catholic bishops—that proposes an end to all abortions except to save the life of the mother. Barrett's personal life reflects her beliefs. At a time when a large percentage of prenatal diagnoses of Down syndrome—67 percent in a 2012 study of U.S. data—result in a choice for abortion, Barrett gave birth when she was about age forty to an affected child, her youngest, Benjamin.

In an email exchange with journalist Margaret Talbot, writing for *The New Yorker*, Penny Nance, head of the conservative Concerned Women for America, expressed her admiration for Barrett, who did not represent classic feminism, but was a mother and accomplished pro-fessional. Barrett, Nance wrote, "decimates the argument that women can't do both, or that women need abortion to 'live their best lives.'"

SUPPORT INDEPENDENT-THINKING WOMEN?
U.S. BISHOPS DRAG THEIR FEET

AS ITS APOSTOLATE for women grows, Endow, the network initiated by Archbishop Gomez and the wealthy Marilyn Coors, is presenting its materials in Spanish for the growing population of immigrant Catholics (70 percent of the Los Angeles archdiocese is Latino), and reaching out to younger women, including at the high school level in a program called Blossom. Archbishop Gomez has also started a group called Given, aimed at young adult women, including young Catholic nuns, to provide "Catholic leadership training." The group was established after surveys showed that increasing numbers of youth identify as "nones," or followers of no religion, many of them ex-Catholics.

But Endow and its ilk are not for everybody.

"It's a concerning group—it's about keeping women in their place," a middle-aged resident of Orange County, California, who is active in her parish told me. This Catholic woman stopped going to Endow retreats in 2019, disillusioned. "It's all about being, not doing. They want you to believe women are holy, but they preach against the secular world that empowers women—it segregates women outside the picture, and it ends up being a kind of indoctrination to make you think that's the view of the Church."

What Endow and Gomez are up against is not only the likes of such independent-thinking Catholic women, but also a small but vigorous population of female Catholics determined to live their faith according to vocations they believe they have, including as priests and deacons. They do not want any longer to wait for the Church to come around. Since 2002, women priests have been ordained—the first by sympathetic male bishops in Europe, and subsequently by their own line of female bishops—until today they number more than 270; they celebrate Mass, baptisms, and weddings, sometimes in houses, or in dedicated churches, or in spaces loaned by other denominations. Many share their services on Zoom. Of these womenpriests, their preferred term in English, the great majority are in the United States.

Rev. Maria Eitz is a slender, mature woman who wore a long dress to celebrate one Mass in San Francisco, with a stone pendant around her neck that caught the light from the tall windows of a Protestant church that opens its doors to Catholics. Eitz preached on social justice, prayed for immigrant children stuck at the border, and quoted Cornel West: "Justice is what love looks like in public." During traditional requests for prayer during Mass, a man in the small congregation—about fifteen men and women—offered, "Bless the women bishops. The men bishops can only seem to speak about one thing—abortion—when so much else needs attention."

Like most other womenpriests, Eitz had obtained a degree in theology (master's, Marquette University) in the years before she studied further for the priesthood with an organization called Roman Catholic Womenpriests-USA (similar organizations exist in other countries). She was ordained by a woman bishop in 2012, and told me she felt the experience was "transformative," especially the moment when she lay down on the floor in prostration, a sign of humility. "It was a very profound event," she said. "I knew I could never go back."

Vatican II did not suggest ordination of women as priests or deacons, nor do all liberal Catholics want them. Pope Francis opposes female ordination. However, a 2015 survey by the Pew Research Center showed that 60 percent of U.S. male and female Catholics approved of the idea. A 2019 NBC survey indicated that 71 percent of Catholic nuns thought the issue warranted further study. (Among male clergy, the survey showed only 24 percent of diocesan priests agreed.) Nothing in Scripture forbids female priests, and the Church's Code of Canon Law can be revised.

"We need equality in the Church, women's leadership and wisdom, and their pastoral ways," said Jean Molesky-Poz, of Berkeley, California, who writes for Catholic publications and has taught in the Graduate Program in Pastoral Ministries at Santa Clara University. "The idea of women priests is emerging, and not just from women who feel called," she said.

Priests who encourage conversation about female ordination may be disciplined by their bishops, stripped of their priesthood, or ex-

communicated. Maryknoll priest Roy Bourgeois, a former naval officer who earned a Purple Heart during the war in Vietnam, and who
founded the School of the Americas Watch that peacefully protested
U.S. training of Latin American military officers who committed
egregious human rights abuses, spoke favorably of women's ordination in appearances on college campuses.

"It was like poking the beehive," Bourgeois told me in a telephone
interview from his home in Columbus, Georgia. "I underestimated
the depth of the sexism and misogyny of the all-male priesthood."
Bourgeois was defrocked in 2012 for continuing to advocate for wom-
en's ordination and expelled from his beloved Maryknoll order.

Since 1975, the Women's Ordination Conference (WOC), a U.S.-
based lobbying group, has tried to convince bishops to modify the
Code of Canon Law so that women may receive the sacrament of
Holy Orders legitimately in the eyes of the Church. In a Zoom interview with Executive Director Kate McElwee from the WOC office
in Rome, I asked about what progress had been made after all these
years. McElwee acknowledged a continuing "disconnect with the
hierarchy." The bishops' attitude against female ordination "impacts
women's lives and livelihoods within the Church, and how fulfilled
they feel in their faith," McElwee said. Catholic women suffer, in
silence or not. Women aspirants to the priesthood often do not want
to wait for a process—trying to change Canon law—with no guarantee of success while living with what they say is a God-given vocation. "We believe it is most important to follow our consciences," Rev.
Martha Sherman of Salem, South Dakota, told me. Sherman was
ordained by a woman bishop in 2013 in St. Cloud, Minnesota.

Officially, the womenpriests are excommunicated from the Church;
they do not recognize the banishments. They do not answer to the
diocesan (male) bishops, they say, but do consider themselves in com-

munion with the pope. They cannot count on support, even in spirit, from U.S. (male) bishops. Without changes in Church law, in their training and practices they lead a semi-clandestine life.

In 2014, Christine Mayr-Lumetzberger, one of the first women ordained as a priest in Europe in 2002, flew from her home in Austria to Brownsburg, Indiana (pop: 22,000), to attend the episcopal ordination of a former Franciscan nun named Nancy Louise Meyer, by another woman bishop, Regina Nicolosi. Mayr-Lumetzberger's original womenpriest cohort is called the Danube Seven, because they received the sacrament on a boat on the river; they included nuns, theologians, and a former first lady of the state of Ohio. Five other women bishops attended Meyer's elevation in Brownsburg.

"We just broke the law," Bishop Meyer told me in an interview. "We have to go outside the institution to be ordained." Her study for the priesthood was "catacombed," she said, kept secret from her family, because they would have objected, and from her employer at the time, the archbishop of Cincinnati.

*　*　*

CATHOLIC WOMEN ARE forbidden from being deacons, too, an ordained ministry which would allow them, like male deacons, to preside at weddings, baptisms, and funerals; to anoint the sick; and to preach during Mass. Fully 60 percent of American Catholic women reported support for the idea of female deacons in a 2017 survey conducted by the Center for Applied Research in the Apostolate (CARA) at Georgetown University.

Delila Vasquez, age sixty, of Fontana, California, has studied theology, taught Confirmation classes, and serves as the CEO of a Catholic professionals' organization. Vasquez told me that when she asked her husband, Roberto, "Would you support me if I want to become a deacon when that opens up for women?" he was taken aback, suggesting the whole family might talk about it first—they have three adult daughters. But Delila and Roberto Vasquez have been married for thirty years and attend Mass regularly, and she is confident he will agree if and when the opportunity presents itself, having heard and seen "my passion."

"I know that in my heart," she said.

Vasquez said she is watching young members of her parish drift away, telling her they find the Church "patriarchal" or "irrelevant." For the Latino Catholic population—Vasquez migrated from Ecuador, and her husband is Mexican American—Vasquez said, "our youth would benefit from seeing women at the altar alongside the priest."

How the altar looks to Latinos is no small consideration. A majority of U.S. Catholics under thirty are Hispanic, and Latinos are the U.S. Church's fastest-growing population. A wife gives formal consent to her husband's ordination as a deacon, and is expected to help in some of his duties, to model a Christian marriage. That is why the assent of Vasquez's spouse is important.

"In the Latin culture the mom has influence," Vasquez said. If women are deacons, "young people could see women in the leadership of the Church. I see it with other denominations where there is a woman preacher. I hear young women describe the preacher as a woman first, and then the role. There's something to be said about that."

For the most part, U.S. bishops appear deaf to the Catholics young and old whom parish workers like Delila Vasquez listen to.

"Women should be invited into every ministry or activity we have that's not doctrinally precluded," said San Diego cardinal Robert McElroy, then a bishop, in a 2019 interview with *National Catholic*

Reporter. But U.S. bishops as a whole turn their backs on women in the diaconate too. In 2019, only a third of U.S. prelates who answered a CARA survey thought the Church should ordain women as deacons, and even fewer (27 percent) thought it would do so. Without leadership from one of the most important bishops' conferences in the world, the USCCB, which is the world's wealthiest, administering the most Catholic educational and health institutions, it is unlikely that the Vatican will move forward on ordaining women as priests or deacons.

THE SILENCING

WHEN VATICAN II encouraged Church participation by laypeople, women began to study for advanced degrees in theology, anticipating more leadership and pastoral roles. Women now make up as much as 50 percent of students in some graduate theology classes, and many professors are women. Some graduates become certified pastoral ministers—for the sick, or for college students, for instance—or educators and other kinds of parish leaders. Some become spiritual directors, trained in theology, Scripture, and psychology, and accompany individuals to see how God is working in their lives, including in times of stress or grief.

Others, like Kristi Laughlin, a social worker, have used their studies and experience in families, or at work, or as members of religious orders, to preach at Mass.

"It was great," Laughlin said, recalling the first time she preached at Holy Spirit Parish in Berkeley in 1996. She focused on the moment in Scripture when Simon Peter recognized Jesus as the Messiah, and Jesus replied by giving him the keys of the kingdom of heaven. "I explained how we are all entrusted with the kingdom," she said, men and women, rich and poor, fit or struggling with illness. "It just gave me such joy."

Over the years, Popes John Paul II and Benedict XVI and ultra-conservative bishops chipped away at the laity's role promoted by the council. Vatican regulations appeared that forbade laypeople from reading the Gospel during Mass, and preaching, unless permitted by the local bishop. U.S. bishops took advantage of the regulations to squeeze out women who were regularly speaking before congregations.

In 2013 when Bishop Michael C. Barber, S.J., took over the Oakland diocese, to which Kristi Laughlin's parish belongs, he took away permission for anyone but a priest or an ordained deacon to reflect on Scripture during Mass. "I was stunned," said Laughlin. Since then, she has preached at the churches of other denominations, but not at a Catholic church.

U.S. bishops have silenced women preachers (and laymen preachers, fewer in number) in other U.S. dioceses. When Archbishop Harry Flynn of St. Paul–Minneapolis prepared to hand over his office to a more conservative successor in 2008, he instructed twenty-nine parishes to end their lay preaching programs, which had been active for a quarter century. In Rochester, New York, women had been giving sermons at parishes since the 1980s while carefully observing, along with their pastors, the letter of canon law by preaching "in dialogue with" the presiding priest, describing their insights as "reflections," not homilies, which are reserved to priests or deacons. A conservative bishop, Salvatore Matano, took over in 2014, and ended the forty-year-old practice.

"It's a tragedy for the women who offer gifts that aren't accepted, and it's a tragedy for the Church that is not taking advantage of all the gifts that are available," theologian Alison M. Benders, a former

associate dean at the Jesuit School of Theology in Berkeley, told me
in an interview. Benders now serves as vice president for mission and
ministry at Santa Clara University.

Recognizing women fully, as priests, deacons, and preachers, with
all the dignity the positions imply, might be an example to the world,
she said.

"It's a tragedy to think that it's OK to categorize and ignore the
full humanity of some people," Benders said. "That's not what our
God does."

9

Our Common Home?

IN MAY 2015 Pope Francis promulgated a landmark encyclical about the environmental crisis and the economic forces that affect it, written with an interfaith panel of scientists and experts in economic development. Called *Laudato Si' (Praise Be)*, the title comes from the thirteenth-century "Canticle of the Sun," written by St. Francis, in praise of God for his creation of the wonders of the earth—Brother Sun, Sister Moon, Brother Fire, Sister Water—and sets the modern letter's tone. Like the glorious song of prayer by his namesake, the letter of Pope Francis evinces a feeling of intimacy with the living earth and its creatures.

But papal encyclicals are not prayers; they are the way a pope puts forth his teachings addressed to problems of the age, which all Catholics are beholden to respect. In the 184 pages of *Laudato Si'*, Francis lays out the holiness and interconnectedness of all creation and suggests responses to the environmental crisis that include a critique of unrestrained capitalism as a cause of the emergency. Trained as a scientist, acting like a statesman, he called for an immediate global dialogue to arrest climate change, and to stop the destruction of the natural world by the hand of man. He directed *Laudato Si'* not only to Catholics, but to "every living person on this planet," with a telling subtitle, "On Care for Our Common Home."

The strength of the scientific, ethical, and theological reasoning in the document, not to mention the authority of the two-thousand-year-old papal institution from which it emerged, had an important effect at a critical time when nations were meeting to set sustainable development goals. The press reacted by calling the letter "bold" (*Los Angeles Times*); "a call to action with scientific rationale . . . written in plain language" (*Chicago Tribune*); and "the most astonishing and perhaps the most ambitious papal document of the past 100 years" (*The Guardian*). Secular attention was widespread, even pleasantly astonished. *The Washington Post* suggested that, in Francis's "masterful grasp" of climate change science, he "unmasks himself . . . as a total policy wonk." The "clarion call," as *USA Today* called the encyclical, "adds an ethical dimension to a debate too often bogged down in warring statistics and economic arguments."

Six months after *Laudato Si'* was published, representatives of 197 countries assembled at COP21, the twenty-first Conference of the Parties (COP) to the United Nations Framework Convention on Climate Change, a long-anticipated meeting that produced the Paris Accords, which legally bind nations to limit greenhouse gasses, which damage the atmosphere and lead to overheating the earth. Later, researchers would say *Laudato Si'* helped to bring forth the accords and other compacts with its moral strength, urgency, and arguments. In the words of scholar Irene Burke, a fellow of Princeton University's Liechtenstein Institute on Self-Determination, the encyclical and experts' work contributed to "political cooperation leading up to pivotal international agreements."

Who did not praise *Laudato Si'*, use it as a template for action, actively promulgate the personal "ecological conversion" that it promotes, or make fundamental climate-conscious changes over which they had control, as the pope so fervently urged?

U.S. bishops.

The American prelates were wary of the encyclical before it even appeared, some of them perhaps concerned about aligning themselves with an environmental movement that contained some activists who suggested population control as a remedy to the climate crisis. Yet in the 1980s U.S. bishops unhesitatingly spoke out on the crisis in the natural world, calling upon parishes and individual Catholics in a pastoral letter "to rise above a preoccupation with material gain" with regard to the energy crisis of the time, to conserve wherever possible and accept "an appropriate share of responsibility for the welfare of creation," even to the point of making "sacrifices." The people of the United States, they said, had so much that they wasted what people in other countries needed.

But by 2015 abortion had become the sole front-burner issue for the United States Conference of Catholic Bishops (USCCB)—everything else seemed less worthy of action. And some bishops just didn't care. For much of the world Church, *Laudato Si'* was one of the most anticipated papal letters in memory, only the second missive from the first non-European pope in more than 1,200 years; yet on the eve of *Laudato Si'*'s release, only 40 of 250 American bishops at the spring meeting of the USCCB in St. Louis attended a workshop on the new encyclical.

The most conservative U.S. bishops spoke directly against the pope's message. Cardinal Raymond Burke disdained the teaching, and the call for "ecological conversion" that rests at its heart. Ecological conversion is the "transformation of hearts and minds toward greater love of God, each other, and creation [and] a process of acknowledging our contribution to the social and ecological crisis," as the global Laudato Si' Movement, founded to inspire and mobilize Catholics along the lines of the encyclical, explains it.

But Burke called ecological conversion "insidious." It was, he said, tantamount to "idolatry."

"What I see behind this is a push for worship of 'Mother Earth,'" he told *The Wanderer*.

Another powerful voice speaking against *Laudato Si'* was Archbishop Carlo Maria Viganò. Although he is not a U.S. prelate, and no longer the Vatican's ambassador to Washington, Viganò maintains close relationships with several conservative U.S. bishops, who fail to condemn his screeds against the pope, and rightist U.S. Catholic media provide a platform for him. "I would like to emphasize that attributing a personal identity to nature, almost endowed with intellect and will, is a prelude to her divinization," warned Viganò in an address to an October 2020 conference in Rome, slamming the pope's emphasis on the interconnectedness of all creation.

The reaction of Catholic conservative media to the letter on the environment ranged from tepid to vicious. The Catholic News Agency, owned by the Eternal Word Television Network, suggested that the faithful should respect the pope, but didn't have to agree with his version of climate change science. R. R. Reno, editor of *First Things*, called *Laudato Si'* "perhaps the most anti-modern encyclical since the Syllabus of Errors, Pius IX's haughty 1864 dismissal of the conceits of the modern era."

MOST EGREGIOUS WAS the way in which U.S. bishops, with few exceptions, have allowed the teaching to languish in silence, turning their collective back on the pope's cry for change for the sake of the planet, the poor, and God's creatures, as if the encyclical would go away, or as if they were making a statement of their own denying the authority of a pope not to their liking. The dismissive, even oppositional, attitude of the U.S. bishops on *Laudato Si'* is not an impression, but a fact quantified by data scientists at Omaha's Creighton University.

In an eye-opening report, researchers using a data set of columns written by bishops from 171 dioceses from June 2014 to June 2019—that is, the year before and the four years after *Laudato Si'* was issued—found that U.S. bishops have effectively ignored the environmental crisis, when they do not deny it. Prelates commonly express their thoughts and teaching to the faithful in the signed columns carried by official diocesan publications, but out of 12,077 columns published by the bishops during the period of the study, only 93, the data showed, a mere 0.8 percent, mentioned climate change at all, and of these, just 56 described it "in terms that suggest it is real or currently happening." Most American Catholics, the researchers found, learned about the pope's thinking about the environment, global warming, and other critical issues in *Laudato Si'* in public, secular media, not Church-connected media.

Some of the U.S. bishops' columns downplayed the pope's authority to teach about climate change. Others "minimized focus on climate change within the Church's broader ecological teachings," the Creighton research report concluded. Compared to only 14 columns on climate change politics, the data showed that bishops opined, in a total of 495 columns, on the politics of abortion (284), health care (118), and immigration (93).

In October 2019 Pope Francis welcomed 185 bishops from around the world to Rome for a synod, a meeting where prelates gather to consider a consequential issue, then present their advice to the pope. Francis was carrying on a long tradition, but he was also doing something new: The Pan-Amazon Synod would be the first in Church history organized around a specific ecological territory, signaling that the pope placed great importance on the vast region whose future was consequential for the health of the planet, and for the continued existence of multiple Indigenous groups.

The Amazon Basin is an expanse of 2.5 million square miles stretching across nine countries sometimes called a "lung" of the planet, so critical is the region's biomass for absorbing carbon dioxide and producing oxygen. But Francis also wanted to focus attention on the Amazon as the homeland of 30 million people, in order to support social justice for its most marginalized inhabitants, and not least to counteract a wave of conversions to fundamentalist evangelical sects, which are often indifferent to saving the rain forest. At the synod, *Laudato Si'* would be alive among the bishops, who would consider ways to make the encyclical concrete across the region, with its endless webs of rivers and scattered populations, where there are so few priests that 90 percent of communities do not have Sunday Mass. (One Amazonian bishop said that if the ratio of priests per square mile in his diocese were applied to Italy, Italy would have only sixty-four priests.)

IN THE AMAZON

ON THE EVE of the meetings, six thousand miles away from Rome in the town of Leticia (pop: 42,000), in the Colombian Amazon, I met with Fr. Rodolfo Piñero in a twilight conversation at the home of the Capuchin missionaries. We had to raise our voices to be heard over the clattering of thousands of multicolored jungle parakeets descending into nearby trees. Piñero, who first came to work in the region in 1992, had participated in some of the three hundred "listening sessions" that had taken place over the previous two years across the Amazon in preparation for the synod, meetings where clergy, nuns, and lay-people spoke of their deepest problems, and suggested their own solutions, many of which were subsequently reflected in the synod agenda. Coordinated by the Pan-Amazonian Ecclesial Network (REPAM), the pre-synod gatherings took place in airy church halls and under thatched roofs. Many participants arrived on foot, by bus, motorcycle, or canoe. REPAM estimated that some eighty-seven thousand local people took part in parishes and the regional gatherings.

Piñero praised the preparatory synod document, which reflected ideas brought up in the listening sessions, such as alleviating the shortage of clergy by ordaining mature married men, preferably Indigenous, and including women in the diaconate—they already performed many church-related rites, like baptism, and often led parish life. Considered controversial elsewhere, such solutions to the shortage of clergy hardly raised an eyebrow in the Amazon. The preparatory synod document was "a correct reflection" of the region and its needs, Piñero said.

The needs touched conservation and inhabitants. Amazonian plant life includes some 390 billion trees in rich diversity—sixteen thousand species—a gift of survival to every person on earth, mitigating the impact of human-caused global warming. But it's a gift at risk from oil and gas companies, industrial loggers, and cattle ranches that feed global markets, including the United States.

Some of the Amazon's four hundred native tribes are nearing extinction, numbering fewer than five hundred people, and others number in the thousands and are thriving. Pope Francis considers the Indigenous to be protagonists of the conservation of their lands; if they persist in the regions where they have lived with their surroundings for generations without destroying them, the natural world has a better chance for survival. Since Vatican II, one important concern has been "inculturation," maintaining the integrity of the Gospel while encouraging sensitivity to the cultural contexts in which the faithful live. How might this work in the Amazon?

ABOUT A THREE-HOUR walk from Leticia through thick forest, the extended family of a Huitoto tribe elder, Warrior of the Jungle, baptized William, age seventy-four, lives in a large, circular house called a *maloca*, with a high conical roof of woven palm, no electricity, and two hearths. Four sturdy columns square the center of the *maloca*'s interior, honoring the jungle, the animals, the water, and the universe. Light slants in through slits in the walls of sticks and wooden boards. This is a contemporary Catholic Indigenous Amazonian household that keeps to traditional customs—just the kind of individuals, along with economically poor nonnatives, often in burgeoning towns, that the Pan-Amazon Synod in Rome aimed to reach and serve.

On the night we met, William sat in a chair carved from a tree trunk and spoke as a thin flame flickered from a wick in a gourd filled with some kind of oil, resting on a stool, its light sending up a small circle of illumination. In a slow, whisper-like voice, he talked about the forest, the connections among men, animals, the elements. "Materialism" was destroying the Amazon, violating the "work of the Creator," he said, adding: "The trees are living beings. That is why they were created. God maintains life. Our lives. God maintains the trees."

Over our hours-long conversation, William occasionally dipped a finger into a small, carved gourd containing a mix of coca powder and dry *yarumo* leaves, and rubbed some inside his mouth. He has a license to grow the coca plant in his farm garden for such use. Along with tobacco, these are substances that the Huitoto believe inspire speech and give strength.

"We are Indigenous people, but we are of a new generation,"

William said. "The world has changed a lot. The new Indigenous have technology." During the day, a neighbor who lived within cell phone range had delivered a message to him. "Children are born with a more forward-looking mentality. Why? Because the world is turning very fast."

Was there any contradiction between his Catholic faith and traditional ways?

"When one is baptized in the Catholic religion, one is Catholic," he said. "We do speak of the earth, of nature—but we don't have any problem [with being Catholic], because everything is the same universe. All is complete. The jungle, the trees, all are created by God. And our Lord Jesus Christ came down to earth to save us from our sins. That's the way it is."

THE SPLASH HEARD ROUND THE WORLD

THE MERE INTRODUCTION of the issues for the synod in its preliminary documents, including those named as important by the Amazon residents, unleashed a firestorm of resistance from conservatives and traditionalists. Priests were celibate and must remain that way, opponents said, so the suggestion of many in the region that mature married men might be ordained was out of the question. The idea of women deacons, even in a remote corner of the world, was the camel's nose under the tent, which could only lead to women's ordination, which was verboten. Indigenous theology? Indigenous customs? An Indigenous rite? Paganism, unacceptable syncretism. For the most conservative Catholics, inculturation, adapting the liturgy with local cultural customs and understandings, was a suspicious concept.

The worst fires in memory burned in the Brazilian Amazon in the weeks before the synod, razing rain forest over an area the size of New

Jersey, generating toxic smoke that darkened skies above cities a thousand miles away from the rain forest, including São Paulo, population
46 million. But the focus that Pope Francis and others wanted to keep
on the region—on the loss of its life forms, on its poor and displaced,
on how creation is seen in the Gospel, on Catholic environmental
thinking and *Laudato Si'*—was sabotaged by ultrarightists who managed to grab the spotlight.

For months ahead of the meetings, they front-loaded opposition
by criticizing the assembly's public working papers. The alt-right international Catholic network of politico-civic organizations called
Tradition, Family, and Property (TFP), which began in 1960 by promoting landed interests in Brazil but has become more influential in
the United States, launched an online Pan-Amazon Synod Watch
that characterized the upcoming synod as a "neo-Communist project."
(TFP president C. Preston Noell and the director of its Washington
bureau, Mario Navarro da Costa, are members of the governing board
of the powerful and secretive Council for National Policy.) Novus
Ordo Watch, an anti–Vatican II Internet apostolate, as it calls itself,
founded in 2002, launched an ongoing, ultimately exhaustive compi-
lation of synod documents, news, and commentary under the rubric
"Welcome to the Jungle."

As the bishops met in their synod, TFP and an anti-abortion coalition called Voice of the Family presented in-person conferences
elsewhere in Rome—TFP's was also live-streamed—where speakers
denied climate change. Addressing the Voice of the Family event,
Notre Dame graduate Michael Voris, who was an award-winning
news reporter and producer for CBS and Fox News affiliates before
establishing the conservative news site Church Militant, advocated
for the resignation of Pope Francis. Delivering an attack on "anti-
Western" liberation theology (to which Pope Francis is not an adher-
ent), Voris called it "born in the bowels of the KGB and unleashed on

South America in a Soviet attempt to destabilize Catholicism on that continent." Liberation theology was behind the synod, he said.

At the TFP session, held in the beautiful eighteenth-century Hotel Quirinale, not far from Trevi Fountain, attendees heard speakers condemn nefarious forces for trying to stop assimilation of native peoples, which they considered a good thing; Indigenous were not among the speakers, nor were they given credit or blame for opposing assimilation, as if the Indigenous themselves had no agency. "The whole wise construction of centuries integrating Indians into society has been dismantled by Liberation Theology missionaries since the seventies, by some members of environmental movements, and by NGOs defending their interests or those of their financiers," the TFP website's roundup reported. For TFP's adherents, the vast rain forest was not worth saving, and it's been that way for a long time. Since the Middle Ages, Catholics "opposed the light of cathedrals . . . to the darkness of the forest inhabited by evil spirits," the TFP site said. "Deforestation is a symbol of civilization."

Two Catholic converts met at these conferences that opposed the synod, and one night over dinner, they hatched a plot to discredit the synod in the eyes of the world. Taylor Marshall, a former Episcopal priest from Texas, and father of eight, was an American radical traditionalist—known by critics as "rad-trads"—who produced a top-fifty Christian podcast and had written a book, *Infiltration: The Plot to Destroy the Church from Within* (i.e., by Marxists, modernists, Masons), published by Sophia Institute Press, which has a publishing agreement with EWTN. The other was Alexander Tschugguel, young (b. 1993), tall, and handsome, who had rallied anti-abortion demonstrators for years at the Austrian version of the March for Life, campaigned against same-sex marriage, disdained the "modernist" Church, and supported the Traditional Latin Mass.

Marshall and Tschugguel objected to video images of the pope and other dignitaries welcoming invited Amazon guests, some in native dress, into Vatican gardens during a synod consecration event. The visitors had planted a tree in honor of St. Francis of Assisi, the patron saint of animals and the environment, whose feast day it had been. Amazonian natives presented the pope with carved wooden images, including one of an unclothed pregnant Amazonian woman, symbolizing fecundity. Tschugguel and Marshall were predisposed to cast aspersions on the Pan-Amazon Synod, given their attendance at the anti-Francis meetings, but now they could say they were scandalized at the "pagan" event in the papal gardens, and considered the figurines idols. Together, Marshall and Tschugguel would divert global attention from the synod and attempt to expose Pope Francis as a liberal usurper of the Seat of St. Peter.

ON THE NIGHT of October 21, 2019, when few people were inside the sixteenth-century Church of Santa Maria in Traspontina (Saint Mary across the Bridge), a few steps from the Vatican walls, Tschugguel slipped through its doors, walked up the aisle, and surveyed the scene in a side chapel, where Amazonian church workers and supporters had met, sung, and prayed during the day. He was looking for the wooden figurines, so his eyes may not have dwelt long on the posters in the chapel, bearing pictures of people murdered as they had fought to protect the rain forest's resources, and the rights of its inhabitants. But they were important to others.

One showed the face of a smiling, silver-haired nun from Ohio named Dorothy Stang, who shared the extreme poverty of the Brazilian jungle residents with whom she worked for almost forty years, harvesting forest products without cutting down trees, defending local people's claims under national land reforms, denouncing threats from loggers and landowners, until February 12, 2005, the day after she had brought human rights complaints to government authorities. Armed hitmen for ranchers who wanted to clear local land for development stopped the nun on a path. As Sister Dorothy began to read aloud the beatitudes from the Bible she carried, according to an eyewitness hiding nearby, they emptied their guns into her head.

Another picture in the side altar showed Xicão Xukuru, *cacique*, or chief, of the 8,500-member Xukuru tribe in Pernambuco, Brazil, a long-haired, clear-spoken leader who waged a nonviolent struggle for recognition of ancestral land rights against incoming settlers who cut down the forest. Xicão Xukuru became a nationwide emblematic figure for Indigenous rights, eventually receiving government recognition for the native homeland, but angering ranchers and settlers in the process. He, too, was assassinated by gunmen, in 1998.

Better known to people outside the Amazon was the man on a third poster, Francisco Alves "Chico" Mendes Filho, the hefty, charismatic son of a Brazilian "Rubber Soldier," one of the tappers who had died by the thousands in the inhospitable jungle during World War II, providing essential war materiel to the Allies. Largely self-taught—the region where he grew up had no schools—Chico Mendes was influenced by priests who practiced liberation theology, and was indefatigable in organizing fellow tappers. He became the figurehead for a struggling rural workers' union movement, which aimed to demarcate Indigenous territories to keep outsiders at bay, and protect the rain forest. Mendes, too, was shot dead, on December 22, 1988, outside his home, by a gunman for a rancher who considered the rubber tappers' organizing to be a threat to plans for expanding grazing land for cattle. Eight years after his assassination, I visited his grandmother and slept at the wood-plank house of his cousin Sebastiao Mendes in the *seringal* where Chico Mendes had grown up and worked, in the municipality of Xapuri. It was easy to see how the lives of the rubber tappers and other Amazonians who survived in relationship with the forest remained arduous, precarious. Before dawn, while walking a soggy trail on rounds with Sebastiao and his teenage son, Antonio, the three of us keeping eyes peeled for ankle-grabbing roots, rattlesnakes, and yellow-headed vipers, young Antonio, wearing rubber-soled tennis shoes, told me with a grin, "We trust to faith, because the snakes bite through your shoes."

Only two days before Tschugguel had entered the Santa Maria in Traspontina church, the posters of the Amazonian martyrs in the chapel had been carried during a Way of the Cross procession from the tomb of St. Peter to the Synod Hall.

WHAT WAS IMPORTANT to Alexander Tschugguel, however, were the wooden carvings that had been in the Vatican garden, now resting in the chapel, including the one representing the woman carrying life that had been gifted to the pope. Tschugguel stole five figurines and spirited them to a first-century bridge in front of the Castel Sant'Angelo, from which, videotaped by an accomplice, he hurled them one by one into the Tiber. Taylor Marshall edited the tape, and made sure it got around, with a soundtrack in which Tschugguel warns that Catholics "are being attacked by members of our own Church."

The offending (to traditionalists) statues were retrieved by carabinieri, and a statuette of an Amazon woman in a canoe held an honored place in the synod meeting hall during the bishops' discussions; yet for audiences in the United States especially, where ultra-right Catholic media had a field day with the story, the damage had been done. In an EWTN segment, reporter Colm Flynn stood in St. Peter's Square with the iconic basilica dome in the background to say the statue "appears to be a pagan fertility icon." Racism, evinced in ridicule of the customary feathers and native dress worn by some

Amazonians come to witness the synod, and lies about the pope's imagined leftist political agenda multiplied on Catholic Twitter. The conservative *LifeSite* called the Tiber episode "the splash heard round the world," and the description stuck like gum on a shoe. A meme of the phrase, showing the carving hitting the water over and over, became available online as a GIF.

Tschugguel was a committed anti-abortion activist, and the female figurine a symbol of fruitfulness, of hope for continued existence, for fast-disappearing natives living in a fast-disappearing habitat. But this fact, as well as the irony, became casualties of the anti-Francis agenda. The "splash heard round the world" sucked the oxygen from much coverage of the urgent, even existential, issues on which the pope desired the world to focus—the climate crisis and economic models that feed it, the poor who suffer from it most, and the earth "herself," as the pope said in *Laudato Si'*, "burdened and laid waste . . . among the most abandoned and maltreated of our poor."

So ubiquitous was the rad-trad version of the Pan-Amazon Synod that secular media on the right, like Fox News, *The Federalist*, and *The American Conservative*, adopted its terms of description, such as "idol," "pagan," and "Pachamama," naming a female goddess revered in the old Inca empire, which had existed in the Andes mountains, not the Amazon, and had nothing to do with the statuettes brought as gifts to Rome. Mainstream U.S. media—*The Wall Street Journal*, *Reuters*—repeated the terms in "he said–she said" reports that smacked of forced efforts at balance, which only gave weight to the fanatic dissembling. The longtime Catholic neoconservative theocon George Weigel, whose work appears widely in Catholic and secular media, eschewed the rad-trad terms, as befits the image of a writer Fox News Radio calls an "intellectual giant," but slammed the synod, characterizing it as "a last effort to rescue 'the project'" of liberation theology, advancing "an eco-version of . . . privileging Third World Experience," an attempt to advance "the progressive agenda globally."

In the weeks after the bishops concluded the synod, Marshall Taylor and the Tradition, Family, and Property organization oversaw a U.S. media tour for Tschugguel, during which he charged that the Amazon synod was a cover for promoting a United Nations agenda of attacking the West as evil, with an Amazon Indigenous liberation theology as a substitute ideal. Traditionalism, he offered, was the answer for the Church.

The USCCB did not defend the pope against the false "Pachamama" narrative, or against harsh criticism over the synod from the right. Bishops elsewhere did. Closing its meeting in Heredia, Costa Rica, in November 2019, the Catholic prelates of the Episcopal Secretariat of Central America and Panama issued a statement of support for the pope and the synod: since Francis was dedicating so much attention to the Amazon's poor, and to "new paths" for the evangelization of its Indigenous, they said, it was "not surprising that the Holy Father has been an object of virulent and insulting attacks, plagued by lies and calumny." The contrast between the reactions of U.S. bishops and their brothers to the south was like the difference between water and whiskey. The Central Americans thanked Francis for the synod, calling it "an ecclesial event that has placed the world's eyes on this vast area, which needs a massive evangelistic effort and colossal strength to be able to implement the many needs of an integral ecology."

WALKING THE WALK—OR NOT

THE ALL-ENCOMPASSING STAND of Pope Francis on the environment is demanding. Human beings must adopt "integral ecology," he said in *Laudato Si'*, calling for deliberate attention to "our

Sister, Mother Earth," in every aspect of life, an "ecological conversion." It will not do merely to consider care for the earth in separate terms of science or ethics, for instance, or practice it piecemeal in behaviors like recycling or carbon trades.

Addressing an assembly of global jurists called the International Association of Penal Law, in Rome, shortly after the synod, the pope said "ecocide" should be considered an international crime against humanity, because a pattern and practice of destroying land and species—ecocide—leads to forced migration of people, displacement, and death. According to the Rome Statute, the treaty that established the International Criminal Court in 1998, the four core international crimes against peace are crimes against humanity, genocide, war crimes, and crimes of aggression. Francis called on the international community to recognize ecocide as a fifth category.

The pope's elevation of "ecological sin" agitated alt-right Catholics most. The synod's final document declared that "acts and habits of pollution and destruction of the harmony of the environment" amounted to a concrete offense committed against God and future generations. Overconsumption, and ignoring predatory models of economic development, were examples of behavior that harmed our relationship with God. For opponents of Francis, the idea of ecological sin was heretical, pantheistic, or absurd, providing fodder for ridicule in conservative and social media: "How many paper towels can a good Catholic use before it becomes a sin?"

For Francis, however, personal accountability for destroying nature was serious. From the beginning of his papacy, he cast climate change and the destruction of natural places as an emergency over which men and women have control, and responsibility. Even before that, as Cardinal Bergoglio of Buenos Aires, the future pope wrote the document adopted by the Fifth General Conference of Latin American Bishops (CELAM), held in Aparecida, Brazil, in 2007, that contains

an entire section on the environment. CELAM's Aparecida document said the region was "affected by the warming of the earth and
climate change caused primarily by the unsustainable way of life of
industrialized countries," warning that the legacy of nature that humanity received from God "often proves to be weak and defenseless
against economic and technological powers." On November 19, 2019,
three weeks after the Pan-Amazon Synod's conclusion, the pope announced that "ecological sin" was being considered for inclusion in the
Catechism of the Catholic Church.

In their joint pronouncements, U.S. bishops do not use the term
"ecological sin," or refer to sins against nature and the environment.
Even when they call for development of an ecological conscience, like
most religious groups do to one extent or another, they undermine the
message with so many caveats and equivocations, that the faithful can
be excused for freezing in place. They began a statement observing the
2021 World Day of Prayer for the Care of Creation with Pope John
Paul II's warning that the world experienced "profound moral crisis *of
which the destruction of the environment is only one troubling aspect.*"
They said environmental problems were "difficult to understand,"
since they deal with "highly complex scientific and technical interactions between natural phenomena, animal and ecosystem behaviors,
and human actions." As if ordinary believers could not discern the effects that fossil fuels and overconsumption have on the environment.
They blamed social media, too, for making the issue supposedly hard
to understand, as well as "the complexity of communication and glo-
balization in the modern world." They concluded their statement with
an invitation to Congress to address environmental problems "with an
emphasis on infrastructure investment."

IN 1981 U.S. bishops declared, "We are no longer called upon simply to tend the Garden God has given us. It is now in our hands to

determine whether our descendants will inherit an earth capable of sustaining them." But the modern USCCB conference has not issued a pastoral statement on conserving fossil fuel energy in more than twenty years. Ecological destruction has become known as an issue important to Pope Francis, linked with his critique of neoliberalism and free market capitalism, but the USCCB neglects environmental advocacy in favor of campaigns over abortion, and denying Holy Communion to politicians with whom they disagree on abortion's legal status, including President Biden.

MONEY, MONEY, MONEY

MONEY IS A strong factor in the U.S. bishops' failure to embrace Pope Francis's teaching on the environment, or to support the call of the international bishops at the Pan-Amazon Synod for "campaigns of divestment from extractive companies responsible for the socio-ecological damage" of the region.

In 2015, some of the largest American Catholic organizations had millions of dollars invested in energy companies, from hydraulic fracturing firms to oil sands producers, according to their own disclosures reviewed by Reuters, the news agency. In another review of documents in Oklahoma and Texas alone, a second Reuters report found 235 oil and gas leasing deals signed with energy and land firms by Catholic Church authorities from 2010 to 2015. The Church offices received a royalty ranging from 15 to 25 percent of the value of what is taken out of the ground, according to the leases cited in the report, which is based on public county records. The Oklahoma City archdiocese, led by Archbishop Paul Coakley, signed three of the new oil and gas leases *after* the publication of *Laudato Si'*. In 2018, Coakley was among six U.S. prelates who defended the "integrity" of the disaffected former papal nuncio Archbishop Carlo Maria Viganò, for whom Coakley had "deep respect," when Viganò called for the resignation of Pope Francis.

The scandal of dioceses owning oil lands came to light again when Nalleli Cobo, a twenty-two-year-old practicing Catholic, received a 2022 Goldman Environmental Prize, known as the Green Nobel, for successfully fighting big oil, beginning with production on land owned by the Church. As a child, Cobo suffered from headaches, asthma, and nosebleeds so severe she had to sleep sitting up. Family members came down with asthma too, and neighbors got sick, so young Nalleli began knocking on doors with her mother in their low income, Latino-majority neighborhood, building a network that campaigned to remove a poisonous oil well looming just feet from their homes. Local and federal investigators had to leave the site after brief visits—they became too ill. Cobo worked into her young adulthood to direct a policy movement in the Los Angeles area—the worst polluted in the country—that led to a ban on new oil exploration, and phasing out of old sites, but not before Cobo was diagnosed with a rare cancer and had to have her reproductive organs removed. The Archdiocese of Los Angeles had leased the land to the offending oil company in Cobo's neighborhood.

"They teach us we must protect God's creation . . . so why are they being hypocrites?" Cobo told *The Guardian* in 2019. "Ultimately the archdiocese is choosing profit over people's health; that's not what Jesus would do, plain and simple."

VISIONS

"YOU NOW HAVE this clash between Pope Francis' vision of the world, and the world that the bishops who run the investments live in," Father Michael Crosby, a Capuchin friar in Milwaukee who advocates socially responsible investing, told *Reuters* for its 2015 reports. "The bishops are a very conservative group, and I'm not hopeful this will be resolved anytime soon."

The USCCB, and financial services that follow its guidelines, sometimes say they don't disinvest from offending enterprises, but aim at "active ownership," holding on to stocks while trying to convince companies to reduce emissions, and to invest in other technologies. But time is too short for this strategy. The Assessment Report of the United Nations Intergovernmental Panel on Climate Change, the definitive measure of global warming, used by governments and entities including the USCCB, said in 2022 that greenhouses gas emissions continue to rise, and existing plans to address climate change are not ambitious enough to limit warming to 2.7°F above preindustrial levels—necessary to avoid even more catastrophic fires, floods, and rising seawaters than we see now. How long do the bishops plan to wait before the companies come around?

The USCCB is invested in the stock market to the tune of some $270 million. Individual entities, from dioceses to schools and universities, even satellite operations like retreat centers, are also heavily invested in the stock market, and thus in the success of capitalism as it is. Catholic institutions may invest their endowments and general funding, from a few hundred million dollars at larger dioceses, for instance, to a billion or more, like the $2.7 billion the Jesuit Boston College manages. But investments that appear difficult to reconcile with climate change, and papal teaching, are made at all levels, sometimes by people who do not even know what their money supports; individual U.S. Church employees, who number in the thousands, including priests, bishops, and laypeople, likely have retirement or pension funds that are also heavily invested in the stock market and, therefore, likely in fossil fuels.

In the absence of a comprehensive data set that shows just how

deeply the U.S. Church is invested in fossil fuels, environmental advocates have made attempts to research the numbers. Kyle Rosenthal, a
2021 graduate of Boston College, coordinates the Catholic Divestment
Network of twenty-seven Jesuit colleges in which students lobby their
university administrations to take investments out of the fossil fuel
industry. Rosenthal told me that he "conservatively" estimates that
the U.S. Catholic Church institutionally, and individuals employed by
it with funds managed through their retirement schemes, hold more
than $49.5 billion in funds invested directly in the stock and bond
markets. "Assuming no divestment, that means likely $4 billion to
$9.5 billion in fossil fuel financing," he said, based on the figures he
has available, and from which he has extrapolated.

"It's not just the youth, but the bulk of people are frustrated that
the environment is not prioritized," Rosenthal said. "The bishops' 'pre-
eminent' issue is abortion, while environmental destruction is actively
killing people daily."

The American bishops' conference clearly believes that investments
have an influence on moral choices, and vice versa, or it would not have
promoted Socially Responsible Investment Guidelines since 1991;
neither would a plethora of self-described Catholic and Christian
investment management firms exist to tailor the investments of the
faithful. The bishops' guidelines decry investment into companies
connected to abortion, euthanasia, assisted suicide, firearms (except
for guns produced for hunters, police, and the military), and pornography, and continues to do so. When the bishops finally completed a
much-awaited revision of the guidelines in 2021, they did not rule out
investment in fossil fuel companies, or others—like some industrial
logging operations—whose work destroys the environment. (They did
add a ban on providers of transgender health care.)

Fossil fuels are barely mentioned in the updated guidelines, which
call in a politic voice for "engagement with" companies regarding cli-

mate change, reducing greenhouse gas emissions, and environmental protection. As they labored over the document so it might be passed during the bishops' fall 2021 conference in Baltimore, only at the last minute—overnight before the vote—did its writers add a footnote suggesting "responsible investments in social and environmental sectors, for example by evaluating progressive disinvestment from the fossil-fuel sector." Bishop David J. Malloy of Rockford, Illinois, chair of the conference's Committee on International Justice and Peace, insisted that the document's working group discussed the subject "extensively," but reckoned "it is not now possible to get a full end" to underwriting fossil fuels. Instead, it would be best to give financial advisors working with the USCCB "room" to determine which investments are appropriate.

MOVING THE MONEY

LIKE TURNING A supertanker on the ocean, reshaping a major investment portfolio takes time and space. The bishops' conference has fiduciary responsibilities, and must assure a reasonable return on its investments. But a major shift of direction also demands will, which appears to be missing in the halls where the U.S. bishops meet.

"We know that the fossil fuels are causing the climate crisis and destroying our planet," said the Vatican's point man on the crisis, Salesian Fr. Joshtrom Kureethadam, speaking from Rome during a 2021 webinar. "Still, we keep on investing [in] the dirty fossil fuels." To continue throwing money at the companies, Kureethadam said, was a "schizophrenic" act.

Despite accelerating global warming, and the Vatican's characterization of divestment from companies that destroy the atmosphere and the natural world as "theological . . . moral . . . and environmental imperatives," as Kureethadam put it, the USCCB drags its feet. Bishop—later Cardinal—Robert McElroy of San Diego, one of the outliers among U.S. prelates for his outspoken fealty to the theology and social teaching of Pope Francis, called its new guidelines "weak" on disinvestment. "I think we're going to have to move to an absolute prohibition on fossil fuels if we're going to give witness to where the world needs to move," he told brother bishops at the Baltimore assembly. Some may have been disinclined to listen, so adamant have conservative bishops become that abortion remains the "pre-eminent" issue for the U.S. Church, while McElroy has said racism, poverty, immigration, and climate change are equally important. "The death toll from abortion is more immediate, but the long-term death toll from unchecked climate change is larger and threatens the very future of humanity," McElroy said in a 2020 speech.

Meanwhile, the first "Catholic" index on a major stock benchmark, the S&P 500 Catholic Values Index, continues to list energy companies. Established in 2015 "for investors who do not want to breach religious norms in their passive investing strategies," constituents are screened to exclude companies that are not aligned with the U.S. bishops' guidelines. That means fossil fuel and other environmentally questionable companies get a free pass.

Besides investments, bishops also depend on individual wealthy Catholics who fund buildings, support favorite programs; implicitly or explicitly, the money comes with the condition that using it does not violate the political and social positions of the benefactors. For U.S. bishops, standing against investment in fossil fuels, or predatory mining and logging, might mean alienating some of their most generous patrons who are in the businesses or profit from investments in them. These are the men and women whose names appear on parish auditoriums, chapels, and schools, and they support the Church in a way the collection basket alone cannot do.

VOICES FROM THE PEWS

AT THE PARISH level, some U.S. Catholics launch pro-environment and *Laudato Si'* action groups, study Church teaching, plant trees, sponsor speakers, share experience about how to consume less, or attempt to draw others into recycling campaigns. But uninvolved bishops are a drag on the cause, and local priests, who answer to the prelates, are often too busy, uninterested, or cautious to actively come to their support.

Betsy Reifsnider, a former environmental justice director at Catholic charities in the Diocese of Stockton, feels thwarted by the bishops. "The church is as politicized as the rest of the country," she lamented to me in a telephone interview. A lifelong Catholic, Reifsnider has spent more than thirty-five years in the environmental field as a regional conservation coordinator for the Sierra Club, a legislative deputy for a Los Angeles City Council member, and leader of two environment advocacy groups—the Mono Lake Committee, and Friends of the River, a conservation organization. She also worked for the federal government as water conservation manager for the region encompassing Northern California, Nevada, and Southern Oregon. To say that Betsy Reifsnider is qualified on the environment is an understatement; to say she is frustrated with the hierarchy of her beloved Church doesn't plumb the depth of her consternation.

She is "shocked," she said, that the USCCB "doesn't make the connection for themselves and for the faithful that working against climate change is to work hard for respect for life. I think they are looking at this one narrow aspect—abortion."

Sometimes local pastors can open the door to making Catholic environmental thinking concrete when a bishop does not actively do so, by supporting parishioners avid to make change happen. Mary Rose LeBaron, a sales professional and Catholic convert, took a six-week online course of study in 2019 with others from the Philippines, Sweden, Germany, and India, learning to be a Laudato Si' Circles animator, part of an international program. Since then she has met regularly with about eighteen members of a group welcomed by the pastor of St. Ignatius parish in San Francisco, although the enthusiasts come from other parishes too. They pray, reflect, share information, change their consumer habits, plant food gardens, organize beach clean-ups, and lobby government representatives on issues like destructive mining. Le Baron told me they discuss *Laudato Si'* and ask, "How do we live it?"

In general, however, "people have not received the tools and resources to easily plug into church teaching [on the environment]," Betsy Reifsnider said. "We are operating in silos. The only reason you know about some things is because we have friends in other parishes."

For years, Reifsnider addressed local audiences as a Catholic climate ambassador, belonging to a corps of volunteers versed in Catholic teaching about the environment whose personal backgrounds range from policy development to organic farming to religious vocation to geo-science. In her experience, Reifsnider said, among ordinary Catholics the gap in understanding is abysmal on certain vital teachings, like environment and abortion, a sign of episcopal failure. Many don't know *Laudato Si'* exists, or know little about it, and most, she reckoned, have "no understanding of ecological sin."

COMFORT ZONES

ON A SUNNY Sunday in March 2022, Bishop Jaime Soto of Sacramento, who has vocally supported *Laudato Si'* around the diocese, donned white vestments and swung holy water from the traditional aspergillum in graceful arcs over solar panels ready for installation at St. Anthony's Church—a small project, but a concrete expression of papal teaching: the panels have a collective capacity of 36.45 kW, expected to supply about 52,000 kWh of clean electricity each year, avoiding the creation of about 1,100 metric tons of carbon dioxide, the equivalent of over 2.7 million miles of driving over the planned life of the system. Savings to the parish allow "greater opportunity for us to fund other critical ministries, including service to the poor, hungry and disadvantaged in our community," a project volunteer told Valley Community Newspapers.

"It's all about the bishop," Fr. Emmet Farrell of San Diego told me. Farrell, a retired priest, is active in Creation Care Ministry teams in his San Diego diocese, made up of volunteer lawyers, doctors, college professors, and others who speak with groups about the Church's teaching on the environment, and in churches if they can. The teams are strongly supported by San Diego cardinal McElroy, said Farrell. "He told us, 'if you get ten good parishes, work with them. Each year can bring in more.'" The diocese counts ninety-eight parishes, but not all are receptive.

Spreading the pope's message "cuts into the comfort zone," said Farrell. "If you're conservative you won't like *Laudato Si'*. It's hard to tell people to change their lifestyle—look at what happened to the prophets—they threw them in the well." Farrell spoke of Dorothy Stang, and Honduran Berta Cáceres, assassinated in 2016, a year after she received the Goldman Environmental Prize for rallying her Indigenous Lenca people to successfully oppose one of the world's largest dam builders, whose project would have inundated their native land. In the San Diego area, pastors are "worried about the collection basket," about giving offense. Yet Farrell said two dozen parishes "have done positive things, a community garden, recycling, promoting LED light bulbs, and more."

San Diego's McElroy was one of two U.S. prelates chosen by Pope

Francis as representatives to the Pan-Amazon Synod. (The other: Boston cardinal Seán O'Malley.) McElroy has extolled the collaborative approach of the Pan-Amazon Synod—grassroots consultation about important issues, listening to all, and "willingness to accept arduous choices"—as a path that can lead the Church in the United States to "move forward from this most painful moment in its history."

In 2022, Pope Francis named McElroy a cardinal. The ultraright Catholic media called it a bad choice. Francis had skipped over the higher ranking Archbishop Salvatore Cordileone of San Francisco, and McElroy's own superior, or metropolitan, Los Angeles archbishop José Gomez, neither of whom speak boldly on confronting the human cost of climate change, for instance.

In 2019, McElroy told an Omaha conference sponsored by the Catholic Climate Covenant, a nonprofit advocacy group, and Creighton University, that he would like to see "a structurally deeper level of commitment" to *Laudato Si'* within the U.S. Conference of Catholic Bishops. "If we don't get this issue right, in the end none of the other issues are going to matter, because human dignity will have been destroyed as we know it if our planet is destroyed," he said.

IN NOVEMBER 2022, when Archbishop José Gómez's term as USCCB president was up, American bishops reinforced their lurch to the right by electing Timothy Broglio, 70, archbishop for the Military Services USA as their leader for the next three years, a tenure that covers the upcoming U.S. presidential election. Oklahoma City Archbishop Paul Coakley, who supported Cardinal Carlo Maria Viganò when the disgraced former papal nuncio called for Pope Francis to resign, was chosen as the new conference secretary—Broglio's former position—beating out Cardinal Joseph Tobin of Newark, one of the pope's strongest supporters. The position gives Coakley leadership of the conference's powerful Committee on Priorities and Plans.

Timothy Broglio, the new American bishops' conference president, is a rightist culture warrior in the fashion of Archbishop Cordileone and Cardinal Burke. When the Pentagon ordered mandatory COVID-19 vaccinations for U.S. military personnel in 2021, Broglio quickly suggested Catholics could request a religious exemption, violating the stand of the pope. Francis embraces ministry to LGBTQ+ persons. Along with Cordileone, Broglio railed against a 2013 Pentagon policy allowing gay domestic partners of active duty armed service members to receive many of the same benefits as military spouses – the decision "undermined marriage," he said. Broglio blames the Church's sex abuse crisis on gay and "effeminate" priests, despite a 2011 study commissioned by bishops that said homosexuality was not a cause.

The new leader of U.S. bishops was formed in the hard-knocks school of Vatican displomacy. He served as the top aide to the Machiavellian Vatican Secretary of State Angelo Sodano from 1990 to 2001, the period when Sodano was trying to disembowel the Latin American bishops' CELAM (in which Francis was a key figure before becoming pope), watering down CELAM's call for promulgating a "gospel of justice...without ambiguity," especially for the poor, its call for rethinking the role of women in the Church, the importance of ecology, and Indigenous spirituality. Sodano, who died in 2022, was also infamous for protecting serial clerical sex abusers including the drug addict and embezzler Marcial Maciel, founder of the Legion of Christ, a religious order that produced many priests. Broglio worked for Sodano, not the other way around, but Broglio was not known to object to his superior's corrupt stands and methods. Neither is he known as a supporter of the initiatives of Pope Francis.

It may be that prophetic voices of certain Catholic prelates will rise above those of the most conservative bishops who now call the tune for the American Catholic Church. Whether that happens in time to reverse the tide of Christian nationalism to which rightist bishops contribute is a matter unresolved. Whether it happens in time to re-focus the American Church on the great issues of our day, and provide moral leadership devoid of political consideration as it is supposed to do, is an open question.

Acknowledgments

MY DEEP APPRECIATION goes to those who allowed themselves to be interviewed and consulted for this book, including several who asked not to be named, so delicate and vexing is the subject of today's Church in the United States. I am thankful to my late parents, Dr. Mary Thérèse Rakowski McConahay and Dr. James Cornelius McConahay, and to Catholic educators, many of them nuns, who taught me the faith, and how to question. Special thanks goes to Rasa Gustaitis and Jean Molesky-Poz for their wise readings and suggestions in the most intensive months of writing, despite the demands of their own projects, and to my indefatigable editorial assistant, Eric Cameron. Thank you to the Alicia Patterson Foundation, particularly Margaret Engel, for a reporting fellowship that helped support my work on this book. Thank you to the librarians of the San Francisco Public Library system and the Mechanics' Institute Library of San Francisco, who soldiered on through the pandemic to provide patrons like me with books and other necessities for our lives and work. Thank you to my loyal agent Andy Ross, and to the exemplary editors at Melville House with whom

I've had the pleasure to work. And thank you to my sister Regina McConahay for providing a floating studio in which to work during a critical phase of writing this book. As always, my deepest personal gratitude goes to Robert DeGaetano and our daughter Maria Angelica DeGaetano for their intellectual contributions and support—I cannot thank them enough.

Sources

1. PLAGUE OF ILLUSION: CATHOLIC CLERICS' PANDEMIC ATTACK ON THE STATE

BOOKS

Hammer, Bonaventure. *The Fourteen Holy Helpers*. Rockford, Illinois: TAN Books, 2009.

Rothschild, Mike. *The Storm Is Upon Us: How QAnon Became a Movement, Cult, and Conspiracy Theory of Everything*. New York: Penguin Random House, 2021.

"Tuchman, Barbara. *A Distant Mirror, the Calamitous 14th Century*. New York: Alfred A. Knopf, 1978."

LEGAL CASES CITED

Roman Catholic Diocese of Brooklyn v. Cuomo, United States Supreme Court, 2020.

DOCUMENTS

"Forming Conscience for Faithful Citizenship." *United States Conference of Catholic Bishops*, 2020. https://www.usccb.org/issues-and-action/faithful-citizenship/forming-consciences-for-faithful-citizenship-title.

"Veritas in Caritate." *St. James the Less Catholic Church*, La Crosse, Wisconsin, April 18, 2021. https://d2y1pz2y630308.cloudfront.net/28828/bulletins/20210418.pdf.

NEWSPAPERS, MAGAZINES

Boorstein, Michelle. "*COVID Kills A Leading Anti-Vaccine Televangelist; Evangelicals Don't Want To Talk About It*." *Seattle Times*, December 3, 2021. https://www.seattletimes.com/nation-world/nation/covid-kills-a-leading-anti-vaccine-televangelist-evangelicals-dont-want-to-talk-about-it.

Boorstein, Michelle. "Marcus Lamb, Head Of Daystar, A Large Christian Network That Discouraged Vaccines, Dies After Getting Covid-19." *Washington Post*, November 30, 2021. https://www.washingtonpost.com/religion/2021/11/30/marcus-lamb-daystar-covid-vaccine-medical-freedom.

Douthat, Ross. "Cardinal Burke: 'I'm Called the Enemy of the Pope, Which I Am Not.'" *New York Times*, November 9, 2019. https://www.nytimes.com/2019/11/09/opinion/cardinal-burke-douthat.html.

Duncan, Robert. "Cardinal Burke: Limiting Muslim Immigration Is Patriotic." *America: The Jesuit Review*, May 21, 2019. https://www.americamagazine.org/politics-society/2019/05/21/cardinal-burke-limiting-muslim-immigration-patriotic.

Gajanan, Mahita, and Gina Martinez. "Here Are the Catholic Church Politics Behind
That Letter Calling on Pope Francis to Resign." *Time*, August 28, 2018. https://time.
com/5380458/pope-francis-resignation-catholic-church.

Gill, John Freeman. "At Old St. Pat's, a History of Defiance." *New York Times*, July 17, 2020.
https://www.nytimes.com/2020/07/17/realestate/at-old-st-pats-a-history-of-defiance.html.

Ismail, Aymann. "We Know Exactly Who the Capitol Rioters Were." *Slate*, January 4, 2022.
https://slate.com/news-and-politics/2022/01/january-6-capitol-riot-arrests-research-
profile.html.

McElwee, Joshua J. "Vatican: Coronavirus Vaccines 'Morally Acceptable' for Catholics."
National Catholic Reporter, December 21, 2020. https://www.ncronline.org/news/vatican/
vaticans-doctrinal-office-coronavirus-vaccines-morally-acceptable-catholics.

McGough, Michael. "Is Pope Francis Purging Conservative Cardinals?" *Baltimore Sun*,
December 17, 2013. https://www.baltimoresun.com/la-ol-pope-burke-conservatives-
20131217-story.html.

Panicali, Michael. "Prayer, Patriotism and Goodwill." *The Tablet* (Brooklyn),
Letters to the Editor, week of January 23, 2021. https://thetablet.org/
letters-to-the-editor-week-of-jan-23-2021/.

Pedroja, Cammy. "Trump CPAC Speech Preceded by 'Divisive' Fired Priest Downplaying
Importance of Science." *Newsweek*, July 12, 2021. https://www.newsweek.com/trump-
cpac-speech-preceded-divisive-fired-priest-downplaying-importance-science-1609035.

Pentin, Edward. "Ex-Nuncio Accuses Pope Francis of Failing to Act on McCarrick's
Abuse." *National Catholic Register*, August 26, 2018. https://www.ncregister.com/news/
ex-nuncio-accuses-pope-francis-of-failing-to-act-on-mccarrick-s-abuse.

Sitman, Matthew. "Why the Pandemic Is Driving Conservative Intellectuals
Mad." *New Republic*, May 21, 2020. https://newrepublic.com/article/157773/
pandemic-driving-conservative-intellectuals-mad.

Timberg, Craig, and Elizabeth Dwoskin. "With Trump Gone, QAnon Groups
Focus Fury on Attacking Coronavirus Vaccines." *Washington Post*, March
11, 2021. https://www.washingtonpost.com/technology/2021/03/11/
with-trump-gone-qanon-groups-focus-fury-attacking-covid-vaccines.

Wadman, Meredith. "Abortion Opponents Protest Covid-19 Vaccines' Use of
Fetal Cells." *Science*, June 5, 2020. https://www.science.org/content/article/
abortion-opponents-protest-covid-19-vaccines-use-fetal-cells.

White, Dawson. "Skipping Mass over Covid-19 Fears A 'Grave Sin,' Wisconsin Archbishop
Warns Catholics." *Kansas City Star*, September 13, 2020. https://www.kansascity.com/
news/nation-world/national/article245704795.html.

PODCASTS
Garofoli, Joe. Interview with San Francisco Archbishop Salvatore Cordileone. *It's All Political*.
Podcast audio. December 1, 2021. https://www.sfchronicle.com/podcasts/article/Listen-
San-Francisco-s-archbishop-talks-Roe-vs-16664263.php.

ONLINE RESOURCES
"Bishop Brennan of Fresno Clears Up His Position on Vaccines." *California Catholic Daily*,
December 14, 2020. https://www.cal-catholic.com/bishop-brennan-of-fresno-clears-up-
his-position-on-vaccines.

"Bishop Urging Catholics Not To Get Vaccine, Says Stem Cells Were Used." YouTube video, 3:24. Posted by NewsNation Now. November 20, 2020. https://www.youtube.com/watch?v=lNVbdffH2os.

Chapman, Michael W. "U.S. Cardinal Burke: To Oppose 'Large-Scale Muslim Immigration' is Patriotic." *CNS News*, May 23, 2019. https://www.cnsnews.com/blog/michael-w-chapman/us-cardinal-burke-oppose-large-scale-muslim-immigration-patriotic.

Cordileone, Salvatore J. "Catholics at the Back of the Line." *First Things*, September 21, 2020. https://www.firstthings.com/web-exclusives/2020/09/catholics-at-the-back-of-the-line.

"COVID-19 Vaccines: Moral & Ethical Concerns." YouTube video, 1:30. Posted by United States Conference of Catholic Bishops. March 4, 2021. https://www.youtube.com/watch?v=9X-vA0NYCZg.

Crist, Carolyn. "Some Medications Also Tied to Religious Vaccine Exemption." *WebMD*, September 18, 2021. https://www.webmd.com/vaccines/covid-19-vaccine/news/20210918/some-medications-also-tied-to-religious-vaccine-exemption.

Daly, Michael. "Trumpy NYC Priest Delivers Toxic Anti-Vaccine Sermon From Pulpit." *Daily Beast*, August 25, 2021. https://www.thedailybeast.com/father-michael-panicali-delivers-anti-vaccine-homily-at-brooklyn-church.

Dickson, Caitlin. "'A Global Conspiracy Against God And Humanity': Controversial Catholic Archbishop Pushes QAnon Themes In Letter To Trump." *Yahoo News*, October 31, 2020. https://www.yahoo.com/video/a-global-conspiracy-against-god-and-humanity-controversial-catholic-archbishop-pushes-q-anon-themes-in-letter-to-trump-134003985.html.

Dunham, Will. "Black Death 'Discriminated' Between Victims." *ABC Science*, January 29, 2008. https://www.abc.net.au/science/articles/2008/01/29/2149185.htm.

Farrow, Mary. "The Fourteen Holy Helpers: Plague Saints for a Time of Coronavirus." *Catholic News Agency*, January 14, 2021. https://www.hbgdiocese.org/the-fourteen-holy-helpers-plague-saints-for-a-time-of-coronavirus.

"Fr. Altman: You Cannot Be Catholic & A Democrat. Period. (Part I)." YouTube video, 9:58. Posted by Alpha News. August 30, 2020. https://www.youtube.com/watch?v=3-7eoTN2vNM.

Heilman, Kim. "Rosary Rally for Fr. Altman." *Musings From The Home: Living Large With Faith And Children*, September 13, 2020. https://musingsfromthehome.com/2020/09/13/rosary-rally-for-fr-altman.

Masci, David, and Gregory A. Smith. "7 Facts About American Catholics." *Pew Research Center*, October 10, 2018. https://www.pewresearch.org/fact-tank/2018/10/10/7-facts-about-american-catholics.

O'Kane, Caitlin. "Catholic Cardinal Who Spread Vaccine Misinformation Now on a Ventilator Battling COVID-19." *CBS News*, August 17, 2021. https://www.cbsnews.com/news/raymond-leo-cardinal-burke-catholic-ventilator-covid-19-misinformation.

Pope Francis. "Extraordinary Moment of Prayer Presided Over by Pope Francis." *Vatican Publishing Library*, March 27, 2020. https://www.vatican.va/content/francesco/en/homilies/2020/documents/papa-francesco_20200327_omelia-epidemia.html.

Reno, R. R. "Say 'No' to Death's Dominion." *First Things*, March 23, 2020. https://www.firstthings.com/web-exclusives/2020/03/say-no-to-deaths-dominion.

Rousselle, Christine. "Springfield, Illinois Bishop Won't Deny Mass to Mask-less Catholics." *Catholic News Agency*, September 2, 2021. https://www.catholicnewsagency.com/news/248864/springfield-catholic-bishop-requests-but-wont-require-masks-at-mass.

"San Francisco Catholics Plan Eucharistic Processions to 'Free the Mass.'" *Catholic News Agency*, September 14, 2020. https://www.catholicnewsagency.com/news/45817/san-francisco-catholics-plan-eucharistic-processions-to-free-the-mass.

Strickland, Bishop J. Twitter post. September 5, 2020, 10:10 AM. https://twitter.com/Bishopoftyler/status/1302293048659935232.

Trump, Donald J. Twitter post. June 10, 2020, 6:17 PM. https://twitter.com/realdonaldtrump/status/1270842639903006720.

United States Grace Force: God Strong. https://usgraceforce.com.

Viganò, Archbishop Carlo Maria. "Archbishop Viganò's Powerful Letter to President Trump: Eternal Struggle Between Good and Evil Playing Out Right Now." *LifeSiteNews*, June 6, 2020. https://www.lifesitenews.com/opinion/archbishop-viganos-powerful-letter-to-president-trump-eternal-struggle-between-good-and-evil-playing-out-right-now.

Viganò, Archbishop Carlo Maria. "Transcript: Steve Bannon's 'War Room' Interview with Abp. Viganò." *LifeSiteNews*, January 4, 2021. https://www.lifesitenews.com/opinion/transcript-steve-bannons-war-room-interview-with-abp-vigano.

2. CHRISTIANIZING AMERICA: THE ROOTS OF THE RELIGIOUS RIGHT

BOOKS

Byrnes, Timothy A. *Catholic Bishops in American Politics.* Princeton, New York: Princeton University Press, 1991.

Millies, Steven P. *Good Intentions: A History of Catholic Voters' Road from Roe to Trump.* Collegeville, Minnesota: Liturgical Press, 2018.

Nelson, Anne. *Shadow Network: Media, Money, and the Secret Hub of the Radical Right.* New York: Bloomsbury, 2019.

Schlafly, Phyllis. *A Choice Not an Echo.* New York: Regnery Publishing, 1964.

Weyrich, Paul M., and William S. Lind. *The Next Conservatism.* South Bend: St. Augustine's Press, 2009.

Weyrich, Paul. "Blue Collar or Blue Blood: The New Right Compared with the Old Right." In Robert W. Whitaker, ed., *The New Right Papers.* New York: St. Martin's Press, 1982.

Weyrich, Paul, and Connaught Marshner, eds. *Future 21: Directions for America in the 21st Century.* Greenwich, Connecticut: Devin-Adair Publishing, 1984.

Williams, Daniel K. *Defenders of the Unborn: The Pro-Life Movement Before Roe v. Wade.* New York: Oxford University Press, 2016.

JOURNALS

Ebin, Chelsea. "Paul Weyrich: The Religious Roots of a New Right Radical." *American Catholic Studies: American Catholic Historical Society*, Vol. 131, no. 3 (Fall 2020): 29-56. https://muse.jhu.edu/article/766312.

"The National Bishops' Conference: An Analysis of its Origins." *The Catholic Historical Review*, Vol. 66, no. 4 (October 1980).

DOCUMENTS

Bernardin, Cardinal Joseph. "A Consistent Ethic of Life: An American-Catholic Dialogue." *Gannon Lecture*, Fordham University, December 6, 1983. https://www.hnp.org/publications/hnpfocus/BConsistentEthic1983.pdf.

Martinez, Mary C. "Architects and Foot Soldiers: The Catholic Influence within the New Christian Right." Syracuse University, Honors Capstone Projects, Spring 2007. https://surface.syr.edu/honors_capstone/589.

Pope Paul VI. "Pastoral Constitution on the Church in the Modern World: Gaudium Et Spes." *Vatican Publishing Library*, December 7, 1965. https://www.vatican.va/archive/hist_councils/ii_vatican_council/documents/vat-ii_cons_19651207_gaudium-et-spes_en.html.

NEWSPAPERS, MAGAZINES

Balmer, Randall. "The Religious Right and the Abortion Myth." *Politico Magazine*, May 10, 2022. https://www.politico.com/news/magazine/2022/05/10/abortion-history-right-white-evangelical-1970s-00031480.

Berman, Ari. "The GOP War on Voting." *Rolling Stone*, August 30, 2011. https://www.rollingstone.com/politics/politics-news/the-gop-war-on-voting-242182.

Boorstein, Michelle. "Draft of U.S. Catholic Bishops' Communion Document Doesn't Mention Biden or Abortion." *Washington Post*, November 2, 2021. https://www.washingtonpost.com/religion/2021/11/02/catholic-bishops-communion-document.

Butterfield, Fox. "Archbishop of Boston Cites Abortion as 'Critical' Issue." *New York Times*, September 6, 1984. https://www.nytimes.com/1984/09/06/us/archbishop-of-boston-cites-abortion-as-critical-issue.html.

Dwyer, Bill. "Wake Up Folks: The Campaign Against Democracy Continues." *Wednesday Journal of Oak Park and River Forest*, November 18,2020. https://www.oakpark.com/2020/11/18/wake-up-folks-the-campaign-against-democracy-continues.

Mincer, Jilian. "Watchdog Finds Much Larger Catholic Influence on U.S. Hospitals." *Reuters*, May 5, 2016. https://www.reuters.com/article/us-usa-healthcare-hospitals/watchdog-finds-much-larger-catholic-influence-on-u-s-hospitals-idUSKCN0XW15L.

O'Harrow, Robert, Jr. "Videos Show Closed-Door Sessions of Leading Conservative Activists: 'Be Not Afraid of the Accusations that You're a Voter Suppressor.'" *Washington Post*, October 14, 2020. https://www.washingtonpost.com/investigations/council-national-policy-video/2020/10/14/367f24c2-f793-11ea-a510-f57d8ce76e11_story.html.

Sawyer, Kathy. "Linking Religion and Politics." *Washington Post*, August 24, 1980. https://www.washingtonpost.com/archive/politics/1980/08/24/linking-religion-and-politics/3d68ea8c-ed85-4d5d-94da-8b429f911a96.

Schmalz, Mathew N. "How the Support of Catholics Helped Donald Trump's Victory." *Fortune*, November 9, 2016. https://fortune.com/2016/11/09/donald-trump-election-2016-catholic-vote.

Simon, Stephanie. "Preacher Built Religious Right into a Political Force." *Los Angeles Times*, May 16, 2007. https://www.latimes.com/archives/la-xpm-2007-may-16-na-falwell16-story.html.

Weiner, Rachel. "Paul Weyrich Dies; Founder of Heritage Foundation." *Huffington Post*, January 18, 2009. https://www.huffpost.com/entry/paul-weyrich-dies-founder_n_152017.

Weyrich, Paul. "An Open Letter to Gov. Burns of Hawaii." *The Wanderer*, March 26, 1970.

Wolfe, Alan. "Mrs. America." *The New Republic*, October 2, 2005. https://newrepublic.com/article/63477/mrs-america.

ONLINE RESOURCES

"A Brief History of USCCB." *United States Conference of Catholic Bishops*. https://www.usccb.org/about/a-brief-history-of-usccb.

"A History of ALEC & The People's Resistance." *ALEC Attacks, Center for Constitutional Rights*, 2019. https://www.alecattacks.org/history-of-alec.

"ALEC Exposed." *The Center for Media and Democracy*. https://www.alecexposed.org/wiki/ALEC_Exposed.

American Legislative Exchange Council. https://alec.org.

Blackwell, Morton C. "A Tribute to Paul Weyrich." *Leadership Institute*. https://www.leadershipinstitute.org/writings/?ID=1.

"Catholic Education." *United States Conference of Catholic Bishops*, 2017. https://www.usccb.org/offices/public-affairs/catholic-education.

Council for National Policy. https://cfnp.org.

Fahmy, Dalia. "7 Facts About Southern Baptists." *Pew Research Center*, June 7, 2019. https://www.pewresearch.org/fact-tank/2019/06/07/7-facts-about-southern-baptists.

"Government Relations." *United States Conference of Catholic Bishops*. https://www.usccb.org/offices/government-relations.

Kaylor, Brian. "A 'Transformative Moment' in SBC Political Activity." *Good Faith Media*, August 20, 2010. https://goodfaithmedia.org/a-transformative-moment-in-sbc-political-activity-cms-16555.

"Knights of Columbus and National Catholic War Council." *United War Work*. https://unitedwarwork.com/groups/knights-of-columbus-and-national-catholic-war-council.

Kummer, Tony. "Pledge to the Christian Flag." *Ministry to Children*, July 2, 2015. https://ministry-to-children.com/christian-flag-pledge.

"National Catholic War Council." *The Catholic University of America, University Libraries*. https://libraries.catholic.edu/special-collections/archives/collections/finding-aids/finding-aids.html?file=nc-war-council.

National Right to Life. https://www.nrlc.org.

Perry, Sarah. "The Department of Education's Intended Revision of Title IX Fails Regulatory and Civil Rights Analysis." *Heritage Foundation*, June 22, 2022. https://www.heritage.org/civil-rights/report/the-department-educations-intended-revision-title-ix-fails-regulatory-and-civil.

Republican Study Committee. https://rsc-banks.house.gov.

"Theocracy Watch." *Wiser Directory*. https://wiser.directory/organization/theocracy-watch.

Weyrich, Paul, and Brian Lamb. "Q&A with Paul Weyrich." *C-SPAN*, March 22, 2005. https://www.c-span.org/video/?185929-1/qa-paul-weyrich.

3. OUR LADY OF THE GRAPES

BOOKS

Chaput, Charles. *Strangers in a Strange Land: Catholic Faith in a Post-Christian World*. New York: Henry Holt, 2017.

Chinnici, Joseph P. *American Catholicism Transformed, From the Cold War Through the Council*. Oxford: Oxford University Press, 2021.

Harrington, Dale. *Mystery Man: William Rhodes Davis – Nazi Agent of Influence*. Dulles, Virginia: Brassey's, 1999.

Mayer, Jane. Dark Money, *The Hidden History of the Billionaires Behind the Rise of the Radical Right*. New York: Doubleday, 2016.

LEGAL CASES CITED

Burwell v. Hobby Lobby Stores, Inc., United States Supreme Court, 2014.

Our Lady of Guadalupe School v. Morrissey-Berru, United States Supreme Court, 2020.

DOCUMENTS

"Bishops, Clergy: End Affiliation with the Napa Institute." *Call to Action*, December 6, 2021. https://www.cta-usa.org/news/napa-institute-letter.

"Business School $3 Million Grant: Business and Economics School to Receive $3 Million." *The Catholic University of America*, Press Release, January 22, 2015. https://communications.catholic.edu/news/2015/01/business-grant.html.

"Koch Industries: Secretly Funding the Climate Denial Machine." *Greenpeace USA*. https://www.greenpeace.org/usa/fighting-climate-chaos/climate-deniers/koch-industries.

Pope Francis. "Post-Synodal Apostolic Exhortation Amoris Laetitia of the Holy Father Francis: On Love in the Family." *Vatican Publishing Library*, March 19, 2016. https://www.vatican.va/content/francesco/en/apost_exhortations/documents/papa-francesco_esortazione-ap_20160319_amoris-laetitia.html.

Pope Paul VI. "Encyclical Letter Humanae Vitae of the Supreme Pontiff Paul VI: On the Regulation of Birth." *Vatican Publishing Library*, July 25, 1968. https://www.vatican.va/content/paul-vi/en/encyclicals/documents/hf_p-vi_enc_25071968_humanae-vitae.html.

NEWSPAPERS, MAGAZINES

"America's Largest Private Companies" *Forbes*, 2021. https://www.forbes.com/largest-private-companies/list.

Busch, Tim. "Teaching Capitalism to Catholics." *Wall Street Journal*, January 22, 2015. https://www.wsj.com/articles/tim-busch-teaching-capitalism-to-catholics-1421970676.

Dias, Elizabeth and Ruth Graham. "Vatican Removes a Prominent Anti-Abortion Activist From the Priesthood." *New York Times*, December 18, 2022. https://www.nytimes.com/2022/12/18/us/vatican-removes-anti-abortion-leader-priesthood.html.

Fink, Richard. "The Structure of Social Change." *Philanthropy Magazine*, Winter 1996. https://www.documentcloud.org/documents/6303746-The-Structure-of-Social-Change-Liberty-Guide.

Gehring, John. "Catholic conservative Napa Institute's profile grows in Washington DC. *National Catholic Reporter*, December 13, 2022. https://www.ncronline.org/news/catholic-conservative-napa-institutes-profile-grows-washington-dc.

Gehring, John. "Napa Institute Expands to Fight the Culture War." *National Catholic Reporter*, August 4, 2021. https://www.ncronline.org/news/people/napa-institute-expands-fight-culture-war.

Gehring, John. "Napa, Koch Funding Sparks Backlash from Notre Dame Professors." *National Catholic Reporter*, December 16, 2021. https://www.ncronline.org/news/people/napa-koch-funding-sparks-backlash-notre-dame-professors.

Jordon, Steve. "Of Two Minds on Economics: Does Teaching at Creighton Institute Contradict Catholic Social Thought?" *Omaha World Herald*, August 10, 2020. https://omaha.com/business/of-two-minds-on-economics-does-teaching-at-creighton-institute-contradict-catholic-social-thought/article_e6a8e72e-130c-5c49-a257-a32f55530905.html.

Kennicott, Philip. "The New Bible Museum Tells a Clear, Powerful Story. And It Could Change the Museum Business." *Washington Post*, November 15, 2017. https://www.washingtonpost.com/entertainment/museums/the-new-bible-museum-tells-a-clear-powerful-story-and-it-could-change-the-museum-business/2017/11/15/6fc76f40-c98e-11e7-8321-481fd63f174d_story.html.

Kroll, Andy. "Exposed: The Dark-Money ATM of the Conservative Movement." *Mother Jones*, February 5, 2013. https://www.motherjones.com/politics/2013/02/donors-trust-donor-capital-fund-dark-money-koch-bradley-devos.

Mayer, Jane. "The Big Money Behind the Big Lie." *The New Yorker*, August 6, 2021. https://www.newyorker.com/magazine/2021/08/09/the-big-money-behind-the-big-lie.

Mayer, Jane. "Is Ginni Thomas a Threat to the Supreme Court?" *The New Yorker*, January 21, 2022. https://www.newyorker.com/magazine/2022/01/31/is-ginni-thomas-a-threat-to-the-supreme-court.

McDermott, Jim. "Senator Dick Durbin on Being Denied Communion over Abortion Stance: 'I Am Careful When I Go to a Church.'" *America: The Jesuit Review*, November 8, 2021. https://www.americamagazine.org/politics-society/2021/11/08/dick-durbin-denied-communion-abortion-241795.

McGurn, William. "The Morality of Charles Koch." *Wall Street Journal*, October 2, 2017. https://www.wsj.com/articles/the-morality-of-charles-koch-1506983981.

Paprocki, Thomas John, and Kevin W. Vann. "Letter to the Editor: A Response to Senator Dick Durbin on Abortion and Holy Communion." *America: The Jesuit Review*, November 15, 2021. https://www.americamagazine.org/faith/2021/11/15/dick-durbin-communion-abortion-241835.

Sanchez, Robert. "Denver's Archdiocese Gets New Leader." 5280: *Denver's Mile High Magazine*, July 18, 2012. https://www.5280.com/2012/07/denvers-archdiocese-gets-new-leader.

Schlumpf, Heidi. "Bishops of the United States, the Basics." *National Catholic Reporter*, June 3, 2019. https://www.ncronline.org/news/accountability/bishops-united-states-basics.

Schlumpf, Heidi. "Matthew Kelly's Companies Do Business with the Nonprofit He Founded." *National Catholic Reporter*, January 16, 2020. https://www.ncronline.org/news/parish/matthew-kellys-companies-do-business-nonprofit-he-founded.

Smith, David. "Inside the Sprawling, Controversial $500M Museum of the Bible." *The Guardian*, October 16, 2017. https://www.theguardian.com/culture/2017/oct/16/inside-the-sprawling-controversial-500m-museum-of-the-bible.

Stone, Peter. "Money and Misinformation: How Turning Point USA Became a Formidable Pro-Trump Force." *The Guardian*, October 23, 2021. https://www.theguardian.com/us-news/2021/oct/23/turning-point-rightwing-youth-group-critics-tactics.

Strauss, Valerie. "The Koch Network Says It Wants to Remake Public Education. That Means Destroying It, Says the Author of a New Book on the Billionaire Brothers." *Washington Post*, October 16, 2019. https://www.washingtonpost.com/education/2019/10/16/koch-network-says-it-wants-remake-public-education-that-means-destroying-it-says-author-new-book-billionaire-brothers.

Sullivan, Amy. "The Catholic Bishops Move Even Further Away from Social Justice." *The New Republic*, September 19, 2012. https://newrepublic.com/article/107541/jonathan-reyes-appointment-usccb-grows-even-more-partisan.

RADIO PROGRAMS

Mohler, Albert. "The Things Worth Dying For: A Conversation with Archbishop Charles Chaput." *Thinking in Public*, August 25, 2021. https://albertmohler.com/2021/08/25/charles-chaput.

Morris, Frank. "Koch Funding on Campus Raises Questions at University of Kansas." *Here & Now*, KCUR, December 17, 2014. https://www.kcur.org/education/2014-12-17/koch-funding-on-campus-raises-questions-at-university-of-kansas.

SONG LYRICS

Brown, Michael. "The John Birch Society." 1961. https://mudcat.org/@displaysong.cfm?SongID=6503,6503&SongID=6503,6503.

ONLINE RESOURCES

"12th Annual Summer Conference." *Napa Institute*, July 2022. http://napa-institute.org/conference/12th-annual-summer-conference.

"About the Napa Institute." *Napa Institute*. https://napa-institute.org/about.

"About Us." *Catholic News Agency*. https://www.catholicnewsagency.com/about.

"About Us." *National Catholic Register*. https://www.ncregister.com/info/about-us.

Alliance Defending Freedom. https://adflegal.org.

Amazing Parish. https://amazingparish.org.

"Archbishop Chaput Tells Synod to Announce Christ Not 'Ideologies and Social Sciences.'" *Catholic News Agency*, October 4, 2018. https://www.catholicnewsagency.com/news/39553/archbishop-chaput-tells-synod-to-announce-christ-not-ideologies-and-social-sciences.

Armiak, David. "Koch Spent Nearly $150 Million in 2020 to Extend His Influence and Promote His Agenda." *Exposed by CMD, Center for Media and Democracy*, November 29, 2021. https://www.exposedbycmd.org/2021/11/29/koch-spent-nearly-150-million-2020.

Arocho Esteves, Junno. "The Joy of Love: Gestures, Spirituality Are Essential in Family Life, Pope Francis Says in His Apostolic Exhortation." *Catholic News Service*, April 21, 2016. https://hawaiicatholicherald.com/2016/04/21/the-joy-of-love.

Augustine Institute. https://www.augustineinstitute.org.

Avery, Dan. "State Anti-Transgender Bills Represent Coordinated Attack, Advocates Say." *NBC News*, February 17, 2021. https://www.nbcnews.com/feature/nbc-out/state-anti-transgender-bills-represent-coordinated-attack-advocates-say-n1258124.

Branded Catholicism. https://brandedcatholicism.wordpress.com.

Brown, Lauretta. "Napa Legal Institute Launches to Help Catholic Groups in the 'Next America.'" *National Catholic Register*, February 28, 2019. https://www.ncregister.com/features/napa-legal-institute-launches-to-help-catholic-groups-in-the-next-america.

Camosy, Charles C. "New Institute Set Up to Help Catholic NGOs Deal with Legal Challenges." *Crux: Taking the Catholic Pulse*, March 1, 2019. https://cruxnow.com/interviews/2019/03/new-institute-set-up-to-help-catholic-ngos-deal-with-legal-challenges.

Chan, Nicholas. "Koch Grant Sparks Debate at SCU Over Philanthropy, Free Speech, Academic Independence." *San Jose Inside*, July 3, 2019. https://www.sanjoseinside.com/news/koch-grant-sparks-debate-at-scu-over-philanthropy-free-speech-academic-independence.

Chaput, Archbishop Charles. "Some Personal Thoughts on the Months Ahead." *Catholic Philly*, August 12, 2016. https://catholicphilly.com/2016/08/archbishop-chaput-column/some-personal-thoughts-on-the-months-ahead.

Dynamic Catholic. https://www.dynamiccatholic.com.

Endow. https://www.endowgroups.org.

FOCUS: Fellowship of Catholic University Students. https://www.focus.org.

Giangravé, Claire. "Pope Francis Addresses the Communion Ban: 'I Have Never Denied the Eucharist to Anyone!'" *Religion News Service*, September 15, 2021. https://religionnews.com/2021/09/15/pope-francis-addresses-the-communion-ban-i-have-never-denied-the-eucharist-to-anyone.

Healing the Culture. https://www.healingtheculture.com.

"Increased Funding, Increased Influence." *UnKoch My Campus*, May 2021. http://www.unkochmycampus.org/funding-report.

"Koch Brothers' Grant to University Sparks Controversy." *Candid: Philanthropy News Digest*, December 18, 2013. https://philanthropynewsdigest.org/news/koch-brothers-grant-to-university-sparks-controversy.

Lawler, Phil. "A Terrific Appointment at the US Bishops' Conference." *Catholic Culture*, September 18, 2012. https://www.catholicculture.org/commentary/terrific-appointment-at-us-bishops-conference.

Levinthal, Dave. "Inside The Koch Brothers' Campus Crusade." *Center for Public Integrity*, March 27, 2014. https://publicintegrity.org/politics/inside-the-koch-brothers-campus-crusade.

Magis Center. https://magiscenter.com.

Millhiser, Ian. "The Supreme Court Stripped Thousands of Teachers of Their Civil Rights." *Vox*, July 8, 2020. https://www.vox.com/2020/7/8/21317223/supreme-court-ministerial-exception-religion-morrissey-berru-samuel-alito.

Mirus, Jeff. "The Catholicization of Social Justice." *Catholic Culture*, September 18, 2012. https://www.catholicculture.org/commentary/catholicization-social-justice.

Montgomery, Peter. "Hobby Lobby: 'Closely Held' Does Not Mean 'Mom and Pop.'" *People for the American Way Foundation*, June 30, 2014. https://www.pfaw.org/blog-posts/hobby-lobby-closely-held-does-not-mean-mom-and-pop.

"More About Chris Stefanick: Chris Stefanick Bio." *Real Life Catholic*. http://www.marioncatholiccommunity.org/uploads/7/0/2/7/70275455/chris_stefanick__bio_.pdf.

"Notre Dame Launches Center for Citizenship & Constitutional Government." *University of Notre Dame College of Arts & Letters*, May 12, 2021. https://al.nd.edu/news/latest-news/notre-dame-launches-center-for-citizenship-constitutional-government.

O'Hare, Kate. "Lawyer Tim Busch Plans for a Catholic Nexus in Orange County."

Breitbart, September 16, 2014. https://www.breitbart.com/local/2014/09/16/lawyer-tim-busch-plans-for-a-catholic-nexus-in-orange-county.

"Our Mission." *Becket: Religious Liberty for All.* https://www.becketlaw org/about-us/mission.

"Our Mission." *The Busch Firm.* http://thebuschfirm.com.

"Papal Teachings on Contraception." *Wijngaards Institute for Catholic Research: Catholics and Contraception.* https://www.catholicsandcontraception.com/papal-teaching-contraception.

"Patriotic Rosary." *Patriotic Rosary.* http://www.patrioticrosary.com/patriotic-rosary.html.

Reinbach, Andrew. "The John Birch Society's Reality." *Huffington Post*, September 12, 2011. https://www.huffpost.com/entry/john-birch-society_b_958207.

"Roman Catholic Diocese of Orange County." *LinkedIn.* https://www.linkedin.com/company/diocese-of-orange.

"Star Trek Into Darkness" (2013). *Internet Movie Database.* https://www.imdb.com/title/tt1408101.

"TalkUp Tuesday: The Crisis of Catholic Communications with David Gibson." YouTube video, 55:45. Posted by Future Church. July 19, 2022. https://www.youtube.com/watch?v=mX5A2ZEvtFs.

"U.S. Bishops File Amicus Curiae Brief Supporting Hobby Lobby and Conestoga Wood Specialties in Supreme Court Cases Challenging HHS Mandate." *United States Conference of Catholic Bishops*, January 28, 2014. https://www.usccb.org/news/2014/us-bishops-file-amicus-curiae-brief-supporting-hobby-lobby-and-conestoga-wood-specialties.

"Vincent Phillip Muñoz: Professor, Political Philosophy." *The Fund for American Studies.* https://tfas.org/staff/vincent-phillip-munoz.

Wells, Christopher. "Pope Francis: Catechesis Is the Echo of the Word of God." *Vatican News*, January 30, 2021. https://www.vaticannews.va/en/pope/news/2021-01/pope-francis-catechesis-is-the-echo-of-the-word-of-god.html.

Whitehouse, Sen. Sheldon. "Time to Wake Up 277: Donors Trust." *Sheldon Whitehouse*, Speeches, December 9, 2020. https://www.whitehouse.senate.gov/news/speeches/time-to-wake-up-277-donors-trust.

"Why The Koch Brothers Find Higher Education Worth Their Money." *Center for Public Integrity*, May 3, 2018. https://publicintegrity.org/politics/why-the-koch-brothers-find-higher-education-worth-their-money.

Wild, Whitney, and Geneva Sands. "Fbi And Dhs Report Finds Deaths At Hands Of Racially Motivated Violent Extremists On The Rise In Us." *CNN*, May 15, 2021. https://www.cnn.com/2021/05/15/politics/fbi-dhs-report-deaths-rise-domestic-violent-extremism/index.html.

4. UNHOLY TRINITY: CLARENCE THOMAS, LEONARD LEO, VIRGINIA THOMAS

BOOKS

Greenhouse, Linda. *Justice on the Brink, The Death of Ruth Bader Ginsburg, the Rise of Amy Coney Barrett, and Twelve Months That Transformed the Supreme Court.* New York: Penguin Random House, 2021.

Hollis-Brusky, Amanda. *Ideas with Consequences, The Federalist Society and the Conservative Counterrevolution.* Oxford: Oxford University Press, 2015.

Posner, Sarah. *Unholy, How White Christian Nationalists Powered the Trump Presidency and the Devastating Legacy They Left Behind.* New York: Random House, 2020.

Stewart, Katherine. *The Power Worshippers: Inside the Dangerous Rise of Religious Nationalism.* New York: Bloomsbury, 2020.

Thomas, Andrew Payton. *Clarence Thomas: A Biography.* New York: Encounter Books, 2001.

Thomas, Clarence. *My Grandfather's Son: A Memoir.* New York: Harper, 2007.

LEGAL CASES CITED

Burwell v. Hobby Lobby Stores, Inc., United States Supreme Court, 2014.

Dobbs v. Jackson Women's Health Organization, United States Supreme Court, 2022.

Georgia v. McCollum, United States Supreme Court, 1992.

Little Sisters of the Poor Saints Peter and Paul Home v. Pennsylvania, United States Supreme Court, 2020.

McDonald v. City of Chicago, United States Supreme Court, 2010.

Trump v. Thompson, United States Supreme Court, 2022.

DOCUMENTS

"Biography: Chief Judge Merrick Brian Garland." Office of U.S. Senator Patrick Leahy. https://www.leahy.senate.gov/imo/media/doc/Judge%20Garland%20Biography.pdf.

U.S. Congress. Senate. Committee on the Judiciary. Nomination of Judge Clarence Thomas to be Associate Justice of the Supreme Court. 102nd Cong., 1st sess., September 10, 11, 12, 13, and 16, 1991. https://www.govinfo.gov/content/pkg/GPO-CHRG-THOMAS/pdf/GPO-CHRG-THOMAS-1.pdf.

U.S. Department of Justice, Office of Public Affairs. "Leader of Oath Keepers and Oath Keepers Member Found Guilty of Seditious Conspiracy and Other Charges Related to U.S. Capitol Breach." November 29, 2022. https://www.justice.gov/opa/pr/leader-oath-keepers-and-oath-keepers-member-found-guilty-seditious-conspiracy-and-other

NEWSPAPERS, MAGAZINES

Associated Press, *Advance Local*. "Ginni Thomas Sent Mark Meadows 29 Texts Trying to Overturn 2020 Election: 'Do Not Concede.'" March 24, 2022. https://www.al.com/news/2022/03/ginni-thomas-sent-mark-meadows-29-texts-trying-to-overturn-2020-election-do-not-concede.html.

Barnes, Robert. "Ginni Thomas Apologizes to Husband's Supreme Court Clerks After Capitol Riot." *Washington Post*, February 2, 2021. https://www.washingtonpost.com/politics/courts_law/ginni-thomas-apology-clarence-thomas-clerks-trump-rally/2021/02/02/a9818cce-6496-11eb-8c64-9595888caa15_story.html.

Blumenfeld, Laura. "The Nominee's Soul Mate." *Washington Post*, September 10, 1991. https://www.washingtonpost.com/archive/lifestyle/1991/09/10/the-nomineess-soul-mate/3e0a9aa9-fdee-41f3-b5be-a6af468d89cc.

Brown, Emma. "Ginni Thomas Pressed 29 Ariz. Lawmakers to Help Overturn Trump's Defeat, Emails Show." *Washington Post*, June 10, 2022. https://www.washingtonpost.com/investigations/2022/06/10/ginni-thomas-election-arizona-lawmakers/.

Dey, Sneha and William Melhado, "Two Constables, Four Police Chiefs and over 3,000 Other Texans Were Members of ihe Oath Keepers, Report Says." *Texas Tribune*, November 7, 2022. https://www.texastribune.org/2022/09/07/texas-oath-keepers-adl/.

Desmond, Joan Frawley. "'Fearless' Justice Clarence Thomas Walks 25 Years in Footsteps of St. Thomas More." *National Catholic Register*, October 31, 2016. https://www.ncregister.com/news/fearless-justice-clarence-thomas-walks-25-years-in-footsteps-of-st-thomas-more.

Feldman, Victor. "'Reclaim New York': Mercer-Funded, Bannon-Guided Campaign Sows Distrust of Local Government." *Berkshire Edge*, August 26, 2017. https://theberkshireedge.com/reclaim-new-york-mercer-funded-bannon-guided-campaign-sows-distrust-in-local-government.

Kroll, Andy. "DonorsTrust—The Right's Dark-Money ATM—Pumps Out Record $96 Million." *Mother Jones*, December 3, 2013. https://www.motherjones.com/politics/2013/12/donors-trust-franklin-center-alec-mercatus-center-dark-money.

Levine, Sam, and Anna Massoglia. "Revealed: Conservative Group Fighting to Restrict Voting Tied to Powerful Dark Money Network." *The Guardian*, May 27, 2020. https://www.theguardian.com/us-news/2020/may/27/honest-elections-project-conservative-voting-restrictions.

Liptak, Adam. "Kavanaugh Recalls His Confirmation at Conservative Legal Group's Annual Gala." *New York Times*, November 14, 2019. https://www.nytimes.com/2019/11/14/us/kavanaugh-federalist-society.html.

Lovelace, Ryan. "Trump Judicial Adviser Leonard Leo Forming New Conservative Advocacy Group CRC Advisors." *Washington Times*, January 8, 2020. https://www.washingtontimes.com/news/2020/jan/8/trump-judicial-adviser-leonard-leo-forming-new-con.

Mayer, Jane. "Is Ginni Thomas a Threat to the Supreme Court?" *The New Yorker*, January 21, 2022. https://www.newyorker.com/magazine/2022/01/31/is-ginni-thomas-a-threat-to-the-supreme-court.

Mencimer, Stephanie. "Tea Party 'Liberty XPO' Fail." *Mother Jones*, September 10, 2010. https://www.motherjones.com/politics/2010/09/tea-party-liberty-xpo-fail.

Mystal, Elie. "Clarence and Ginni Thomas, the Supreme Court's Unethical 'It' Couple." *The Nation*, February 9, 2022. https://www.thenation.com/article/politics/ginni-clarence-thomas.

O'Harrow, Robert, Jr., and Shawn Boburg. "A Conservative Activist's Behind-the-Scenes Campaign to Remake the Nation's Courts." *Washington Post*, May 21, 2019. https://www.washingtonpost.com/graphics/2019/investigations/leonard-leo-federalists-society-courts.

Shoaib, Alia. "The Estranged Wife of Indicted Leader of Oath Keepers Tells CNN He Is a 'Dangerous Man' and 'Complete Sociopath.'" *Business Insider*, January 15, 2022. https://www.businessinsider.com/oath-keepers-leaders-wife-says-he-is-a-complete-sociopath-cnn-2022-1.

Toobin, Jeffrey. "The Conservative Pipeline to the Supreme Court." *The New Yorker*, April 10, 2017. https://www.newyorker.com/magazine/2017/04/17/the-conservative-pipeline-to-the-supreme-court.

FILMS

Pack, Michael, director. *Created Equal: Clarence Thomas in His Own Words*. Manifold Productions, 2020. 1 hr., 55 min.

ONLINE RESOURCES

Council for National Policy. https://cfnp.org.

Diana Davis Spencer Foundation. https://ddsfoundation.org.

Elsman, Dale. "Rep. Slaughter, Public Interest Groups Release New Evidence That Federalist Society Annual Dinners Are, Indeed, Fundraisers." *Common Cause*, January 30, 2014. https://www.commoncause.org/media/rep-slaughter-public-interest-groups-release-new-evidence-that-federalist-society-annual-dinners-are-indeed-fundraisers.

Fang, Lee. "Inside the Influential Evangelical Group Mobilizing to Reelect Trump." *The Intercept*, May 23, 2020. https://theintercept.com/2020/05/23/coronavirus-evangelical-megachurch-trump/.

Hurley, Bevan. "'You Can't Make That Make Sense': Supreme Court Expert Rails Against Justice Clarence Thomas for Potential Conflict of Interest." *Yahoo News*, January 22, 2022. https://news.yahoo.com/t-sense-supreme-court-expert-183114656.html.

Kirzinger, Ashley, Cailey Muñana, Audrey Kearney, Mollyann Brodie, Gabriela Weigel, Brittni Frederiksen, Usha Ranji, and Alina Salganicoff. "Abortion Knowledge and Attitudes: KFF Polling and Policy Insights." *Kaiser Family Foundation*, January 22, 2020. https://www.kff.org/womens-health-policy/poll-finding/abortion-knowledge-and-attitudes-kff-polling-and-policy-insights.

Maguire, Robert. "$1 Million Mystery Gift to Trump Inauguration Traced to Conservative Legal Activists." *Open Secrets*, May 14, 2018. https://www.opensecrets.org/news/2018/05/mystery-gift-to-trump-inauguration-from-conservative-activists/.

Maguire, Robert. "$80 Million Dark Money Group Tied to Trump Supreme Court Advisor, Leonard Leo." *Citizens for Responsibility and Ethics in Washington*, October 23, 2020. https://www.citizensforethics.org/reports-investigations/crew-investigations/80-million-dark-money-group-tied-to-trump-supreme-court-advisor-leonard-leo.

Michaelson, Jay. "The Secrets of Leonard Leo, the Man Behind Trump's Supreme Court Pick." *Daily Beast*, July 24, 2018. https://www.thedailybeast.com/the-secrets-of-leonard-leo-the-man-behind-trumps-supreme-court-pick.

Olear, Greg. "Leo the Cancer: Leonard Leo, Opus Dei & the Radical Catholic Takeover of the Supreme Court." *Prevail*, February 26, 2021. https://gregolear.substack.com/p/leo-the-cancer.

Ruse, Austin. "The Littlest Suffering Souls, Part 2: Margaret Leo of McLean." *The Catholic Thing*, May 31, 2013. https://www.thecatholicthing.org/2013/05/31/the-littlest-suffering-souls-part-2-margaret-leo-of-mclean.

Schwartz, Brian. "Inside the Consulting Firm Run by Ginni Thomas, Wife of Supreme Court Justice Clarence Thomas." *CNBC*, April 5, 2022. https://www.cnbc.com/2022/04/05/inside-the-consulting-firm-run-by-ginni-thomas-wife-of-supreme-court-justice-clarence-thomas.html.

Sarah Scaife Foundation. http://www.scaife.com/sarah.html.

Seipel, Brooke. "$1 Million Donation to Trump Inauguration Traced To Conservative Legal Activists: Report." *The Hill*, May 15, 2018. https://thehill.com/homenews/administration/387713-1-million-donation-to-trump-inauguration-traced-to-conservative-legal.

Swan, Jonathan and Alayna Treene. "Leonard Leo to Shape New Conservative Network." *Axios*, January 7, 2020. https://www.axios.com/leonard-leo-crc-advisors-federalist-society-50d4d844-19a3-4eab-af2b-7b74f1617d1c.html.

"Text: House Democrats Call for Justice Thomas's Recusal on Health Law Constitutionality." *Kaiser Health News*, February 9, 2011. https://khn.org/news/text-weiner-calls-for-justice-thomas-to-recuse.

United States Commission on International Religious Freedom. https://www.uscirf.gov.

5. THE PIZZA KING AND PRINCES OF THE CHURCH

BOOKS

Duffner, Jordan Denari. *Islamophobia, What Christians Should Know (and Do) about Anti-Muslim Discrimination*. Maryknoll, New York: Orbis Books, 2021.

Leonard, James. *Living the Faith, A Life of Tom Monaghan*. Ann Arbor: University of Michigan, 2012.

Monaghan, Tom, with Robert Anderson. *Pizza Tiger*. New York: Random House, 1986.

Silverstein, Ken. *Private Warriors*. New York: Verso, 2000.

Stinnet, Peggy. *A Call to Deliver, Tom Monaghan, Founder of Domino's Pizza and the Miracles and Pilgrimage of Ave Maria University*. Franklin, Tennessee: Clovercroft Publishing, 2015.

Weigel, George. *Faith, Reason, and the War against Jihadism: A Call to Action*. New York: Knopf Doubleday, 2009

JOURNALS.

Arkin, William M. "A Tale Of Two Franks." *Bulletin of the Atomic Scientists*, Vol. 51, no. 2 (March/April 1995): 80.

LEGAL CASES CITED

Abbott v. Abbott, United States Supreme Court, 2010.

Acts 17 Apologetics v. City of Dearborn, United States District Court for the Eastern District of Michigan, 2011.

Americans for Prosperity v. Bonta, United States Supreme Court, 2021.

Catholic League v. City of San Francisco, United States Ninth Circuit Court of Appeals, 2010.

Mauricio v. Daugaard, on Petition for Writ of Certiorari to the Supreme Court of the State of South Dakota, 2017.

Stand Up America Now v. City of Dearborn, United States District Court for the Eastern District of Michigan, 2013.

T.A. (Amador) v. McSwain Elementary School District, United States District Court for the Eastern District of California, 2008.

DOCUMENTS

"Open Letter to the Bishops of the Catholic Church." Easter Week, 2019. https://www.documentcloud.org/documents/5983408-Open-Letter-to-the-Bishops-of-the-Catholic.html.

"Philosophy of the Curriculum." *Ave Maria University Catalogue* (2020–2021): 49. https://www.avemaria.edu/wp-content/uploads/2020/07/Academic-Catalogue-2020-2021-FINAL.pdf.

NEWSPAPERS, MAGAZINES

Cave, Damien. "Far From Ground Zero, Obscure Pastor Is Ignored No Longer." *New York Times*, August 25, 2010. https://www.nytimes.com/2010/08/26/us/26gainesville.html.

Donahue, Bill. "Hail Mary." *Mother Jones*, March/April 2007. https://www.motherjones.com/politics/2007/03/hail-mary.

Elliott, Andrea. "The Man Behind the Anti-Shariah Movement." *New York Times*, July 30, 2011. https://www.nytimes.com/2011/07/31/us/31shariah.html.

Etehad, Melissa. "After Nice, Newt Gingrich Wants to 'Test' Every Muslim in the U.S. and Deport Sharia Believers." *Washington Post*, July 15, 2016. https://www.washingtonpost.com/news/morning-mix/wp/2016/07/15/after-nice-newt-gingrich-wants-to-test-every-american-muslim-and-deport-those-who-believe-in-sharia.

"Evangelists Awarded $300,000 in Lawsuit Against City of Dearborn." *The Arab American News*, May 31, 2013. https://www.arabamericannews.com/2013/05/31/Evangelists-awarded-300000-in-lawsuit-against-City-of-Dearborn.

Gass, Nick. "Two Killed in Dallas Outside Muhammad Cartoon-Contest Event." *Politico*, May 4, 2015. https://www.politico.com/story/2015/05/two-killed-in-dallas-outside-muhammad-cartoon-contest-event-117592

Hudson, John. "The Roots of Breivik's Rage." *The Atlantic*, July 25, 2011. https://www.theatlantic.com/international/archive/2011/07/roots-breiviks-rage/353232/.

Kirkpatrick, David D. "Deadly Mix in Benghazi: False Allies, Crude Video." *New York Times*, December 28, 2013. https://www.nytimes.com/2013/12/29/world/middleeast/searching-for-truth-in-benghazi.html.

Leech, Nick. "How Dearborn, Michigan Became The Heart Of Arab America." *The National*, July 5, 2017. https://www.thenationalnews.com/arts-culture/how-dearborn-michigan-became-the-heart-of-arab-america-1.117177.

Light, Jonathan. "City of Dearborn Settles Lawsuit—Apologizes to Acts17." *Dearborn Free Press*, May 7, 2013. https://www.dearbornfreepress.com/2013/05/07/city-of-dearborn-settles-lawsuit-apologizes-to-acts17.

McCarthy, Tom. "Steve Bannon's Islamophobic Film Script Just One Example of Anti-Muslim Views." *The Guardian*, February 3, 2017. https://www.theguardian.com/us-news/2017/feb/03/steve-bannon-islamophobia-film-script-muslims-islam.

Malik, Siddique. "Gingrich Is 'Discombobulating." *Louisville Courier-Journal*, July 20, 2016. https://www.courier-journal.com/story/opinion/contributors/2016/07/20/malik-gingrich-discombobulating/87145872/.

Morell, Michael. "The Real Story of Benghazi." *Politico Magazine*, May 11, 2015. https://www.politico.com/magazine/story/2015/05/the-real-benghazi-cia-insiders-account-117828.

Partlow, Joshua, and Ernesto Londono. "Mob Protesting Koran Burning Kills 7 at U.N. Compound in Kabul." *Washington Post*, April 2, 2011. https://www.washingtonpost.com/world/12-killed-in-attack-on-un-compound-in-northern-afghanistan/2011/04/01/AFrb5iHC_story.html.

Pearce, Matt. "Reports: Terry Jones Arrested with 2,998 Kerosene-Soaked Korans." *Los Angeles Times*, September 11, 2013. https://www.latimes.com/nation/nationnow/la-na-nn-terry-jones-korans-20130911-story.html.

Persaud, Trevor. "Dispute in Dearborn." *Christianity Today*, August 18, 2010. https://www.christianitytoday.com/ct/2010/september/1.17.html.

Shane, Scott. "In Islamic Law, Gingrich Sees a Mortal Threat to U.S." *New York Times*, December 21, 2011. https://www.nytimes.com/2011/12/22/us/politics/in-shariah-gingrich-sees-mortal-threat-to-us.html.

ONLINE RESOURCES

Alliance Defending Freedom. https://adflegal.org.

American Center for Law and Justice. https://aclj.org.

American Freedom Defense Initiative. https://afdi.us.

Americans for Prosperity. https://americansforprosperity.org.

Ave Maria Mutual Funds. https://www.avemariafunds.com.

Becket Fund for Religious Liberty. https://www.becketlaw.org/about-us.

Bennett, Daniel. "The Rise of Christian Conservative Legal Organizations." *Religion & Politics*, June 10, 2015. https://religionandpolitics.org/2015/06/10/the-rise-of-christian-conservative-legal-organizations.

Bridge, A Georgetown University Initiative. https://bridge.georgetown.edu.

"Cardinal Raymond Burke Endorses Thomas More Law Center for Its Important Service Restoring Christian Culture." *Thomas More Law Center*, August 10, 2017. https://www.thomasmore.org/press-releases/cardinal-raymond-burke-endorses-thomas-law-center-important-service-restoring-christian-culture.

Center for Religious Law and Freedom. https://www.clsreligiousfreedom.org.

Chaput, Charles J. "A Little Wisdom from Bernard." *First Things*, October 21, 2021. https://www.firstthings.com/web-exclusives/2021/10/a-little-wisdom-from-bernard.

"CNN: Mayor: No Sharia Law In Dearborn." YouTube video, 5:50. Posted by CNN. October 11, 2010. https://www.youtube.com/watch?v=y3V57aLHfes.

Duss, Matt. "Neocon 'Team B' Author Yerushalmi: 'Islam Was Born in Violence; It Will Die That Way.'" *ThinkProgress*, September 20, 2010. https://archive.thinkprogress.org/neocon-team-b-author-yerushalmi-islam-was-born-in-violence-it-will-die-that-way-f2758ed0b16e.

First Liberty Institute. https://firstliberty.org.

Geller Report. https://gellerreport.com.

Giangravé, Claire. "Pope Francis Dismisses 'Heresy' Charges for His Commitment to Christian-Muslim Dialogue." *Religion News Service*, March 8, 2021. https://religionnews.com/2021/03/08/pope-francis-dismisses-heresy-charges-for-his-commitment-to-christian-muslim-dialogue.

"History: Hamada Silkworks (Magnenerie Mourgue d'Algue)." *The Silk Valley*. https://thesilkvalley.com/history.

Jensen, Tom. "Trump Supporters Think Obama Is a Muslim Born in Another Country." *Public Policy Polling*, September 1, 2015. https://www.publicpolicypolling.com/wp-content/uploads/2017/09/PPP_Release_National_90115.pdf.

Jihad Watch. https://www.jihadwatch.org.

Liberty Counsel. https://lc.org.

National Legal Foundation. https://nationallegalfoundation.org.

O'Rourke, Ciara. "State Rep. Leo Berman Says Judges [In] Dearborn, Michigan Practice

Shariah Law." *PolitiFact*, May 14, 2011. https://www.politifact.com/factchecks/2011/
	may/14/leo-berman/state-rep-leo-berman-says-judges-dearborn-michigan.

Pacific Justice Institute. https://pacificjustice.org.

Raddatz, Martha. "General Petraeus: Burn a Quran Day Could 'Endanger Troops.'"
	ABC News, September 6, 2010. https://abcnews.go.com/WN/Afghanistan/
	burn-quran-day-sparks-protests-afghanistan-petraeus-endanger/story?id=11569820.

"Sharia Law in the US Debunked Myth 1." YouTube video, 4:05. Posted by acts17appalling. July
	10, 2010. https://www.youtube.com/watch?v=DXvJJuxAFxY.

"State Legislation Restricting Use of Foreign or Religious Law." *Pew Research Center*, April 8,
	2013. https://www.pewforum.org/2013/04/08/state-legislation-restricting-use-of-
	foreign-or-religious-law.

Taylor, Vanessa. "A Guide to the 2021 Supreme Court—and How It's Likely to Rule
	on Today's Biggest Issues." *Mic*, June 7, 2021. https://www.mic.com/impact/
	supreme-court-justices-political-leanings-a-guide-to-the-2021-court-81060330.

"Testimonial: Former Congressman LTC Allen West." *Thomas More Law Center.* https://www.
	thomasmore.org/testimonial/former-congressman-ltc-allen-west.

"Testimonial: Pat Buchanan, Conservative Political Commentator, Author, & Syndicated
	Columnist." *Thomas More Law Center.* https://www.thomasmore.org/testimonial/
	pat-buchanan-conservative-political-commentator-author-syndicated-columnist-2.

"Thomas More Law Center Wins Landmark First Amendment Case for Every American in the
	U.S. Supreme Court." *Thomas More Law Center*, July 1, 2021. https://www.thomasmore.org/
	press-releases/thomas-more-law-center-wins-landmark-first-amendment-case-for-every-
	american-in-the-u-s-supreme-court.

Thomas More Society. https://thomasmoresociety.org.

"UPDATE: ACLU Says Jones Ruling Was 'Blatantly Unconstitutional." *Patch*, April 23, 2011.
	https://patch.com/michigan/dearborn/terry-jones-to-file-suit-protest-in-dearborn-next-friday.

Viganò, Archbishop Carlo Maria. "The Great Reset: The Latest Great Lie." *Queen of Angels*,
	August 1, 2021. https://www.qoa.life/blogs/news/archbishop-vigano-the-great-reset-
	the-latest-great.

6. MINISTRY OF PROPAGANDA

BOOKS

Borghesi, Massimo. *Catholic Discordance: Neoconservativism vs. the Field Hospital Church of Pope
	Francis.* Translated by Barry Hudock. Collegeville, MN: Liturgical Press Academic, 2021.

Clermont, Betty. *The Neo-Catholics, Implementing Christian Nationalism in America.* Atlanta:
	Clarity Press, 2009.

Himmelstein, Jerome L. *To the Right: The Transformation of American Conservatism.* Berkeley:
	University of California Press, 1990.

Huntington, Samuel P. *The Clash of Civilizations and the Remaking of World Order.* New York:
	Touchstone, 1997.

Senèze, Nicolas. *Comment l'Amérique veut changer de pape.* Paris: Bayard Editions, 2019.

Simon, William E., with John M. Caher. *A Time for Reflection: An Autobiography.* Washington,
	D.C.: Regnery Publishing. 2004.

Vallely, Paul. *Pope Francis: The Struggle for the Soul of Catholicism.* New York: Bloomsbury USA, 2015.

DOCUMENTS

"The Challenge of Peace: God's Promise and Our Response—Pastoral Letter on War and Peace by the National Conference of Catholic Bishops of the United States." *Bulletin of Peace Proposals*, Vol. 15, no. 3 (1984): 244-51. https://www.jstor.org/stable/44481133.

"Economic Justice for All: Pastoral Letter on Catholic Social Teaching and the U.S. Economy." *National Conference of Catholic Bishops*, November 1986. https://www.usccb.org/upload/economic_justice_for_all.pdf.

Mahony, Cardinal Roger. "Ethical Dimensions of a World Without Nuclear Weapons." *Kroc Institute for International Peace Studies*, University of Notre Dame, October 25, 2011. http://nuclearfiles.org/menu/key-issues/ethics/issues/religious/2011-1025_Cardinal_Talk_NotreDame.pdf.

Novak, Michael, and Michael Joyce. "Toward the Future: Catholic Social Thought and the U.S. Economy—A Lay Letter." Lay Commission on Catholic Social Teaching and the U.S. Economy, January 1, 1984. https://philpapers.org/rec/NOVTTF.

Pope Francis. "Apostolic Exhortation Evangelii Gaudium of the Holy Father Francis to the Bishops, Clergy, Consecrated Persons and the Lay Faithful on the Proclamation of the Gospel in Today's World." *Vatican Publishing Library*, November 11, 2013. https://www.vatican.va/content/francesco/en/apost_exhortations/documents/papa-francesco_esortazione-ap_20131124_evangelii-gaudium.html.

NEWSPAPERS, MAGAZINES

Barnhardt, Ann. "Calling All Bishops That Are Still Catholic —The Die Is Cast: Bergoglio Must Be Deposed." *The Remnant*, February 29, 2016. https://remnantnewspaper.com/web/index.php/fetzen-fliegen/item/2347-calling-all-bishops-that-are-still-catholic-the-die-is-cast-bergoglio-must-be-deposed.

Douhat, Ross. "The Slow Road to Catholic Schism." *New York Times*, September 14, 2019. https://www.nytimes.com/2019/09/14/opinion/sunday/the-slow-road-to-catholic-schism.html.

Dulle, Colleen. "Explainer: The Story Behind Pope Francis' Beef with EWTN." *America: The Jesuit Review*, September 30, 2021. https://www.americamagazine.org/faith/2021/09/30/pope-francis-ewtn-arroyo-media-241547.

Fraga, Brian. "As Catholic News Service Closes, Ideological and Evangelical Outlets Stand to Fill the Void." *National Catholic Reporter*, June 14, 2022. https://www.ncronline.org/news/catholic-news-service-closes-ideological-and-evangelical-outlets-stand-fill-void.

Gibson, David. "In Closing Catholic News Service, US Bishops Undermine Their Pastoral Work." *National Catholic Reporter*, May 12, 2022. https://www.ncronline.org/news/opinion/closing-catholic-news-service-us-bishops-undermine-their-pastoral-work.

Horowitz, Jason. "Pope Says It's 'An Honor That the Americans Attack Me.'" *New York Times*, September 4, 2019. https://www.nytimes.com/2019/09/04/world/africa/pope-americans-attack.html.

Joyce, Kathryn. "Deep State, Deep Church: How QAnon and Trumpism Have Infected the Catholic Church." *Vanity Fair*, October 30, 2020. https://www.vanityfair.com/news/2020/10/how-qanon-and-trumpism-have-infected-the-catholic-church.

Kelley, Tina. "In Quiet Fields, Father Ritter Found His Exile; After Scandal, Covenant House Founder Had a Simple, Solitary Life Upstate." *New York Times*, October 22, 1999. https://www.nytimes.com/1999/10/22/nyregion/quiet-fields-father-ritter-found-his-exile-after-scandal-covenant-house-founder.html.

Mayer, Jane. "How Right-Wing Billionaires Infiltrated Higher Education." *Chronicle of Higher Education*, February 12, 2016. https://www.chronicle.com/article/how-right-wing-billionaires-infiltrated-higher-education.

Morlino, Bishop Robert C. "Encountering Christ Through Life Changes." *Diocese of Madison Catholic Herald*, December 25, 2013. https://madisoncatholicherald.org/bishop-column-15.

Moses, Paul. "Piety, Populism, and 'Patriots.'" *Commonweal*, January 8, 2021. https://www.commonwealmagazine.org/piety-populism-and-patriots.

O'Loughlin, Michael J. "Catholic News Service Closure Opens the Door to Partisan and Ideological Church Coverage, Catholic Journalists Warn." *America: The Jesuit Review*, May 12, 2022. https://www.americamagazine.org/faith/2022/05/12/catholic-news-service-closure-bishops-242974.

Roebuck, Jeremy, and David Gambacorta. "For Archbishop Chaput and Pope Francis, Envoy's Letter a Reminder of Past Tensions." *The Philadelphia Inquirer*, August 28, 2018. https://www.inquirer.com/philly/news/pennsylvania/philadelphia/archbishop-chaput-and-pope-francis-catholic-church-vigano-letter-20180828.html.

Simon, William E. "The Media's War on the Catholic Church." *Crisis Magazine*, May 1, 1996. https://www.crisismagazine.com/1996/the-medias-war-on-the-catholic-church.

Spadaro, Antonio. "Evangelical Fundamentalism and Catholic Integralism: A Surprising Ecumenism." *La Civiltà Cattolica*, July 13, 2017. https://www.laciviltacattolica.it/articolo/evangelical-fundamentalism-and-catholic-integralism-in-the-usa-a-surprising-ecumenism.

Spadaro, Antonio. "'Freedom Scares Us': Pope Francis' conversation with Slovak Jesuits." *La Civiltà Cattolica* En. Ed., Vol. 5, no. 10 (October 2021). https://www.laciviltacattolica.com/freedom-scares-us-pope-francis-conversation-with-slovak-jesuits.

Steinfels, Peter. "Bishops Raise Morality Issue on 'Star Wars.'" *New York Times*, June 26, 1988. https://www.nytimes.com/1988/06/26/us/bishops-raise-morality-issue-on-star-wars.html.

Walker, Andrew T. "The Problem with Catholic Integralism in One Tweet." *Providence Magazine*, Institute on Religion and Democracy, November 27, 2019. https://providencemag.com/2019/11/problem-catholic-integralism-tweet-adrian-vermeule.

Wineke, William R., and Lisa Schuetz. "Morlino Urges a 'Moral Minimum,' Madison Seems to Show 'Virtually No Public Morality,' Catholic Bishop Writes." *Wisconsin State Journal*, February 7, 2004. https://archive.ph/20130411021021/http://www.highbeam.com/doc/1G1-113029002.html.

Winters, Michael Sean. "Archbishop Chaput Calls Pope Francis a Liar." *National Catholic Reporter*, October 25, 2021. https://www.ncronline.org/news/opinion/archbishop-chaput-calls-pope-francis-liar.

Winters, Michael Sean. "On The Latin Mass, Pope Francis Pulls Off the Band-Aid." *National Catholic Reporter*, July 16, 2021. https://www.ncronline.org/news/opinion/distinctly-catholic/latin-mass-pope-francis-pulls-band-aid.

Winters, Michael Sean. "Wanted: A Shepherd for the Windy City." *The Tablet*, July 24, 2014. https://www.thetablet.co.uk/features/2/2940/wanted-a-shepherd-for-the-windy-city.

RADIO PROGRAMS

Neuhaus, Father Richard John. "In Support of Pre-Emptive War Doctrine." *All Things Considered*. National Public Radio. March 16, 2006. https://www.npr.org/templates/story/story.php?storyId=5284809.

ONLINE RESOURCES

"About." *Ethics and Public Policy Center*. https://eppc.org/about.

"About First Things." *First Things*. https://www.firstthings.com/about.

Arkansas Catholic. https://www.arkansas-catholic.org.

Brockhaus, Hannah. "The Amazon Synod, By the Numbers." *Catholic News Agency*, October 11, 2019. https://www.catholicnewsagency.com/news/42524/the-amazon-synod-by-the-numbers.

Burke, Cardinal Leo. "Cardinal Burke's Full Interview with Spanish Magazine Vida Nueva: 'It Seems to Many that the Church's Ship Has Lost Its Compass.'" *Rorate Caeli*, November 7, 2014. https://rorate-caeli.blogspot.com/2014/11/cardinal-burkes-full-interview-with.html.

"Celebrating the Life of Rev. Richard John Neuhaus." *The Catholic University of America*, March 14, 2018. https://communications.catholic.edu/news/2018/03/neuhaus.html.

Church Militant. https://www.churchmilitant.com.

Cocozzelli, Frank L. "How Roman Catholic Neocons Peddle Natural Law into Debates about Life and Death." *Political Research Associates*, June 8, 2008. https://politicalresearch.org/2008/06/08/how-roman-catholic-neocons-peddle-natural-law-debates-about-life-and-death.

"Committee on Communications." *United States Conference of Catholic Bishops*. https://www.usccb.org/committees/communications/who-we-are.

D'Souza, Dinesh. Twitter post. March 17, 2022, 5:30 PM. https://twitter.com/DineshDSouza/status/1504616231239835660.

De Souza, Father Raymond J. "Michael Novak (1933–2017): Large in Life, With an Even Larger Heart." *Michael Novak*, February 24, 2019. https://www.michaelnovak.net/news/2019/2/24/michael-novak-1933-2017-large-in-life-with-an-even-larger-heart.

Faith Catholic. https://www.faithcatholic.com.

Giangravé, Claire. "In Reforming the Priesthood, Pope Francis Insists on Middle Ground." *Religion News Service*, February 17, 2022. https://religionnews.com/2022/02/17/in-reforming-the-priesthood-pope-francis-insists-on-middle-ground.

LifeSite News. https://www.lifesitenews.com.

"Mission Statement." *The Institute on Religion and Democracy*. Archived via Wayback Machine, February 12, 2006. https://web.archive.org/web/20060212160904/http://www.ird-renew.org/site/pp.asp?c=fvKVLfMVIsG&b=356299.

Pelletier, Rodney. "The Sword of Islam." *Church Militant*, March 25, 2021. https://www.churchmilitant.com/news/article/the-sword-of-islam.

Ratner, Lizzy. "Olin Foundation, Right-Wing Tank, Snuffing Itself." *Observer*, May 9, 2005. https://observer.com/2005/05/olin-foundation-rightwing-tank-snuffing-itself.

"The Shifting Religious Identity of Latinos in the United States." *Pew Research Center*, May 7,

2014. https://www.pewresearch.org/religion/2014/05/07/the-shifting-religious-identity-of-latinos-in-the-united-states.

Weigel, George. "There's a Pony in Here Somewhere: A Post-Synodal Reflection." *Ethics & Public Policy Center*, October 28, 2019. https://eppc.org/publication/theres-a-pony-in-here-somewhere-a-post-synodal-reflection.

Weinandy, Thomas. "Is Pope Francis a Heretic?" *First Things*, May 7, 2019. https://www.firstthings.com/web-exclusives/2019/05/is-pope-francis-a-heretic.

"World Over – 2013-12-12 – Cardinal Burke Exclusive, Donohue, Royal, Fr. Murray with Raymond Arroyo." YouTube video, 55:51. Posted by EWTN. December 13, 2013. https://www.youtube.com/watch?v=Edq69fJLnXo.

7. THE BISHOPS AND BLACK CATHOLICS

INTERVIEW BY THE AUTHOR
Name withheld, February 2022.

BOOKS

Benders, Alison M. *Recollecting America's Original Sin, A Pilgrimage of Race and Grace.* Collegeville, Minnesota: Liturgical Press Academic, 2022.

Du Mez, Kristin Kobes. *Jesus and John Wayne: How White Evangelicals Corrupted a Faith and Fractured a Nation.* New York: Liveright Publishing, 2020.

MacLean, Nancy. *Democracy in Chains: The Deep History of the Radical Right's Stealth Plan for America.* New York: Penguin, 2017.

Massingale, Bryan N. *Racial Justice and the Catholic Church.* Maryknoll, New York: Orbis Books: 2010.

Segura, Olga M. *Birth of a Movement: Black Lives Matter and the Catholic Church.* Maryknoll, New York: Orbis Books, 2021.

LEGAL CASES CITED

Shelby County v. Holder, United States Supreme Court, 2013.

DOCUMENTS

"Bishop Joseph Francis, SVD. Anniversary Edition." Imani (Faith), Archdiocese of Newark, Office of African American, African & Caribbean Apostolate n.d. https://www.rcan.org/sites/default/files/files/Newsletter%2C%20Bishop%20Francis%20Edition(1).pdf.

"Discrimination and Catholic Conscience." *Pastoral Letters of the United States Catholic Bishops*, Volume II (1941–1961), November 14, 1958: 201–207. https://www.usccb.org/issues-and-action/cultural-diversity/african-american/resources/upload/Discrimination-Christian-Conscience-Nov-14-1958.pdf.

Massingale, Fr. Bryan N. "2021 Pax Christi USA 'Teacher of Peace' Award Acceptance Remarks." *Pax Christi USA*, July 31, 2021. https://paxchristiusa.org/wp-content/uploads/2021/08/2021-Pax-Christi-USA-Teacher-of-Peace-Award-Acceptance-Remarks.pdf.

"Open Wide Our Hearts: The Enduring Call to Love—A Pastoral Letter Against Racism." *United States Conference of Catholic Bishops*, November 2018. https://www.usccb.org/resources/open-wide-our-hearts-enduring-call-love-pastoral-letter-against-racism.

"Statement of U.S. Bishop Chairmen in Wake of Death of George Floyd and National Protests." *United States Conference of Catholic Bishops.* May 29, 2020. https://www.usccb.org/news/2020/statement-us-bishop-chairmen-wake-death-george-floyd-and-national-protests.

"Statement of U.S. Bishops' President on George Floyd and the Protests in American Cities." *United States Conference of Catholic Bishops,* May 31, 2020. https://www.usccb.org/news/2020/statement-us-bishops-president-george-floyd-and-protests-american-cities.

"Statement on National Race Crisis." *Pastoral Letters of the United States Catholic Bishops,* Volume III (1962–1974), April 25, 1968: 156–160. https://www.usccb.org/issues-and-action/cultural-diversity/african-american/resources/upload/Statement-on-National-Race-Crisis-April-25-1968.pdf.

"What We Have Seen and Heard: A Pastoral Letter on Evangelization From the Black Bishops of the United States." *United States Conference of Catholic Bishops,* September 9, 1984. https://www.usccb.org/issues-and-action/cultural-diversity/african-american/resources/upload/what-we-have-seen-and-heard.pdf.

NEWSPAPERS, MAGAZINES

Buchanan, Larry, Quoctrung Bul, and Jugal K. Patel. "Black Lives Matter May Be the Largest Movement in U.S. History." *New York Times,* July 3, 2020. https://www.nytimes.com/interactive/2020/07/03/us/george-floyd-protests-crowd-size.html.

Davidson, Madeleine. "White Christians in the US Helped Build, Sustain White Supremacist Nation, Author Says." *National Catholic Reporter,* September 19, 2020. https://www.ncronline.org/news/justice/white-christians-us-helped-build-sustain-white-supremacist-nation-author-says.

Duvall, Tessa. "Fact Check 2.0: Separating the Truth from the Lies in the Breonna Taylor Police Shooting." *Louisville Courier Journal,* June 16, 2020. https://www.courier-journal.com/story/news/crime/2020/06/16/breonna-taylor-fact-check-7-rumors-wrong/5326938002.

Fraga, Brian. "Black Catholics Respond with Dismay as Gomez Calls Protests 'Pseudo-Religions.'" *National Catholic Reporter,* November 5, 2021. https://www.ncronline.org/news/justice/black-catholics-respond-dismay-gomez-calls-protests-pseudo-religions.

Gardner, Amy, Kate Rabinowitz, and Harry Stevens. "How GOP-Backed Voting Measures Could Create Hurdles for Tens of Millions of Voters." *Washington Post,* March 11, 2021. https://www.washingtonpost.com/politics/interactive/2021/voting-restrictions-republicans-states.

Gehring, John. "Napa Institute Expands to Fight the Culture War." *National Catholic Reporter,* August 4, 2021. https://www.ncronline.org/news/people/napa-institute-expands-fight-culture-war.

Gordon-Reed, Annette. "Slavery and the Legacy of White Supremacy." *Foreign Affairs,* January/February 2018. https://www.foreignaffairs.com/articles/united-states/2017-12-12/americas-original-sin.

Horan, Daniel P. "The Bishops' Letter Fails to Recognize that Racism Is a White Problem." *National Catholic Reporter,* February 20, 2019. https://www.ncronline.org/news/opinion/faith-seeking-understanding/bishops-letter-fails-recognize-racism-white-problem.

"NCR's Newsmaker of 2021: Archbishop Gomez, a Failed Culture Warrior." *National Catholic Reporter,* December 17, 2021. https://www.ncronline.org/news/opinion/ncrs-newsmaker-2021-archbishop-gomez-failed-culture-warrior.

Seitz, Bishop Mark J. "El Paso's Bishop Mark Seitz: Black Lives Matter." *National Catholic Reporter*, June 4, 2020. https://www.ncronline.org/news/opinion/el-pasos-bishop-mark-seitz-black-lives-matter.

Stunson, Mike. "Catholic Priest Compares Black Lives Matter to 9/11 Terrorists in Michigan Sermon." *Kansas City Star*, September 15, 2020. https://www.kansascity.com/news/nation-world/national/article245744050.html.

Zapor, Patricia. "At Black Catholic Symposium Mass, Cardinal Gregory Says a Lesson for Contemporary Times is 'Live the Fullness of Life Now.'" *Catholic Standard*, October 13, 2021. https://cathstan.org/news/faith/at-black-catholic-symposium-mass-cardinal-gregory-says-a-lesson-for-contemporary-times-is-live-the-fullness-of-life-now.

RADIO PROGRAMS

Cone, Rev. James H. "Black Liberation Theology, in its Founder's Words." *Fresh Air from WHYY*. National Public Radio. March 31, 2008. https://www.npr.org/templates/story/story.php?storyId=89236116.

ONLINE RESOURCES

Anderson, Monica, Skye Toor, Lee Raine, and Aaron Smith. "An Analysis of #BlackLivesMatter and Other Twitter Hashtags Related to Political or Social Issues." *Pew Research Center*, July 11, 2018. https://www.pewresearch.org/internet/2018/07/11/an-analysis-of-blacklivesmatter-and-other-twitter-hashtags-related-to-political-or-social-issues.

"Archbishop Asks Catholics to Fast, Pray for Pelosi Over Abortion Issue." *Catholic News Service*, September 30, 2021. https://www.catholicnews.com/archbishop-asks-catholics-to-fast-pray-for-pelosi-over-abortion-issue.

"Biden Makes Clear Rebuke of White Supremacy in Inaugural Address." *Associated Press*, January 21, 2021. https://www.nbcnews.com/news/nbcblk/biden-makes-clear-rebuke-white-supremacy-inaugural-address-n1255155.

"Biography: Most Reverend José H. Gomez." *LA Catholics*. https://archbishopgomez.org/biography.

Burch, Brian. "Peek At These Numbers." *CatholicVote*, November 11, 2019. https://catholicvote.org/peek-at-these-numbers.

"CatholicVote Announces the Top Ten Courage Awards for 2021." *CatholicVote*, December 29, 2021. https://catholicvote.org/catholicvote-announces-the-top-ten-courage-awards-for-2021.

"CatholicVote Launches $9.7 Million Campaign to Expose Joe Biden's Anti-Catholic Record and Policies." *CatholicVote*, September 17, 2020. https://www.prnewswire.com/news-releases/catholicvote-launches-9-7-million-campaign-to-expose-joe-bidens-anti-catholic-record-and-policies-301133618.html.

Cohen, Li. "Police in the U.S. Killed 164 Black People in the First 8 Months of 2020. These are their names. (Part II: May–August)." *CBS News*, September 10, 2020. https://www.cbsnews.com/pictures/black-people-killed-by-police-in-the-us-in-2020-part-2.

"Demand a Secure Border Now." *Judicial Watch*. https://www.judicialwatch.org/petitions/demand-secure-border-now.

Flynn, JD. "Indiana Priest's Suspension After Black Lives Matter Letter Divides Catholics." *Catholic News Agency*, July 9, 2020. https://www.catholicnewsagency.com/news/45117/indiana-priests-suspension-after-black-lives-matter-letter-divides-catholics.

"Ginny Thomas' Republican Connections Raise Ethics Concerns for Scotus." *American Oversight*. https://www.americanoversight.org/ginni-thomas-republican-connections-raise-ethics-concerns-for-scotus.

Gomez, Archbishop José H. "After El Paso." *LA Catholics*, August 13, 2019. https://archbishopgomez.org/blog/after-el-paso.

Gomez, Archbishop José H. Facebook post. "#TheVoicesofLA: Leadership Roles for Women in the Catholic Church." October 9, 2018. https://www.facebook.com/archbishopgomez/videos/176244229919995.

Gomez, Archbishop José H. "Reflections on the Church and America's New Religions." *LA Catholics*, November 4, 2021. https://archbishopgomez.org/blog/reflections-on-the-church-and-americas-new-religions.

"James Augustine Healy: From Slave to Scholar to Shepherd." *Roman Catholic Diocese of Portland*. n.d. https://portlanddiocese.org/harvest/healy-slave-scholar-shepherd.

Jenkins, Jack. "Conservative PAC Sues Biden Administration, Targeting Nuns, Liberal Catholics in Records Request." *Religion News Service*, February 10, 2022. https://religionnews.com/2022/02/10/conservative-pac-targets-nuns-liberal-catholics-in-records-lawsuit.

Jensen, Kurt. "Speaker: Black Lives Matter Is About 'Conversation, Interchange, Action.'" *Catholic News Service*, October 10, 2021. https://cruxnow.com/cns/2021/10/speaker-black-lives-matter-is-about-conversation-interchange-action.

Jones, Sam. "US Crisis Monitor Releases Full Data for 2020." *US Crisis Monitor*, February 5, 2021. https://acleddata.com/2021/02/05/us-crisis-monitor-releases-full-data-for-2020.

Mahony, Cardinal Roger M. "Commentary: Catholic Responsiveness to Voter Suppression." *Catholic News Service*, May 8, 2021. https://www.catholicnews.com/commentary-catholic-responsiveness-to-voter-suppression.

Mohamed, Besheer, Kiana Cox, Jeff Diamant, and Claire Gecewicz. "Faith Among Black Americans." *Pew Research Center*, February 16, 2021. https://www.pewforum.org/2021/02/16/faith-among-black-americans.

"On Supreme Court Decision on Voting Rights: 'Participation in Political Life Is A Right and Moral Obligation' State U.S. Bishops." *United States Conference of Catholic Bishops*, July 3, 2013. https://www.usccb.org/news/2013/supreme-court-decision-voting-rights-participation-political-life-right-and-moral.

Pope Francis. "Fratelli Tutti: Encyclical Letter of the Holy Father Francis on Fraternity and Social Friendship." *Vatican Publishing Library*, October 3, 2020. https://www.vatican.va/content/francesco/en/encyclicals/documents/papa-francesco_20201003_enciclica-fratelli-tutti.html.

Pope Francis. "Video Message of the Holy Father Francis on the Occasion of the Fourth World Meeting of Popular Movements." *Vatican Publishing Library*, October 16, 2021. https://www.vatican.va/content/francesco/en/messages/pont-messages/2021/documents/20211016-videomessaggio-movimentipopolari.html.

Reaves, Jayme R. "What Is Public Theology?" *Jayme R. Reaves blog*, October 23, 2016. https://www.jaymereaves.com/blog/2016/10/22/what-is-public-theology.

Silva, Cynthia. "'White Supremacy, Racism': Remembering the El Paso Massacre that Targeted Latinos." *NBC News*, August 3, 2021. https://www.nbcnews.com/news/latino/white-supremacy-racism-remembering-el-paso-massacre-targeted-latinos-rcna1580.

"Voting Laws Roundup: July 2021." *Brennan Center for Justice*, July 22, 2021. https://www.brennancenter.org/our-work/research-reports/voting-laws-roundup-july-2021.

"Who We Are." *LA Catholics*. https://lacatholics.org/who-we-are.

Williams, Thomas D. "L.A. Archbishop Decries Rise of Globalism, Anti-Christian 'Elite Leadership Class." *Breitbart*, November 5, 2021. https://www.breitbart.com/faith/2021/11/05/l-a-archbishop-decries-rise-of-globalism-anti-christian-elite-leadership-class.

8. CATHOLIC WOMEN, CATHOLIC GIRLS

INTERVIEWS BY THE AUTHOR

Alison Benders, Peg Bogle, Roy Bourgeois, Maria Eitz, Kristi Laughlin, Kate McElwee, Nancy Louise Meyer, Jean Molesky-Poz, Brenda Noriega, Martha Sherman, Kara Speitz, Delila Vasquez, and Diana Wear.

Name withheld, February 2022.

BOOKS

Allen, John L., Jr. *Opus Dei: An Objective Look Behind the Myths and Reality of the Most Controversial Force in the Catholic Church*. New York: Doubleday, 2005.

Cruz, Rafael. *A Time for Action: Empowering the Faithful to Reclaim America*. Washington, DC: WND Books, 2016.

Cummings, Kathleen Sprows. *A Saint of Our Own, How the Quest for a Holy Hero Helped Catholics Become American*. Chapel Hill: University of North Carolina Press, 2019.

Whitehead, Andrew L., and Samuel L. Perry, *Taking America Back for God, Christian Nationalism in the United States*. New York: Oxford University Press, 2020

Zagano, Dr. Phyllis. *Women: Icons of Christ*. New York: Paulist Press, 2020.

DOCUMENTS

Bopp, Jr., James, National Right to Life Committee General Counsel, Courtney Turner Milbank, and Joseph D. Maughon. "NRLC Post-Roe Model Abortion Law". June 15, 2022. https://www.nrlc.org/wp-content/uploads/NRLC-Post-Roe-Model-Abortion-Law-FINAL-1.pdf.

Jaime L. Natoli, Deborah L. Ackerman, and Suzanne McDermott. "Prenatal Diagnosis of Down Syndrome: A Systematic Review of Termination Rates (1995–2011)." National Institutes of Health, National Center for Biotechnology Information. https://pubmed.ncbi.nlm.nih.gov/22418958/.

NEWSPAPERS, MAGAZINES

Brown, Emma, Jon Swaine, and Michelle Boorstein. "Amy Coney Barrett Served as a 'Handmaid' in Christian Group People of Praise." *Washington Post*, October 6, 2020. https://www.washingtonpost.com/investigations/amy-coney-barrett-people-of-praise/2020/10/06/5f497d8c-0781-11eb-859b-f9c27abe638d_story.html.

Talbot, Margaret. "Amy Coney Barrett's Long Game." *The New Yorker*, Feb. 14&21, 2022. https://www.newyorker.com/magazine/2022/02/14/amy-coney-barretts-long-game.

ONLINE RESOURCES

Archbishop José H. Gomez. "#TheVoicesofLA: Leadership Roles for Women in the Catholic Church." Facebook, October 9, 2018. https://www.facebook.com/watch/?v=176244229919995.

"Biography: Most Reverend José H. Gomez." *LA Catholics*. https://archbishopgomez.org/biography.

Crary, David. "U.S. Hispanic Catholics Are Future, but Priest Numbers Dismal." *AP News*, March 14, 2020. https://apnews.com/article/az-state-wire-phoenix-tx-state-wire-race-and-ethnicity-in-state-wire-0cd91a02ad1bfe947d77c3e1a2c313a8.

Endow. https://www.endowgroups.org.

The GIVEN Institute. https://giveninstitute.com.

Girls' Blossom Summer Camp. https://www.santiagoretreatcenter.org/copy-of-blossom-girls-camp.

Roman Catholic Womenpriests—USA Western Region History. https://romancatholicwomenpriests.org/westernregionnew/history/

Women's Ordination Conference. https://www.womensordination.org

9. OUR COMMON HOME?

INTERVIEWS BY THE AUTHOR

Farrell, Rev. Emmet, Mary Rose LeBaron, Rev. Rodolfo Piñero, Betsy Reifsnider, Kyle Rosenthal, and William Warrior of the Jungle.

Name withheld, June 2022.

BOOKS

Pope Francis. *Encyclical on Climate Change and Inequality: On Care for Our Common Home*. New York: Melville House Books, 2015.

DOCUMENTS

"Amazonia: New Paths for the Church and for an Integral Ecology." *Preparatory Document of the Synod of Bishops for the Special Assembly of the Pan-Amazon Region*, August 6, 2018. https://press.vatican.va/content/salastampa/en/bollettino/pubblico/2018/06/08/180608a.html.

Archbishop Paul S. Coakley and Bishop David J. Malloy. "Statement on Upcoming World Day of Prayer for the Care of Creation." *United States Conference of Catholic Bishops*, September 1, 2021. https://www.usccb.org/resources/statement-upcoming-world-day-prayer-care-creation-september-1-2021.

"Bishops' Statements on the Environment." *United States Conference of Catholic Bishops*. https://www.usccb.org/resources/bishops-statements-environment.

Burke, Irene. "The Impact of Laudato Si' on the Paris Climate Agreement." *Liechtenstein Institute on Self-Determination at Princeton University White Papers*, No. 3, August 2018. http://arks.princeton.edu/ark:/88435/dsp013b591c298.

"Climate Change 2022: Impacts, Adaption and Vulnerability." *Intergovernmental Panel on Climate Change*, 2022. https://www.ipcc.ch/report/sixth-assessment-report-working-group-ii.

Danielsen, Sabrina, Daniel R. DiLeo, and Emily E. Burke. "U.S. Catholic bishops' silence and denialism on climate change" *Environmental Research Letters*, Volume 16, Number 11. Published 19 October 2021.

"Instrumentum laboris: Amazonia: New Paths for the Church and for an Integral Ecology." *Synod of Bishops for the Special Assembly of the Pan-Amazon Region*, June 17, 2019. https://press.vatican.va/content/salastampa/it/bollettino/pubblico/2019/06/17/0521/01081.html.

"Paris Agreement." *United Nations Framework Convention on Climate Change*, 2015. https://unfccc.int/sites/default/files/english_paris_agreement.pdf.

Pope Benedict XVI. "Letter of His Holiness Benedict XVI to the Bishops of Latin America and the Caribbean." *Latin American Episcopal Council*, June 29, 2007. https://www.celam.org/aparecida/Ingles.pdf.

Pope Francis. "Encyclical Letter Laudato Si' of the Holy Father Francis on Care for Our Common Home." *Vatican Publishing Library*, May 24, 2015. https://www.vatican.va/content/francesco/en/encyclicals/documents/papa-francesco_20150524_enciclica-laudato-si.html.

"Reflections on the Energy Crisis: A Statement by the Committee on Social Development and World Peace." *United States Catholic Conference*, April 2, 1981. https://www.usccb.org/issues-and-action/human-life-and-dignity/environment/upload/reflections-energy-crisis.pdf.

"Socially Responsible Investment Guidelines for the United States Conference of Catholic Bishops." *United States Conference of Catholic Bishops*, November 2021. https://www.usccb.org/resources/Socially%20Responsible%20Investment%20Guidelines%202021%20(003).pdf.

NEWSPAPERS, MAGAZINES

"Amazon Rainforest is Home to 16,000 Tree Species, Estimate Suggests." *The Guardian*, October 18, 2013. https://www.theguardian.com/environment/2013/oct/18/amazon-rainforest-tree-species-estimate.

Arocho Esteves, Junno. "Pope Francis: Catechism Will Be Updated to Define Ecological Sins." *America: The Jesuit Review*, November 15, 2019. https://www.americamagazine.org/faith/2019/11/15/pope-francis-catechism-will-be-updated-define-ecological-sins.

Brachear Pashman, Manya. "Pope Francis Makes Chicago Catholics See Green." *Chicago Tribune*, June 18, 2015. https://www.chicagotribune.com/news/ct-pope-francis-climate-change-encyclical-met-20150618-story.html.

"Brazilian Rancher Gets 30 Years in Killing of the Environmentalist Nun Dorothy Stang." *New York Times*, May 16, 2007. https://www.nytimes.com/2007/05/16/world/americas/16iht-brazil.1.5733266.html.

Crary, David. "San Diego Bishop Mcelroy Named by Pope Francis as a Cardinal." *The Hill*, May 29, 2022. https://thehill.com/news/ap/ap-u-s-news/san-diego-bishop-mcelroy-named-by-pope-francis-as-a-cardinal.

DiLeo, Daniel R., Sabrina Danielsen, and Emily E. Burke. "Study: Most US Catholic Bishops Kept Silent on Francis' Climate Change Push." *National Catholic Reporter*, October 19, 2021. https://www.ncronline.org/news/earthbeat/study-most-us-catholic-bishops-kept-silent-francis-climate-change-push.

Ducey, Charlie. "Alexander Tschugguel's Bid to Save the Church in Europe." *Ethika Politika*, November 27, 2019. https://www.ethikapolitika.org/2019/11/27/save-the-church-in-europe.

Editorial Board. "The Pope's Clarion Call on Climate: Our View." *USA Today*, June 18, 2015. https://www.usatoday.com/story/opinion/2015/06/18/pope-francis-climate-change-encyclical-editorials-debates/28941183.

Faiola, Anthony, Michelle Boorstein, and Chris Mooney. "Release of Encyclical Reveals Pope's Deep Dive into Climate Science." *Washington Post*, June 18, 2015. https://

www.washingtonpost.com/local/how-pope-franciss-not-yet-official-document-on-climate-change-is-already-stirring-controversy/2015/06/17/ef4d46be-14fe-11e5-9518-f9e0a8959f32_story.html.

Fier, Don. "Interview with Cardinal Burke…He Is With Us: Trusting in the Lord in Turbulent Times." *The Wanderer*, December 26, 2019. https://thewandererpress.com/catholic/news/frontpage/interview-with-cardinal-burke-he-is-with-us-trusting-in-the-lord-in-turbulent-times.

Goodstein, Laurie. "Pope Francis May Find Wariness Among U.S. Bishops on Climate Change." *New York Times*, June 14, 2015. https://www.nytimes.com/2015/06/14/us/pope-francis-may-find-wariness-among-us-bishops-on-climate-change.html.

"The Guardian View on Laudato Si': Pope Francis Calls for a Cultural Revolution." *The Guardian*, June 18, 2015. https://www.theguardian.com/commentisfree/2015/jun/18/guardian-view-on-laudato-si-pope-francis-cultural-revolution.

Hansen, Luke. "Top Five Takeaways from the Amazon Synod." *America: The Jesuit Review*, November 11, 2019. https://www.americamagazine.org/faith/2019/11/11/top-five-takeaways-amazon-synod.

Lakhani, Nina. "Nalleli Cobo: The Young Activist Who Led Her La Neighborhood Against Big Oil." *The Guardian*, November 10, 2021. https://www.theguardian.com/society/2021/nov/10/nalleli-cobo-the-young-activist-who-led-her-la-neighbourhood-against-big-oil.

Lavelle, Devin. "A Brighter Future at St. Anthony." *Valley Community Newspapers*, March 10, 2022. http://www.valcomnews.com/a-brighter-future-at-st-anthony.

McConahay, Mary Jo. "Catholics in the Amazon Await the Synod's Decisions." *National Catholic Reporter*, October 23, 2019. https://www.ncronline.org/news/earthbeat/catholics-amazon-await-synods-decisions.

McElroy, Bishop Robert W. "Bishop Mcelroy: US Church Is Adrift, Synodality Can Renew It." *National Catholic Reporter*, November 7, 2019. https://www.ncronline.org/news/opinion/bishop-mcelroy-us-church-adrift-synodality-can-renew-it.

Roewe, Brian. "Complaint Seeks to Push Boston College to Drop Fossil Fuel Stocks." *National Catholic Reporter*, December 17, 2020. https://www.ncronline.org/news/earthbeat/complaint-seeks-push-boston-college-drop-fossil-fuel-stocks.

Roewe, Brian. "Vatican Official: Church Divestment from Fossil Fuels Is 'Moral Imperative.'" *National Catholic Reporter*, May 20, 2021. https://www.ncronline.org/news/earthbeat/vatican-official-church-divestment-fossil-fuels-moral-imperative.

Sadowski, Dennis. "Bishops Approve New Socially Responsible Investment Guidelines." *National Catholic Reporter*, November 17, 2021. https://www.ncronline.org/news/justice/bishops-approve-new-socially-responsible-investment-guidelines.

Yardley, William, and Tom Kington. "Pope Francis, in Leaked Draft Letter, Calls for Curbing Global Warming." *Los Angeles Times*, June 15, 2015. https://www.latimes.com/world/europe/la-fg-sej-vatican-climate-change-20150615-story.html.

ONLINE RESOURCES

"Archbishops Decry Military Gay Benefits plans." *Catholic News Service*, February 15, 2013. https://www.catholicnewsagency.com/news/26597/archbishops-decry-military-gay-benefits-plan.

"Amazon: People & Communities." *WWF*. https://www.worldwildlife.org/places/amazon.

"Amazon Rainforest: The World's Most Biodiverse Region." *Nature & Culture International.* https://www.natureandculture.org/ecosystems/amazon-rainforest.

Archbishop Viganò. "Catholic Identity Conference: Vatican II & the New World Order." Transcript. *The Archbishop Viganò Archive*, October 24, 2020. https://www.catholicity.com/vigano/2020-10-24.html.

"Background Briefing: Amazon tribes." *Survival International.* https://www.survivalinternational.org/about/amazontribes.

Bourne, Lisa. "Oklahoma Archbishop: I've 'Deepest Respect' for Viganò. His Claims Demand 'Deeper Examination.'" *LifeSiteNews*, August 31, 2018. https://www.lifesitenews.com/news/oklahoma-archbishop-ive-deepest-respect-for-vigano-his-claims-demand-deepe.

Campos, Staci P. "US Bishops Are Considering Guidelines for Socially Responsible Investment." *TAC Lawna*, November 17, 2021. https://tac-lawna.org/us-bishops-are-considering-guidelines-for-socially-responsible-investment.

"Catholic Climate Ambassadors." *Catholic Climate Covenant.* https://catholicclimatecovenant.org/program/catholic-climate-ambassadors.

"CELAM: In Wake of Santo Domingo, Political Struggle Between Vatican, Local Church Continues. NCR." *National Catholic Reporter*, January 22, 1993. https://www.thefreelibrary.com/CELAM%3a+in+wake+of+Santo+Domingo%2c+political+struggle+between+Vatican%2c...-a013417525.

Cosgrave, Jenny. "Mass Appeal? S&P Launches 'Catholic Values' Index." *CNBC*, August 20, 2015. https://www.cnbc.com/2015/08/20/mass-appeal-sp-launches-catholic-values-index.html.

Harris, Elise. "Central American Bishops Defend Francis over Amazon Synod, 'Pachamama.'" *Crux*, December 1, 2019. https://cruxnow.com/church-in-the-americas/2019/12/central-american-bishops-defend-francis-over-amazon-synod-pachamama.

"Laudato Si' Circles." *Laudato Si' Movement.* https://laudatosimovement.org/act/laudato-si-circles.

Laudato Si' Movement. https://laudatosimovement.org.

McElroy, Bishop Robert W. "A Church in Crisis Moves to the Future." St. Mary's University, MacTaggart Catholic Intellectual Tradition Lecture Series, November 6, 2019. https://mediaspace.stmarytx.edu/media/The+Most+Reverend+Robert+W.+McElroy+++The+MacTaggart+Catholic+Intellectual+Tradition+Lecture+Series%2C+November+6%2C+2019/1_477nc2z1/143878661.

Mena, Adelaide. "Infallible? Informal? How Binding Is the New Encyclical On Catholics?" *Catholic News Agency*, June 19, 2015. https://www.catholicnewsagency.com/news/32194/infallible-informal-how-binding-is-the-new-encyclical-on-catholics.

Molino, Jorge. "Angelo Sodano's Background: the Godfather of the Vatican." *Pressenza*, May 31, 2022. https://www.pressenza.com/2022/05/angelo-sodanos-background-the-godfather-of-the-vatican/.

"Nalleli Cobo: 2022 Goldman Prize Winner." *Goldman Environmental Prize.* https://www.goldmanprize.org/recipient/nalleli-cobo.

Pan-Amazon Synod Watch. https://panamazonsynodwatch.info.

Reno, R. R. "The Return of Catholic Anti-Modernism." *First Things*, June 18, 2015. https://www.firstthings.com/web-exclusives/2015/06/the-return-of-catholic-anti-modernism.

Roewe, Brian. "Bishop McElroy Calls for Deeper Level of Commitment on Addressing Climate Change from the US Bishops." *Millenial Journal*, August 5, 2019. https://millennialjournal. com/2019/08/05/bishop-mcelroy-calls-for-deeper-level-of-commitment-on-addressing-climate-change-from-the-us-bishops.

Smith, Peter and David Crary. "US Catholic Bishops Elect Timothy Broglio as New President." *Associated Press*, November 15, 2022. https://apnews.com/article/religion-539937dc8c2369d 10a247428119d34f4.

"U.S. Bishops Vote for USCCB Secretary and Committee Chairmen at Fall Plenary Assembly." USCCB Public Affairs Office, November 16, 2022. https://www.usccb.org/news/2022/ us-bishops-vote-usccb-secretary-and-committee-chairmen-fall-plenary-assembly.

Valdmanis, Richard. "Exclusive: In Clash with Pope's Climate Call, U.S. Church Leases Drilling Rights." *Reuters*, September 22, 2015. https://www.reuters.com/article/us-pope-usa-drilling/exclusive-in-clash-with-popes-climate-call-u-s-church-leases-drilling-rights-idUSKCN0RM0AY20150922.

Valdmanis, Richard. "Insight—Pope's Climate Push at Odds with U.S. Catholic Oil Investments." *Reuters*, August 12, 2015. https://www.reuters.com/article/uk-usa-catholic-fossilfuels-insight/insight-popes-climate-push-at-odds-with-u-s-catholic-oil-investments-idUKKCN0QH0ED20150812.

Voris, Michael. "Amazon Synod Will Replace Universal Church with 'Globalist Church.'" *LifeSiteNews*, October 4, 2019. https://www.lifesitenews.com/news/ amazon-synod-will-replace-universal-church-with-globalist-church-michael-voris.

Weigel, George. "Letters from the Synod—2019: #9." *First Things*, October 28, 2019. https:// www.firstthings.com/web-exclusives/2019/10/letters-from-the-synod-2019-9.

White, Christopher. "Activist Says Idea of 'Ecological Sin' Boils Down to, 'We Consume Too Much.'" *Crux*, November 4, 2019. https://cruxnow.com/church-in-the-usa/2019/11/04/ activist-says-idea-of-ecological-sin-boils-down-to-we-consume-too-much.

Index

264

INDEX